The EGYPTIANS

CYRIL ALDRED

The EGYPTIANS

Third edition, revised and updated by
Aidan Dodson

with 140 illustrations, 12 in color

 Thames & Hudson

Ancient Peoples and Places
FOUNDING EDITOR: GLYN DANIEL

Frontispiece: The face of the gold mummy-mask of Tutankhamun, with stone-inlaid eyes, and other features highlighted in colored glass.

First published in the United Kingdom in 1961
by Thames & Hudson Ltd, London
Second edition published in the United States of America in 1984
by Thames & Hudson Inc., 500 Fifth Avenue, New York,
New York 10110

thamesandhudsonusa.com

Third edition, revised by Aidan Dodson, 1998
Reprinted 2005

Library of Congress Catalog Card Number 98-60040
ISBN- 13: 978-0-500-28036-2
ISBN- 10: 0-500-28036-3

Printed and bound in Singapore by C.S. Graphics

Contents

Preface

The revision of a classic text is always a daunting task, and Cyril Aldred's *The Egyptians* certainly merits classic status. First published in 1961, and revised by Aldred himself in 1984, it well deserved reviewers' enthusiasm. However, in the years that have passed since the appearance of both editions, there have been many new discoveries and, just as important, many new ways of looking at old evidence, which have brought about some significant changes in the way that aspects of Egyptian history and culture are now interpreted.

In revising the book, I have generally taken care to leave Aldred's words intact wherever possible, and make changes only where the progress of research has made his interpretation untenable. In addition, I have expanded some areas to reflect new discoveries, and rewritten and rearranged one chapter to better mirror modern conceptions. Finally, I have thoroughly revised the bibliography to include the most recent reliable works in various areas, and sometimes omit those that have not stood the test of time.

I must thank the publishers for inviting me to undertake this revision, which I dedicate to the memory of Cyril Aldred, whose writings were pivotal for me in my earliest years as a fledgling Egyptologist.

Yate, South Gloucestershire   AIDAN DODSON

1 (*pp. 6–7*) The Great Temple, hewn out of the living rock to a depth of over 60 m at Abu Simbel on the west bank of the Nile, is dedicated to Ramesses II and the three national gods of Egypt in his time, Amun of Thebes, Ptah of Memphis and Re-Herakhty of Heliopolis.

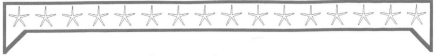

Introduction

The chronology

Our knowledge of the ancient Egyptians and their history is derived from various sources. There are the disjointed reports of some classical writers, notably Herodotus, who according to some authorities may never have visited more than the area around the Greek trading centre at Naukratis in the 5th century BC, and evidently relied heavily upon the reports of earlier travellers such as Hecataeus of Miletus. The Old Testament has bequeathed us a few biased references to events which were seldom contemporary. Scanty accounts also exist from other foreign sources, such as the Hittite state records and the archives of Babylonia and Assyria.

The evidence from Egypt itself is of two kinds, the literary and the archaeological. There are for instance the written records in temple inscriptions, tomb autobiographies, lists of rulers, letters and reports of all kinds. Although nearly all this material is greatly damaged and incomplete, some of it is of great value, such as the laconic annals of early kings on the fragmentary Palermo Stone. Many of the official pronouncements which the pharaohs left for posterity are no more than propaganda designed to sustain the god-like status of the ruler by putting a favourable gloss on events during his reign. Even in the rare instances where set-backs are reported, as for instance, the demoralized state of the nation at the accession of Tutankhamun, or the dangerous isolation of Ramesses II at the Battle of Qadesh, the occasion is used to reveal the divine might of the king in overcoming adversity.

It is in fact doubtful whether the Egyptians had any idea of history as modern Westerners understand it. In most cases, however, a certain check upon the official account, where it exists, can be exercised by reading between the lines, and trimming the outline here and there to a more plausible shape through our understanding of the mental workings of the ancient editors. The discipline is similar to that employed by modern intelligence services to discover their opponents' concealed intentions and resources.

In this work of detection every scrap of information, some of it from the most unlikely sources, such as a work-roster or an ancient graffito, must be fitted patiently into a complicated mosaic. But the problem of finding out what exactly happened in ancient Egypt is truly formidable, and is not lessened by the uneven wealth of records, which often tend to confuse the

2

2 The Palermo Stone is inscribed with the annals of selected kings of the first five dynasties. The front face shown here has in the top row the names of predynastic kings of whom nothing is recorded except their names. The lower registers are divided into compartments by year signs recording events by which the year was remembered. Below in each exergue is entered the height in cubits that the Nile reached in that particular year. In the bands separating each register is inscribed the name of the king whose annals are recorded below it.

picture with intractable detail in some areas, and to obscure it altogether with an entire absence of data in others.

An example of such a system in action can be seen from the modern reconstruction of the chronology of pharaonic Egypt. For this purpose, historians accept as a framework the scheme adopted by Manetho, the High Priest in Heliopolis who in the 3rd century BC wrote a history of Egypt. For the sake of uniformity they also often render the names of the pharaohs in his Greek versions, where they exist, a system which is followed here, thus *Amenophis* rather than *Amenhotep*, *Amenhetep*, *Amunhotpe* etc. Manetho's work has not survived except in a few extracts and as a list of kings and their years of rule preserved in the writings of early Christian chronographers. He divided into thirty-one dynasties the entire chronicle of events from the unification of Upper and Lower Egypt under Menes, the first pharaoh, to the conquest of Alexander the Great in 332 BC. His lists and lengths of the reigns, however, have had to be extensively modified because of corruptions in the ancient texts and the discovery of more reliable documents of an earlier date, in addition to evidence and greater detail from contemporary monuments.

Thus fragments of the stela, or its copies, in the collections at Palermo, Cairo and London (the Palermo Stone), recording selected events during the five centuries from Menes to Neferirkare of the Fifth Dynasty, throw a faint and flickering light on some of the obscurer reigns. Another such stela has recently been identified, reused as a sarcophagus lid. It once bore the chronicles of the kings of the Sixth Dynasty, and although in very poor condition is likely to allow us to undertake major revisions of our conception of this period. The king-list in the temple of Sethos I at Abydos represents a roster of those monarchs to whom Sethos wished offerings to be made; they are arranged chronologically, beginning with Menes, but omit some monarchs for political, or other, reasons that are less easy to ascertain. A greatly damaged and reconstructed papyrus in Turin (the Turin Canon) gives a much more detailed 'administrative' list, drawn up under Sethos I's successor, Ramesses II. Fragments of other king-lists made at this same period have also survived, but all are incomplete and tendentious, and the correct order of successions is dubious in places.

Other documents have permitted greater detail to be supplied in the case of individual kings. Thus a series of dated labels from pottery food-jars excavated in the ruins of the palace of Amenophis III at Western Thebes, has shown that he survived at least into the last days of his thirty-eighth regnal year. The exact length of the reign of Sethos II in years, months and days is known from an entry in a diary kept by a scribe in charge of workmen decorating the king's tomb.

Egyptologists have further grouped Manetho's dynasties into larger time-spans, coinciding with periods when a distinct cultural pattern prevailed, separated by obscure interludes of political upheaval.

Dynasty	Period	Approximate Date BC
I–II	Archaic	3050–2663
III–VI	Old Kingdom	2663–2195
VII–XIa	First Intermediate	2195–2066
XIb–XIII	Middle Kingdom	2066–1650
XIV–XVII	Second Intermediate	1650–1550
XVIII–XX	New Kingdom	1550–1064
XXI–XXV	Third Intermediate	1064–664
XXVI	Saite	664–525
XVII–XXXI	Late Period	525–332
Ptolemaic	Hellenistic	332–30
Imperial	Roman	30 BC–AD 395

Some scholars have applied principles of naming after their political seats to the naming of epochs within the obscure Intermediate Periods, where it is possible to define more narrowly a certain interval of rule. Thus *Herakleopolitan* is often used to describe the Ninth and Tenth Dynasties, whereas *Hyksos* is applied to the Fifteenth and Sixteenth Dynasties.

In the New Kingdom, the Nineteenth and Twentieth Dynasties are often referred to as *Ramesside* after the predominant name of their kings. The reign of Akhenaten (*c.* 1360–1343) is generally designated the *Amarna* period from the name of his residence-city at modern Tell el Amarna.

From the Middle Kingdom, the Egyptians dated events to the reign of a particular king from his first year of rule onwards, beginning again with each change of ruler. Before then, events were dated to a specific year in a king's reign by reference to an outstanding occurrence in that year, such as his accession, his first smiting the Easterners (see ill. 45) and so on. From the time of the Second Dynasty, however, it became customary to date events to a biennial occasion, the census of cattle. If odd years had to be recorded they were referred to as, 'the year after the nth numbering of all oxen etc.', and this system prevailed until the end of the Old Kingdom, after which, with the government divided among a number of petty rulers, no single centralized scheme could succeed.

The exact length of a reign has been preserved in very few instances. For some periods it is even uncertain whether the full list of kings and their proper order of succession have survived. The chronology of Egypt has therefore had to be established by modern scholars, largely by working forwards and backwards from one or two fixed points determined from chance recordings of astronomical phenomena. Thus the heliacal rising of the star Sirius (see p. 89), noted in regnal year seven of Sesostris III, can be calculated to have occurred in 1872 BC. A similar sighting, reported on the ninth day of the third month of *shomu* (see p. 89) in the ninth year of Amenophis I has been used to fix his accession within a twenty-six-year time-span. Unfortunately, recent work has cast some doubt over the methodologies used, and accordingly there must remain considerable doubt about the absolute dating of events prior to 664 BC.

It is now becoming clear that much of the detailed chronology built up in past decades is badly flawed, and that a general lowering of dates, even beyond the minima which have become accepted, may be necessary. Indeed, there have been attempts to lower New Kingdom dates by whole centuries. These are undoubtedly wrong, but there seems definite scope for dropping some by as much as half a century. The chronology used in this book represents a conservative reading of the emerging data.

The various 'scientific' dating methods – carbon-14, thermoluminescence, dendrochronology – have had little impact on the chronological reconstruction of pharaonic Egypt since, even in their most refined forms, their margins of error are generally in excess of the uncertainties in the 'historical' dating scheme. On the other hand, when one moves into the area of prehistory their importance increases dramatically. Together with 'archaeological' methods, particularly based on the seriation of pottery types, they provide the basis upon which the sequence of Predynastic cultures can be assessed.

1 · The loss and recovery of pagan Egypt

Decline and coma

In AD 130, during the golden summer of the Roman Empire, Hadrian, with his empress Sabina and a numerous retinue, toured his domains in Egypt. The visit was notable for a number of events, apart from the great singularity that an emperor in Rome had chosen to explore his personal estate. Hadrian disputed in Greek with professors at the Museum of Alexandria, and building work on towns and temples was initiated or re-invigorated throughout the land. A tragic incident occurred when his catamite, the handsome Bithynian youth Antinous, drowned himself in the Nile to avert from the Emperor some mysterious calamity forecast by an oracle. At the site of this disaster, near modern Sheikh Abada in Middle Egypt, Hadrian founded the city of Antinoë in his honour, and its ruins were still extensive at the beginning of the last century.

The Emperor and his suite also camped for several days in the plain at Western Thebes before the two monolithic quartzite colossi which were all that remained visible of the gigantic mortuary temple of Amenophis III, built some fifteen centuries earlier. In Classical times the northern statue was held to represent the Homeric Memnon slain at the siege of Troy, since occasionally as its fissured stone warmed up in the rays of the rising sun, it emitted a low moaning note, as though the dead hero were greeting his mother Eos, the dawn. She in turn responded by shedding tears which fell as the morning dew. Memnon did not fail to salute Hadrian, even before the sun rose, and with a clearer note like the sound of a gong at the second hour, and yet a third time later, showing how beloved was the Emperor among the gods. The court poetess, Balbilla, commemorated the occasion in Greek verses which are inscribed on the left leg of the colossus.

These are the last pictures we receive of a pharaoh exercising his governance in the land of Egypt. Half a century later, an earth tremor demolished the upper half of the statue of Memnon; and although it was crudely repaired, it never spoke again.

During the same period, despite persecution, Christianity had established itself at Alexandria, where St Mark had preached his gospel, and where his remains were entombed until the Venetians removed them to Venice in AD 829. Alexandria became the chief centre of Christian thought, until

Byzantium eclipsed it in the 5th century. In the 2nd century, Christianity spread throughout the Delta and from there to the rest of Egypt, steadily ousting the old pagan religion and its cultural manifestations, including the writing of the native language in hieroglyphic and hieratic scripts, although demotic writing continued in use for the business of everyday life until the 5th century AD. Such learning had by this late period become little more than the secret lore of a few priestly adepts; but with their displacement by the new activist presbyters, their pagan learning expired with them. It lingered a little longer at the great centre of Isis-worship on the island of Philae in the First Cataract, where the last hieroglyphic inscription was carved in AD 394. Three years earlier, the triumph of Christianity had been consummated in the destruction by the zealous patriarch Theophilus of the Serapeum of Alexandria, the great temple of the universal cult of Serapis, introduced by the Ptolemies seven centuries earlier. By the 5th century AD the ancient learning had so far been forgotten that the explanations of hieroglyphic writing offered at that time by Horapollo were so wide of the mark as to have succeeded only in misleading subsequent scholars.

In the previous century the practice had arisen of writing the contemporary spoken Egyptian in the letters of the Greek alphabet, supplemented by seven characters derived from the demotic script to indicate sounds not represented in Greek speech. This script is called Coptic, after the Copts, the Christian descendants of the ancient Egyptians, and was chiefly employed in the writing of Biblical and ecclesiastical literature. Indeed, the ancient language is still used for chanting and praying in the Coptic Church, though it has not been generally spoken or understood since the 16th century when it died out in favour of Arabic. Its resurrection as a literary language and its philological study have been the work of European scholars, since the Jesuit Athanasius Kircher began publishing his pioneer researches in AD 1636.

The adoption of Christianity by the Egyptians was as much political as religious in its motivation. The Imperial prefects from the time of Augustus onwards had ruthlessly exploited Egypt as a source of cheap grain for feeding the unruly mob at Rome. The xenophobia and resistance that such oppression provoked found the simple doctrines of the Early Church particularly congenial. Moreover, Coptic religious thought embraced a concept which had been cherished in Egypt since earliest pagan times, that the Son of God was wholly divine, and every human element had been absorbed by his divinity. The Egyptian Church adhered fervently to this belief, even when the Council of Chalcedon in AD 451 promoted the rival doctrine that Christ combined a human with a divine nature.

The Monophysite dogma of the Copts was regarded as a heresy by the Eastern Orthodox Christians, and alienated the Egyptians from their Byzantine rulers. In AD 641 they welcomed the armies of the Caliph Omar as their deliverers from an intolerable torment. The Islamic Arab invaders at first treated the Copts with generosity and forebearance; but the Copts' arrogance and intransigence soon alienated their conquerors and resulted in further oppression and indoctrination.

The Copts had desecrated the monuments of their pagan past, plundering them for building stone, hammering out the figures of gods from the walls, or covering them with plaster and whitewash in order to convert ancient shrines into Christian churches. The Mohammedans no less eyed askance the monuments of their ancient past with new-found revulsion as the work of the Devil, and abandoned them to encroaching sands when they did not quarry them for convenient stone, or eviscerate them in search of the treasures they were popularly thought to conceal, or squat among their ruins in mud brick villages. In the face of this indifference and even hostility, the study of Egypt's pagan past had to await a change of mind elsewhere, and this arose in Europe at the end of the Middle Ages when scholars returned to the inspiration of the literature of Greece and especially Rome. The revival of Classical learning, however, meant that the Egyptian past was known only as it was reflected in the writings of Greek and Roman authors, many of whose manuscripts became available with the fall of Constantinople in AD 1453 and the dispersal of Byzantine scholars to the West.

Students of ancient Egypt were not well served by the writings of Classical authors. The first Greek visitors to Egypt in the 7th century BC were overawed by a wealthy and unified power in contrast to their own warring congeries of rival city states. In seeking their own antecedents in a civilization that seemed to have existed since the beginning of time, they clutched gratefully at any straw that appeared familiar in a turbulent flood of novelties. Thus they heard the name of modern Luxor pronounced as something like 'ta'ipe' (the Sanctuary), and thought it must be the original of their Thebes. Similarly, Abodu, the town where the god Osiris was paramount, they recognized as their Abydos. They also tried to identify the gods of their pantheon with equivalents among the deities of Egypt, but they never really understood Egyptian religion and were inclined to see in inexplicable acts and beliefs a more profound significance than actually existed.

For Herodotus in the 5th century BC Egypt was remarkable for the number of marvels which it contained, and because more monuments which defied description were to be found there than anywhere else. Yet the inhabitants in their manners and customs seemed to have inverted the general practices of mankind. In his observations, he often goes sadly astray; but his remarks suffice to paint a picture of a nation apart, talented but perverse.

Other Classical travellers, such as Diodorus Siculus and Strabo, found it difficult to reconcile what seemed to them childish beliefs with stupendous technical achievements, and they thought that an esoteric wisdom must lie behind the appearance of foolishness. Thus originated the myth of the superior and mysterious wisdom of the ancient Egyptians, which has persisted until very recently, for is it not mentioned in Holy Writ 'that Moses was learned in the wisdom of the Egyptians' (Acts 7, 22), and only the wisdom of Solomon exceeded it (I Kings 4, 29–31)?

Roman writers, such as Plutarch, Apuleius and Iamblichus, were more concerned with this wisdom as expressed in religious ideas, particularly those of the widespread Isis cult. Early Christian writers, such as Eusebius, Lactantius and Clement of Alexandria, described Egyptian religious beliefs and practices merely to expose their falsity. The only pagan Egyptian to speak with some authority, Manetho, is unfortunately for the most part silent since his history has been lost, apart from brief extracts in the writings of the Jewish historian, Josephus, and early Christian chronographers. The passages quoted by Josephus, however, do not inspire much confidence that Manetho's chronicle would have differed widely from the farrago of myths reported by Herodotus, despite the learned Egyptian's ability to consult the ancient records of his people, and to compile a list of rulers in chronological order.

It is unfortunate that as Renaissance scholars became familiar with the works of Classical authors, they should also have fallen under the spell of the Neoplatonists who in Alexandria in the 3rd century AD developed Platonic ideas with oriental mysticism, particularly as expounded in the writings of Plotinus, Porphyry, Iamblichus and others. An obsession with the meaning of symbols is characteristic of the Renaissance Neoplatonists. Horapollo's *Hieroglyphica* of the later 5th century AD was intensively studied since his exposition of Egyptian hieroglyphs was particularly concerned with a mystical interpretation of these picture-signs. The works of other Classical commentators were also combed for further elucidation, and only confirmed the view that Egyptian hieroglyphs conveyed abstract moral and philosophical ideas of profound significance, despite the extreme paucity of actual specimens of the script. The few examples that were available were almost exclusively carved upon obelisks carried off to Rome in Imperial days. Some of these were still standing, while others, together with various Egyptian

3 The head of a queen from a sphinx made in the middle years of the Twelfth Dynasty. It was removed from Egypt in Roman times to adorn an Imperial villa, probably that of Hadrian at Tivoli, and acquired in 1771 by Gavin Hamilton for Lord Shelburne.

monuments imported to adorn art galleries attached to Imperial baths and villas, were brought to light during building operations throughout the 16th and subsequent centuries. 3

The history of Egyptology in Europe over the next two centuries is an attempt to interpret hieroglyphic writing according to the esoteric Neoplatonist ideas, and the gradual emergence of a school of sceptics during the Age of Reason with a more rational attitude to the subject. In this long progression from mysticism to intellectual comprehension many scholars made small but significant contributions, notably Warburton and Young in Britain; Zoëga and Niebuhr in Denmark; Montfaucon, Barthelemy, and Silvestre de Sacy in France; and Åkerblad in Sweden. By the end of the 18th century, Egyptian studies were ready to take a new direction.

Reawakening

In 1798 this new course was set by a sudden and dramatic coup. Napoleon Bonaparte, at the head of a French army, dusted off a plan of campaign which the German philosopher Gottfried Leibniz had earlier urged upon Louis XIV in his anxiety to divert Le Grand Monarque from his territorial ambitions in continental Europe. This embraced the mounting of an expedition to Egypt, with the construction of a canal across the isthmus of Suez as one of its objectives. But Napoleon decided also upon the study of the Egyptian past in the process. His exhortation to his troops at the Battle of the Pyramids, 'Soldiers, forty centuries look down upon you', rings up the curtain on the Romantic discovery of Egypt. The baggage train of his army included nearly 200 savants whose business it was to explore, describe, and even to excavate. No such scientific expedition had till then visited any ancient site, and it set a pattern for several such missions in the new century. While Napoleon's adventure was militarily ill-fated, it firmly established French ascendancy in the cultural affairs of Egypt. The thirty-six illustrated volumes of the *Description de l'Egypte* in which Vivant Denon (1747–1825) and his collaborators described the monuments that they found in Egypt appeared between 1809 and 1823 (2nd edition) and created the liveliest stir. For almost the first time, scholars in the seclusion of their libraries could study copies of ancient monuments and texts existing in the land of Egypt itself, and were no longer dependent upon the meagre trickle of miscellaneous antiquities that had come into the cabinets of dilettanti during the 18th century as a result of visits to Alexandria and Grand Cairo. Well may the French have struck a medal in 1826 to commemorate the issue of these volumes, showing in Neo-Classical fashion a French soldier removing the veil from the awakening Isis.

By the Capitulations of Alexandria, the British seized possession of the Rosetta Stone, a large fragment of basalt inscribed with a text in Greek, demotic and hieroglyphic scripts, which a French officer had unearthed while digging a trench at Rosetta in the Western Delta. This antiquity, now in the British Museum, carried the bilingual text which scholars sought as a means of discovering the key to the hieroglyphic system of writing. Various students now took halting steps along the path of decipherment, but the credit for the first valid decipherment of hieroglyphs goes to the Frenchman Jean François Champollion (1790–1832), the virtual founder of Egyptology as a serious discipline. To his many natural gifts, Champollion added an extensive knowledge of Coptic as well as other Oriental languages, and from his eventual recognition that hieroglyphs were merely a means of expressing in picture-signs a language which also survived in a greatly modified form written in Greek characters, his progress was rapid. In September 1822, his celebrated *Lettre à M. Dacier*, read at a meeting of the Academie des Inscriptions et Belles Lettres in Paris, first gave the world the correct system for deciphering Egyptian hieroglyphs. The phenomenal progress that his studies had made in the short space of ten years before his death in 1832 at the early age of forty-one, is seen in his *Précis* (1824) and in the grammar and materials for a dictionary that he left for posthumous publication. Almost at a blow the scientific study of the ancient Egyptians had begun: for the first time since Theodosius I, they could speak for themselves.

Champollion's successors carried the study of the ancient language to ever greater degrees of refinement so that today philology is a vast and separate study within the Egyptological ambit. The researches of Lepsius, Birch, Goodwin, Brugsch, Chabas, de Rougé, Maspero, Stern, Erman and others in the 19th century, consolidated the ground won, and embraced also the intensive study of the hieratic and demotic scripts, as well as Coptic. In the present century the work of many philologists, but notably that of Möller, Griffith, Sethe, Gunn and Gardiner, have resulted in an ability to read most Egyptian texts with grammatical precision, even when the meaning is not entirely clear to our modern understanding. The greatest lack is in the documents themselves, the texts that have survived being but a fortuitous sampling of the ancient literature. Official inscriptions with historical implications carved in hieroglyphs on temples, stelae and other monuments, are not uncommon for some periods but are almost entirely lacking for others. Funerary and religious texts, often of baffling obscurity, are found written in hieroglyphic and hieratic scripts on temple walls, tomb chambers, coffins and papyrus rolls. A meagre selection of poems and stories has survived from a restricted period, largely because they were set as exercises for schoolboys to copy. Wisdom texts, satires, meditations, lamentations and prophecies also exist. Works of a semi-scientific nature throw light on the ancient understanding of surgery, medicine and mathematics. A single papyrus roll (the Wilbour Papyrus), giving a cadastral survey of Middle Egypt in the 12th century BC, has provided some insight into topography, taxation, the raising of summer crops, land-owning and ancillary matters. Opinions vary whether an incomplete account of a mission to the Lebanon in the 11th century BC to buy cedar wood – the 'Report of Wenamun' – is an official report or a work of fiction. The duties and responsibilities of a vizier are set out in a number of texts inscribed in some tombs of the earlier Eighteenth Dynasty. Other documents record contracts, lawsuits and the findings of royal commissions set up to investigate allegations of tomb-robbing; and a conspiracy in a royal harem. Official and private correspondence, unfortunately all too rare, has also been recovered. A mass of miscellaneous texts, mostly fragmentary, scribbled on flakes of limestone, shards of pottery and scraps of papyrus, or carved as graffiti on rocks and quarry walls, has been instrumental in piecing together all sorts of information relating to the course of history and the life of individuals at various periods.

A free accession of new material is, of course, always required, but further great finds of secular papyri, similar to those from the Theban area during the first half of the last century, seem unlikely; and future studies will have to focus upon a more accurate and intensive study of the documents already to hand. Unexpected discoveries can be made in such unpromising fields as accounts, receipts and lists of various sorts. The recent accurate publication, mostly by the scholars of the French Institute in Cairo, of the voluminous but difficult texts carved on the walls of the great Ptolemaic temples of Upper Egypt, has enabled students to achieve a better understanding of earlier fragments relating to temple architecture and administration, besides much religious mythology and ritual. More meticulous translations of the ancient records have led to new evaluations and interpretations, and the pace of change in our knowledge of ancient Egypt is still brisk.

Explorations and discoveries

From the first, Champollion had realized that the crying need in his time was for more and accurate copies of inscriptions on the monuments still visible in Egypt, and in 1828, with the Italian scholar, Ippolito Rosellini (1800–43), he embarked on a year-long survey. He was followed by others, notably by the great Prussian expedition of Richard Lepsius (1810–84) in 1842–45. A vast store of inscriptional material from Egypt, Nubia and the Sudan was published between 1849 and 1859 in the twelve massive volumes of Lepsius' *Denkmaeler aus Aegypten und Aethiopen*, consisting of plates only. The text appeared posthumously in five volumes between 1897 and 1913. This still remains a fundamental work and will never be entirely superseded as some of the monuments it records have since been destroyed or mutilated. Its accuracy, unhappily, like that of its predecessors, is of a limited kind.

Precise delineation and a sympathetic interpretation are found elsewhere, however, in the work of some other copyists, notably that of Robert Hay (1799–1863) and the team of artists whom he employed during several visits to Egypt before 1838, when they copied monuments and drew plans. Hay's invaluable manuscripts and notes have, unfortunately, never been published except in extracts in other men's works. A similar fate befell the manuscripts

4

4 The great Prussian Expedition, led by Karl-Richard Lepsius from 1842–5, was a supremely well-prepared and equipped operation that made a record of Egyptian and Sudanese sites and monuments that is still of great value. Here, they celebrate the birthday of their king, Friedrich Wilhelm IV, atop the Great Pyramid of Giza.

and drawings of the Breton scholar, Achille Prisse d'Avennes (1807–79), which repose unpublished in the Bibliothèque Nationale in Paris.

Another copyist, who like Hay and Prisse worked for his own delectation, independently of any officially sponsored mission, was John Gardner Wilkinson (1797–1875), who in 1821 went to Egypt for his health's sake, like so many visitors in the 19th century, and spent the next decade there copying and investigating the monuments. The results of his labours were largely embodied in his *Manners and Customs of the Ancient Egyptians* (1837), with its quaint and appealing woodcuts. This work had a considerable influence in popularizing Egyptology among the educated classes of Victorian Britain and is still not without its value.

Later in the century several expeditions shared in the work of recording surface monuments with a progressive degree of accuracy. In particular, the Egypt Exploration Fund (later Society), founded in 1882 by a band of amateurs in Britain who were deeply disturbed at the continuing destruction of the antiquities of Egypt, set itself the task of recording the more important of the extant monuments. The work which Howard Carter, Aylward Blackman and Norman and Nina Davies produced for the Fund is deserving

5

of the highest praise. So no less is the promptitude with which the Fund published these records worthily and inexpensively. Other missions have emulated and sometimes surpassed the standards set by the Fund, even if they have not matched its speed and low costs. The careful copying of monuments is still among the most valuable work undertaken by foreign missions in Egypt, notably by the Oriental Institute of the University of Chicago, and the German and French Institutes in Cairo, in addition to the Egypt Exploration Society, and employs all the resources of photography and other modern techniques for securing and publishing a faithful record. Much, however, still remains to be done in this particular field.

The French expedition of 1798 had set a fashion for visiting Egypt and this burst into more feverish life at the end of the Napoleonic Wars, which had interrupted the tradition of the educational Grand Tour. By 1815 vistas had widened to include the Near East. A curiosity was rekindled about the Levant which had been in abeyance since the cessation of pilgrimages to the Holy Land in the Middle Ages. The spirit of enquiry was also stimulated by a resurgence of piety on the part of European Christendom with its reformed doctrines, evangelical fervour and missionary zeal. Visits to the Biblical Lands became not only an object of idle curiosity but also an act of faith.

At the same time, the Albanian coffee-merchant-turned-soldier, Mohammed Ali (1769–1849), by a combination of ruthless cunning and sheer ability had made himself master of Egypt, suppressed the Mameluke beys, already defeated by Napoleon, and won a virtual independence from his Turkish overlord in Istanbul. His rule was marked by the creation of an effective army, the expansion of Egypt into Asia and the Sudan, and

5 The priest Userhet, his wife and mother, sit under the shade of a sycamore-fig in Paradise, while the goddess of the tree offers them a platter of dainties and pours cool draughts of water into their cups. The bird-souls of the deceased hover above them or drink water from a T-shaped pool.

improvements in irrigation-works and agriculture. As he and his successors became more Westernized, many European doctors, engineers, bankers, merchants, missionaries and the like were assisting in the travail of Egypt as a modern power.

But some of these accoucheurs were also interested in the antiquities that since the French expedition and the discovery of the Rosetta Stone had awakened Europe to the importance of actual objects as well as the inscriptions upon them. Even before Champollion had discovered how hieroglyphs should be read, the consuls of the various powers, particularly Henry Salt (1780–1827) of Britain and Bernardino Drovetti (1775–1852) of France, together with their agents, were vying with each other in amassing bigger and better *antikas*. It was this rivalry that filled the museums of London, Leyden, Paris, Turin and other cities of Europe with huge monuments which even today give the layman almost his only acquaintance with Egyptian antiquity. During this period of 'unbridled pillage' almost as much was destroyed as was preserved. Tombs were opened with battering-rams or gunpowder; precious written records were reduced to disjointed scraps; hardly anything was secured with its pedigree intact. Into this spoiling of the ancient Egyptians their descendants entered with as much zest as anyone, being only too eager to sell chance finds that they neither understood nor cherished. In the process, antiquities were divided among several collectors, the head of a statue being acquired by one agent and the body by his rival. Papyri were cut up and the parts sold separately, thereafter to live apart for ever. Mohammed Ali, too, was not averse to bestowing gigantic monuments, such as colossi and obelisks, upon foreign powers that he wished to favour, on the understanding that they would go to the trouble and expense of removing them.

In 1854 an event occurred which was to have far-reaching effects on the rediscovery of the Egyptian past. A young French official of the Louvre, Auguste Mariette (1821–81), was commissioned to go to Egypt and collect Coptic manuscripts, but while on a visit to Saqqara, thinking that he recognized half-buried in the sands monuments which seemed to mark an ancient site described by Strabo, coolly renounced his mission and 'almost furtively' began to dig. This enterprise, which took him four years to complete, uncovered the vast Serapeum (the tomb of the sacred Apis bulls) and greatly enriched the Louvre with antiquities of different periods. It also sealed his destiny, for in 1858 the Khedive Said appointed him conservator of monuments, and thereafter his life was dedicated to the excavation and preservation of the antiquities of Egypt on her own soil. The creation and development of an antiquities service to promote and regulate proper archaeological exploration and the establishing of a national museum to display, conserve, and facilitate the study of Egyptian antiquities, were the life-work of Mariette, who relentlessly carried out his mission in the face of obstacles from all sides – the intrigues of dealers and officials who were doing well out of the unregulated sale of *antikas*, the jealousies of other scholars

6 Seated statue of Ramesses II, made early in his reign, wearing the Blue Crown and holding the crook sceptre: acquired by J. J. Rifaud for Drovetti, from Karnak. Nefertari, the chief queen of Ramesses, appears on a smaller scale by his left leg and their son (not shown) by his right leg.

who thought they could do better, and the indifference and treachery of the Khedive himself. The frustrations that Mariette suffered in his work would have broken the health and spirit of a lesser man; and in his energy and resilience, he may be said to have met fully the challenge of his time.

Mariette's innovations were in the spheres of policy and administration. His methods are indistinguishable from those of his rivals; too much was attempted and his resources dissipated among too many sites; supervision was poor, inadequate field-notes were kept and very little was published. While Mariette's labours cannot be under-estimated, much of what he achieved would have been lost if his immediate successor, another

Frenchman, Gaston Maspero (1846–1916), had not followed him as director-general in 1881. Maspero's long and diplomatic though interrupted tenure of office saw the firm consolidation of the shaky foundations of the antiquities service and the training of Egyptians to play an increasing part in its concerns. The building of a worthy museum and the proper publishing of results were also actively pursued.

By the eighties of the century, the exertions of such scholars, and their works of popularization, had created new patrons of Egyptology – the educated middle classes of Europe and America, many of whom had visited the Nile Valley, and who banded together in learned societies, were prepared to give the financial support that hitherto had been provided only by wealthy individuals or state coffers. A lot of this good was done by stealth; and it was thought desirable to confront a public, brought up with a deep reverence for the Classics and the Bible, with aims that would arouse an immediate response. Thus the prime object of the newly created Egypt Exploration Fund was to excavate in Egypt 'with a view to the further elucidation of the History and Arts of Ancient Egypt, and to the illustration of the Old Testament narrative . . . also to explore sites connected with early Greek History.'

These latter objectives were faithfully observed in the early expeditions of the Fund which in 1884 commissioned for their explorations at Tanis a comparatively unknown surveyor, Flinders Petrie (1853–1942), who was destined to revolutionize the technique of excavation in Egypt. Petrie was a man of no systematic education but with the most remarkable natural gifts which he dedicated entirely during his long lifetime to the pursuit of Egyptian and Palestinian archaeology. Applying the principles of excavation first invented in Britain by General Pitt-Rivers, and developing them in an Egyptian *milieu*, he broke entirely with the traditions of the old *déblayeurs*, who were concerned only with uncovering substantial buildings from encroaching sands, or moving colossal monuments into museums. He paid attention to the many unconsidered trifles that had previously been overlooked or despised, the scribbles on potsherds, the broken bits of amulets and rings, fragments of crude domestic pottery, loose beads, discarded drill cores, all the dross and rubbish of antiquity; and he showed that in their context they had a story to tell. Many of his innovations are now so much the accepted practice of field archaeology that it is difficult to believe that they were once revolutionary, such as the use of melted wax to secure fragile objects *in situ*; or the discovery of foundation deposits as a means of dating buildings and defining their limits even when they have been razed to the ground; or the study of the stylistic development and degeneration of artifacts as a means of dating; indeed the typology of such things as weapons, pottery, stone vessels and beads owes a great deal to him. For half a century he followed the routine of excavating a site in the winter months and publishing the results in the following summer. His publications are an almost inexhaustible mine of information and are indispensable despite the faults occasioned by haste and often the exercise of a too imaginative leap to conclusions. In his time he trained two generations of excavators, most of whom he outlived, and his methods were adopted and developed by others.

The techniques followed by Petrie and his pupils revolutionized fieldwork in Egypt and have resulted in considerable refinement in excavation methods, requiring the collaboration of several specialists and the incorporation of statistical analyses in the marshalling of data. The computer is now inevitably being recruited for much of this work. New exploration is likely to involve urgent rescue-work on sites threatened by extinction, or sondages aimed at confirming earlier conclusions, or resolving problems of interpretation. A great deal, in fact, still requires to be done; almost the whole of the prehistoric period, for instance, demands expert investigation, and the need for skilled archaeologists is as clamant as ever.

In recent years, a number of new approaches have come upon the scene, above and beyond traditional excavation. A much greater emphasis is now placed upon survey methods, in which the maximum information is gained from an area without the destruction inherent to excavation, although this of course remains a fundamental means of recovering an ancient site. A means of penetrating below the surface without even lifting a trowel exists in various remote-sensing techniques, such as resistivity measurement. These detect anomalies below the ground that can indicate the presence of buildings, tombs and other features. They have been successfully applied in the Valley of the Kings, Saqqara and a number of other locations; at Memphis, drill cores across the locality have taught us vast amounts about the development of that great city.

Yet more 'new' approaches include ethnoarchaeology and experimental archaeology. These harness the observation of modern handling of archaic problems, and practical attempts to reproduce ancient results. The British expedition to Tell el Amarna under Barry J. Kemp has seen much work in these directions, including the brewing of ancient Egyptian beer, following the excavation of a brewery, sponsored by a modern British equivalent.

Changes in the Egyptian antiquities service's regulations in 1936 led to a reduction in the number of foreign missions working in the country, with their activities effectively stopped by the outbreak of war three years later. Egyptian archaeologists, on the other hand, made some important discoveries between 1939 and 1945 and in subsequent years. Foreign work was, however, slow in recommencing owing to post-war economic difficulties, the political problems that followed the Egyptian revolution and the Suez Crisis of 1956, and the case of an American excavator's alleged theft of antiquities from his site at Dahshur in 1957.

In 1960, however, the threat to the ancient sites in Nubia and the Sudan that arose through the proposed creation of a vast lake behind the High Dam at Aswan in 1971 induced the authorities to relax their conditions, and foreign missions were cordially invited to take part in a crash programme to rescue the doomed monuments. Much of the old fruitful co-operation between the foreign expeditions and the native antiquities services was restored. International experts collaborated in recording and moving the threatened temples, and other monuments, to places of safety. Other missions excavated sites threatened by total immersion, uncovering new information in the process, and publishing their results. In return, they received a proportion of the finds not retained by the national museums in Cairo and Khartoum. Important antiquities from other sites in Egypt and some of the dismantled temples from the threatened riverine area were offered in return for the services rendered. In this way, for example, the shrine of Pedesi and Pihor from Dendur has been re-erected in New York, and a colossal sandstone head of Akhenaten from Karnak is now proudly displayed in the Louvre. Such co-operation has happily continued since this huge rescue operation, and continues to be welcomed in view of fresh threats to the ancient sites in Egypt itself, with the rapid encroachment of agriculture and industrialization, not to mention the general rise in subsoil water as a result of perennial irrigation.

There are still aspects of the Egyptian heritage, however, both ancient and medieval that arouse concern. It is not sufficient to excavate with skill and record with accuracy. Publication and conservation are also important; and the antiquities rescued from oblivion must be made readily available for exhibition and study. Such obligations which Egypt shares with other advanced nations are a drain upon resources. The Egyptian Museum is now badly crowded and its material in store not easily accessible. The same conditions prevail at the many local magazines scattered on the important sites, despite the building of a fine new museum at Luxor. The monuments themselves are suffering from the constant attentions of thousands of visitors and a rise in industrial pollution. A number of recent earthquakes have also undermined the structures of certain monuments, and flash floods caused further damage to Theban tombs. Yet another threat is posed by the astronomical prices commanded by Egyptian artifacts on the international art market. High-level corruption has seen scenes cut from the walls of sealed and protected monuments, to re-emerge shorn of all identifying features in the salerooms of Europe, America and Japan.

On a brighter note, the new Nubian Museum at Aswan should soon open its doors to visitors and, after many false starts, the site for a new museum has been acquired near the Pyramids of Giza. Built to the highest modern display standards, it will complement rather than replace the old museum in the centre of Cairo, which will become more of a study centre. The funding for this, however, remains a problem in a country struggling with poverty and over-population. Only with the full co-operation and goodwill of the international community can this, and other, projects to safeguard Egypt's heritage come to full fruition – co-operation which is owed to a land that possesses so much of mankind's cultural patrimony.

2 · The ancient places

Sudan and Nubia

The heavy monsoon rains that fall on the Abyssinian tableland each year from May to September swell the waters of the Blue Nile and change it into an immense mountain torrent, rising in spate and sweeping all before it. The raging flood grinds the boulders in its bed and carries the finer red-brown silt in suspension for thousands of miles. At the modern town of Khartoum, the Blue Nile is joined by the White Nile which flows from the natural reservoir of the great lakes of Central Africa and provides a steady flow of clear water throughout the summer months. Almost 200 miles north of Khartoum the last great tributary, the Atbara, rising in the Abyssinian plateau, pours its flood into the Nile during the rainy season. At other times it shrinks into a number of pools within its sandy bed. By the middle of June the inundation formerly reached Aswan and continued to rise in Egypt until the beginning of September when it slowly fell, and had disappeared by the following spring. This is the river system which the Egyptians since prehistoric times have tried to control, and which they have only succeeded in taming with the recent building of the Aswan High Dam.

From the Atbara northwards, the main stream flows in a vast sweep between tawny hills of Nubian sandstone. Its passage through this hot, fly-bitten region, is impeded at five major points by reefs of hard igneous stone, polished black by the action of sun and spray, and forming the cataracts or turbulent rapids amid craggy islands. Between the Fourth and Third Cataracts stands Gebel Barkal, the southernmost boundary of Egypt at the time of its greatest expansion in the New Kingdom when the dependencies of Wawat (Nubia) and Kush (the lower Sudan) were under the charge of an Egyptian 'prince' or viceroy, appointed by the pharaoh. From here northwards lie the sand-engulfed ruins of the outposts of empire which the Egyptians built at this period at Sesebi, Sulb and Amara.

About 15 miles north of this point, the traveller reaches the southernmost shore of Lake Nasser, the great artificial lake that has been formed by damming the Nile near Aswan, 300 miles to the north. Lake Nasser has drowned all the ancient sites on the banks of the Nile and effectively expunged Nubia from the map of Africa. Many of the visible monuments, such as the two great speos (rock-cut) temples at Abu Simbel, have been removed to higher ground in various enclaves, or to the museum precincts

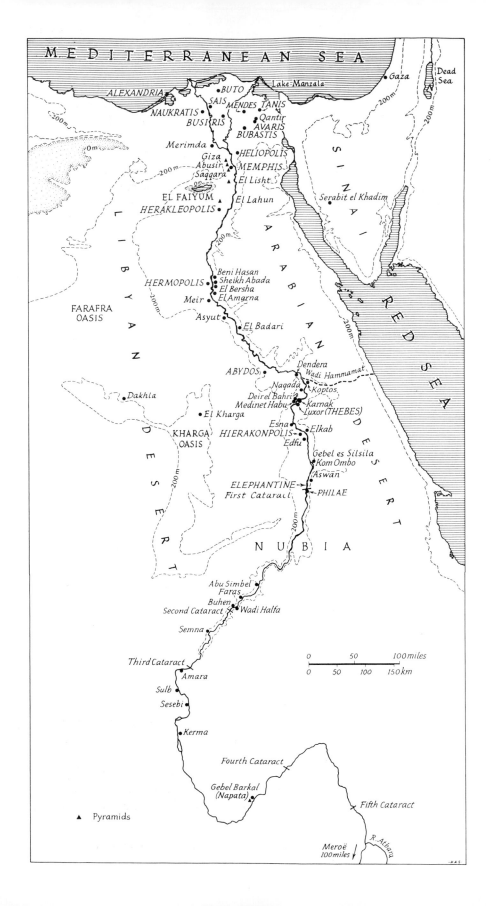

MEDITERRANEAN SEA

Gaza

Dead Sea

Lake Manzala

ALEXANDRIA
BUTO
SAIS
MENDES TANIS
NAUKRATIS
Qantir
BUSIRIS
AVARIS
BUBASTIS

Merimda
HELIOPOLIS

Giza
Abusir
MEMPHIS
Saqqara
El Lisht

EL FAIYUM
El Lahun
HERAKLEOPOLIS

Serabit el Khadim

Beni Hasan
HERMOPOLIS
Sheikh Abada
El Bersha
Meir
El Amarna
Asyut
El Badari

FARAFRA OASIS

ABYDOS
Dendera
Wadi Hammamat
Dakhla
Naqada
Koptos
Deir el Bahri
Medinet Habu
Karnak
El Kharga
Luxor (THEBES)

Esna
Elkab
KHARGA OASIS
HIERAKONPOLIS
Edfu
Gebel es Silsila
Kom Ombo
Aswan

ELEPHANTINE
First Cataract
PHILAE

N U B I A

Abu Simbel
Faras
Buhen
Second Cataract
Wadi Halfa
Semna

Third Cataract
Amara
Sulb
Sesebi

Kerma

Fourth Cataract

Gebel Barkal
(Napata)
Fifth Cataract

Meroë
100 miles

R. Atbara

MEDITERRANEAN SEA

LIBYAN   DESERT

ARABIAN   DESERT

SINAI

RED SEA

0   50   100 miles
0   50   100   150 km

▲ Pyramids

at Khartoum and elsewhere. Only the Egyptologist keeps alive any remembrance of the seven great mudbrick forts which the Egyptians built in the Second Cataract, all the way from Semna-South to Buhen near Wadi Halfa, to protect their southern frontier and to regulate the import of tropical products from Central Africa during the Middle Kingdom. The only vestiges of them that now remain are two reconstructed stone garrison chapels at Khartoum, and at Berlin two stelae and scraps of papyrus despatches that the commanders sent to each other as situation reports. The ruins of these trading forts, with their massive walls of mud brick, have now disintegrated under 10 m of Nile water.

Upper Egypt

About 4 miles south of Aswan, the northern extremity of Lake Nasser is marked by the High Dam opened in 1971. From this giant reservoir the Nile, now carefully controlled, flows into the channel that it has worn throughout the ages in a great sill of granite, which interrupts the broad mass of Nubian sandstone. The action of the water has eroded the granite barrier into a string of rocky islands of which Elephantine is the most northerly. In this frontier region of granite outcrops and rocks sculptured by the swirl of the rapids into fanciful abstract shapes, inscriptions cut into the stone mark the passage of ancient viceroys and other officials to and from their seats of government further south, and give imperfect echoes of the march of events in this region and far beyond it.

Many of the graffiti were carved with propitiatory prayers to the gods of the cataract by travellers anxiously preparing to undertake the hazardous passage of the rapids, or to set off along the desert road on the western bank so as to by pass the river barriers. Other graffiti commemorate the successful completion of great works in the quarries of the vicinity, such as the extraction of obelisks and colossi. Not a few of the inscriptions, which vary from mere scribbles to handsome stelae, give valuable historical data.

The granites, basalts and quartzites of the Aswan region have always been the main sources of hard stone in Egypt. Impressive evidence of the ancient workings is found in the northern quarry on the east bank where an unfinished obelisk still lies undetached in its giant trench. It is over 41 m long and weighs some 1170 tons, i.e. six times as much as the 'Cleopatra's Needle' on the Thames embankment in London. A series of fissures in the granite matrix, which were only revealed as the work reached a late stage, obliged the engineers to abandon their project. Massive monuments that were even heavier, such as the colossus of Ramesses II in his mortuary temple, or another at Tanis, were successfully extracted and moved hundreds of miles to the north.

8

The quarrying operations were important to the east bank which also had the function, like so many frontier settlements, of acting as an entrepot and customs house for imports from the south. The name of Aswan derives from

7 (left) Sketch map of Egypt and Nubia showing the main sites (Greek place-names are in capitals, modern Arabic names in lower case type).

the Egyptian word for a 'trade' or 'market' and indeed a *suq* of sorts still exists in the town.

The natural political and defensive boundary was on the island of Elephantine in the middle of the river just below the cataract. This was the southernmost extent of Egypt proper. 'From Elephantine to the marshes of the Delta' was the Egyptian equivalent of 'from Dan to Beersheba', and it was proverbial that a native from the island would be unintelligible to the marsh-dwellers, probably because he would speak the Nubian language which, with the Nubian race, still persists as far as Gebel es Silsila to the north.

Elephantine maintained a frontier fortress and a garrison from early times. A Jewish cohort was stationed here during Persian times in the 6th century BC, and got on bad terms with the local populace through religious disputes, as we learn from Aramaic papyri found on the site. In the later Old Kingdom (*c.* 2663–2195 BC), the pharaoh's peace was kept by the local barons who bore the title of Keeper of the Gateway of the South. These marcher lords are among the earliest African explorers who have left any account of their adventures. They led trading caravans and punitive expeditions far into the southern hinterland and recorded some of their experiences in the tombs which they built for themselves along a hill terrace on the western bank. Thus we read of the exploits of Harkhuf, who brought back a dancing pygmy to the delight of his young king; and of Sabni, who set out to recover the body of his father, Mekhu, slain on another expedition, and when he succeeded, buried him in a tomb next to his own.

As the southern boundary was pushed further south in the Middle and New Kingdoms, the importance of Elephantine as a frontier fortress declined, though it rose again to pre-eminence when the provinces of Nubia and Kush were lost at the end of the New Kingdom (*c.* 1064 BC). It was, however, always renowned for its religious significance. The Nile was believed to well up every year from a cavern beneath the island to produce the inundation, and this miracle was accomplished by a ram-head aspect of the Creator, the god Khnum, who ruled the entire cataract region and, indeed, other localities on the Nile where the water was impeded by rocks or other obstructions. He was accompanied by two goddesses to form a triad, his consort Satis, and his daughter Anukis who was mistress of the large island of Seheil with its quarries, temples and numerous graffiti. A restored Nilometer with its calibrated steps leading down from the high bank to the low water-level still bears witness to the importance of Elephantine in the use of the Nile flood.

It was customary in the Eighteenth Dynasty, at least, for kings to celebrate their second jubilees by erecting little peripteral temples on Elephantine in honour of the Khnum triad. An example built by Amenophis III in the 14th century BC was still standing almost intact when the French expedition visited the island in AD 1799. Twenty years later it had been demolished to provide stone for a new quay. Pillars from similar shrines with the names of

8 (*left*) A granite obelisk, still lying attached to its bed in the north quarry at Aswan. As work progressed, fissures were revealed that would have made its removal in one piece impossible. Eventually abandoned, the obelisk probably dates to the reign of Tuthmosis III, and may have been the intended mate of the 'single obelisk' eventually erected by Tuthmosis IV at Karnak.

9 (*right*) Relief of the Creator in his aspect of Khnum, the ram-headed god of the Cataract, who controlled the Inundation of the Nile, embracing Tuthmosis IV.

Amenophis II and Tuthmosis IV can be seen in the foundations of the temple at the southern end of the island where various kings have added their constructions over several centuries, the most recent being that of the Emperor Trajan. By this time, however, Elephantine had lost its primacy as the seat of the inundation to the island of Bigga, 8 miles to the south, where tradition affirmed that the left leg of the god Osiris had been buried, and where his tomb was situated. The drowned Osiris was believed to float in the Nile at each flood time when he became the 'Lord of the Inundation'. The legend was fostered by the presence of the cult of Isis, the wife of Osiris, on the adjacent island of Philae which became the centre of the cult of Isis and the Horus-child, and a place of pilgrimage for her worshippers throughout the Roman world.

The temples on Philae, now rebuilt on the adjacent island of Agilkia, are the first of a series of magnificent stone buildings that arose on ancient foundations at Kom Ombo, Edfu and Esna in Ptolemaic and Roman times as far as Dendera 115 miles to the north. These vast edifices in their huge proportions, their unstinted use of sandstone and granite, their elaborate floriated capitals, their astronomical ceilings, their scrupulous detail and technical triumphs, have a solemn grandeur. They were built according to an architectural plan which was supposed to have been revealed in a codex that fell from heaven at Saqqara in the days of Imhotep. The most complete

10 of them is the temple of the falcon god Horus at Edfu, built between 237 and 57 BC, the most perfectly preserved monument of the ancient world. Its many inscriptions have bequeathed a wealth of information about the founding of such temples, their construction and use, the daily ritual, the festivals and their dates, the duties of the various priests, even the dimensions of each chamber, its name and purpose, besides myths of very ancient origin.

11 Its companion temple of the goddess Hathor at Dendera was linked to Edfu by a new-year festival. Amid scenes of wild rejoicing on both banks of the river, the image of Hathor was brought in her gilded barge, like Cleopatra in her meeting with Antony on the Cydnus, to repose in the birth-temple at Edfu. As a result of this union, a divine child, Horus, Uniter of Upper and Lower Egypt, was engendered. The temple of Dendera deeply impressed the French expedition, and through the engravings in their *Description* influenced the design of contemporary architecture and the applied arts. Unfortunately, however, the reliefs on these temples are ill-

10 Colonnaded court of the Temple of Horus at Edfu, showing the rear of the two great towers of the entrance pylon lacking their cornices. Begun in 237 BC by Ptolemy III, it was completed by Ptolemy XIII, having taken 180 years to build.

11 The Temple of Dendera was dedicated to the worship of the goddess Hathor, whose symbol the sistrum (cf. ill. 128) forms the design of the columns in its hypostyle halls. The main structure, which goes back in its origins to the reign of Pepy II, was rebuilt by the Ptolemies and Emperors, and work was still in progress in the reign of Diocletian.

proportioned, a lifeless interpretation of traditional formulae copied as an esoteric mystery. The hieroglyphic texts, too, are ugly and congested, the 'typography' is confused and the individual signs distorted to mere ornamentation.

At Edfu the yellow Nubian sandstone gives way to the pinkish nummulitic limestone from which the Nile has scoured its ancient bed, and for the next 350 miles the river flows between verges of rich alluvial soil hemmed in on both sides by arid desolation. On the west lies the Western or Libyan Desert, an immense eroded tableland broken by lines of shifting sand-hills and by a string of fertile depressions which run almost parallel to the Nile. These oases are watered by subterranean wells supplied from the Nile water-table and their inhabitants have traded their produce with Egypt from earliest times.

The Arabian desert on the east presents an awe-inspiring landscape as it thrusts a protective range of barren mountains rising to over 2000 m between the Nile Valley and the Red Sea. It is scored by deep *wadis*, or dry water-courses, which on occasions can become raging torrents as sudden and violent storms break out over the desert hills especially in winter. During such occurrences, rainwater may collect in natural cisterns, and a rich desert flora develops rapidly and carpets the stony ground for a season until scorched to extinction again. A number of springs, too, support a sparse vegetation and make a scanty subsistence possible for the flocks of the wandering bedouin. Protected by these inhospitable deserts Egypt exists for most of its length as a narrow strip of cultivated land, seldom more than 7 miles in width and often much less.

A dozen miles north of Edfu, at Kom el Ahmar and Elkab, lie the ruins of the twin cities Nekhen and Nekheb, on opposite banks of the Nile, which together probably formed the capital of Upper Egypt in prehistoric times. The former site was first dug at the end of the 19th century, and revealed antiquities of the highest importance in the study of the Predynastic and Archaic Periods. A long-term programme of work still underway has greatly expanded our knowledge of the growth of what was one of the very earliest of Egyptian cities. Named Hierakonpolis by the Greeks, the town had a falcon god as its local deity, and may have been the natal town of the kings who were ultimately to unite Egypt. Elkab, on the other hand, was presided over by a vulture, Nekhebet ('she-of-Nekheb'), who came to be regarded as the patron genius of the whole of Upper Egypt and is frequently associated with her counterpart, the cobra goddess Edjo of Buto and Lower Egypt in heraldic devices.

Elkab is notable for its stout walls of mud brick still standing, though the considerable space that they enclose, larger than the town site, is something of an enigma. Here too in the eastern hills are tombs of worthies who during the 16th century BC played an important part in the wars of their Theban overlords against the Hyksos power in the far north. Texts inscribed on their chapel walls and two of their statues are valuable records of the early Eighteenth Dynasty. The most impressive of the tombs, however, despite some ancient and modern damage, is that of Paheri dating to the early reign of Tuthmosis III. Its carefully sculptured low reliefs, which still retain much

12

12 The cliffs behind the city of Elkab were first employed for the burial of local grandees in the Twelfth Dynasty. This practice increased in the Thirteenth–Seventeenth Dynasties, with which the local governors had close links. The most famous tomb is that of Paheri, who was mayor during the reigns of Tuthmosis II and III. Like most tombs in the necropolis, it comprises a single room, decorated in painted low-relief, in this case showing oxen ploughing the fields.

13 The Great Temple of Amun at Karnak, looking westward across the Sacred Lake. To the left are the south buildings, comprising Pylons VII to X, while on the right is the obelisk of Hatshepsut, the Hypostyle Hall and, in the distance, Pylon I.

of their colour, give interesting scenes from Paheri's life as governor of the locality, but are more remarkable for the amusing, even punning, captions to the various incidents represented, including a jingle, first identified by Champollion, that the herdsmen sing as they drive the cattle around the threshing-floor – 'Thresh away, oxen tread the grain faster: straw for yourselves, corn for your master.'

Thebes

From Elkab the Nile describes a huge S-bend as far as Koptos, about 120 miles farther north, and almost midway between these two points on the east bank stands the modern town of Luxor, which with the adjoining village of Karnak and other localities forms the site of Thebes, the southern capital at the period of Egypt's greatest development during the New Kingdom. To Belzoni, the Italian adventurer, who acted as the agent of the British Consul Henry Salt early in the 19th century, the remains of Karnak and Luxor were 13 like those of 'a city of giants, who after long conflict were all destroyed, leaving the ruins of their various temples as the only proofs of their former existence.' After more than a century of clearances and excavations, the picture is still true, and though much as been uncovered, cleaned and restored, a great deal remains to be investigated and interpreted.

It is, however, on the west bank, with its many ruined temples and ceme- 14 teries, that the most intensive exploration has been made during the past century. It is from these realms of the dead that the bulk of the antiquities have come that grace the collections of Europe, America and Egypt itself.

14 The First Pylon of the mortuary temple of Ramesses III at Thebes, its cornice destroyed, with the slots for the twin flag poles visible on each side of the entrance. The main relief on the northern tower shows the king wearing the Red Crown of Lower Egypt sacrificing northern foes to Re-Herakhty, as the god of Lower Egypt. On the southern tower, the king wearing the White Crown slaughters southern enemies before Amun-Re as the patron god of Upper Egypt. The decoration of Egyptian temples was carefully orientated.

So many documents from this same source have contributed to our view of the Egyptian past that we are now in danger of interpreting Egyptian history with a distinctly Theban bias.

At Thebes the flanking hills on each bank retire to leave a wide belt of cultivation and even the sober Baedeker is moved to a lyrical appreciation of the scene:

> The verdant crops and palms which everywhere cheer the traveller as soon as he has quitted the desert, the splendid hues that tinge the Valley every morning and evening, the brilliant, unclouded sunshine that bathes every object even in the winter season, lend to the site of Ancient Thebes the appearance of a wonderland, richly endowed with the gifts of never-failing fertility.

Perhaps it was the luminous quality of the atmosphere in this locality that induced the Thebans to conceive of Amun, their city god, as having sovereignty over air and light. A Theban poet under Ramesses II wrote a series of poems in praise of the city and its god, but gets carried away by his theme and makes the unsupportable claim that it is the most ancient city in the world.

Thebes rose to prominence only in the Middle Kingdom when its local princes fought their way to supreme power and ruled as pharaohs over a reunited Egypt. Throughout its history Thebes remained a centre of resistance to alien rule from the north. After the expulsion of the Hyksos by its princes, it won great prestige and wealth as the birthplace of the new dynasts. It was here that the pharaohs now had their tombs hewn in the rock of a lonely wadi on the west bank, the Valley of the Kings, dominated by a pyramidal hill, 'The Peak'. The wadi was used for the burials of kings from Tuthmosis I down to the end of the Twentieth Dynasty, when Ramesses XI left his tomb unfinished there. In addition, during the Eighteenth Dynasty, a number of very favoured private individuals were granted burial chambers there, although their mortuary chapels remained amongst those of their peers, on hillsides facing the Nile. These chapels, which honeycomb the hills, together with many burial chambers, are of great importance, as their painted walls have bequeathed us some memorial of their names and many lively scenes of contemporary life and aspirations.

During the Nineteenth and Twentieth Dynasties, a few members of the king's family were also buried in the valley, although most were interred in a new Valley of the Queens, some way to the south. However, amongst these princely tombs in the Valley of the Kings was the largest rock tomb ever cut in Egypt. Made for the sons of Ramesses II, KV 5 contains over a hundred chambers, even though much of the sepulchre remains uncleared (1997).

All the pharaohs' tombs in the Valley of the Kings were pillaged at various times during the New Kingdom itself, especially towards the end of the period, with one exception: that of Tutankhamun escaped anything more than superficial robbery, and survived to be discovered in 1922. The despoiled bodies of other royalties were hidden away by officials in two mass burials, two of which were only discovered in the 19th century; interestingly, it appears that these very same officials were responsible for relieving the tombs of what precious material remained in them before transferring their occupants to places of safety.

The mortuary temples which complemented the royal tombs stood in a row a mile away in the plain, facing the Nile and overlooked by the tomb-chapels of the nobility. They stretch from Gurna in the north to Medinet Habu in the south, and include those of almost all pharaohs from the early Eighteenth Dynasty down to the latter part of the Twentieth, by which time the king was permanently resident in the Delta. While a few are well preserved, most were dismantled in antiquity as their cults failed, leaving in some cases only scanty foundations and fragmentary reliefs and sculpture.

The rise of Thebes naturally increased the influence and wealth of Amun, whose great temple at Karnak became a sort of national shrine to which kings of all subsequent periods added their chapels and endowments. The brief but momentous reign of the so-called heretic pharaoh Akhenaten in the 14th century BC encouraged the eclipse of the many local gods of Egypt in favour of his sole god, the Aten: but none suffered more grievously than the wealthy Amun whose images were smashed, whose shrines were desecrated and whose priests were dispersed. Amun, however, recovered, though slowly, under subsequent kings; and in time his estate became the most wealthy of institutions, exercising considerable power in the land, particularly Upper Egypt, until late times.

Even early in the Eighteenth Dynasty, Thebes had ceased to be the pharaoh's chief residence, and thereafter it gradually became the holy city of Amun, the king of the gods, and therefore a focus for pilgrimages. In the ancient world the feasts of the gods were momentous affairs of which the modern Christian Easter and Christmas are but echoes. The celebrations of the festivals of Amun were sufficiently important to bring rulers to Thebes to take part in these joyous events. Thus the feast of Opet, during which the Amun triad were towed in their resplendent barges, amid rejoicings on both canal banks, from Karnak to Luxor during the second month of Inundation, was an occasion when the god gave oracular judgments on human affairs not capable of resolution by normal means. Several kings found it expedient to attend these events when their assumption of power, or nomination to the throne, received divine approval. A faint echo of the occasion survives in the annual trundling of the boat of the local saint, Sheikh Abu'l Haggag, from his mosque in the Luxor temple, around the town on a horse-drawn cart.

The west bank at Thebes was also within the domain of Amun, who had first manifested himself at the creation of the world in the form of the primeval snake, Kneph, residing in an underground cavern at Medinet Habu. The barque of Amun, containing his veiled image or fetish, was taken across the river in the second month of summer for a festival commemorated every year at Deir el Bahri, and every decade at Medinet Habu. Thus Amun of Thebes united the world of the living on the east bank and the realms of the dead on the west. But in the latter region, he also shared his power with the goddess Hathor, the patroness of the deserts in which the necropoleis were situated. She was manifest as a wild cow, or a comely queen wearing cow's horns on her crown, and her image is encountered frequently in the temples and tombs of Western Thebes.

The sunset of Thebes was long and blood red. In the 7th century BC it was sacked by the Assyrians. The Persians under Cambyses assailed it a century and a half later. Under the Ptolemies, the rival centre of Ptolemais eclipsed it in power and privilege, though it recovered some self-esteem for a time during the rebellion against Ptolemy V. It again revolted under Ptolemy X and was recaptured after a lengthy siege which wrought great damage. Undeterred by its unlucky fate, it opposed the oppressive rule of the Romans in 30 BC and was thoroughly devastated for its pains. Of the 'hundred gated Thebes' mentioned by Homer, only a dozen damaged pylons among the temple ruins now remain.

Abydos

Some 100 miles north of Thebes as the Nile flows, lies Abydos, the next ancient site of importance, near the modern village of el Araba in an area which is rich in prehistoric cemeteries. Somewhere within its bounds, probably near Girga, was This, the seat of the immediate ancestors of the first pharaohs. The kings of the First Dynasty built their tombs and associated funerary enclosures there, surrounded by the graves of their retainers. The royal tombs themselves, whose sequence begins before the unification, comprised brick-lined chambers, in pits and with minimal superstructures. Over a mile away, however, huge panelled enclosures of mud-brick enclosed structures associated with the funerary rituals, and provided the prototypes for later royal mortuary buildings.

The local god was originally a black dog-like animal known as the 'Chief of the Westerners', i.e. the Lord of the Dead; but by the Eleventh Dynasty, his position and titles had been entirely absorbed by another god, Osiris, who was probably a human manifestation of the same chthonic power. Osiris is represented as a king in his mummy wrappings, wearing the characteristic conical White Crown of Upper Egypt. As a death god of Upper Egypt he was identified with similar deities in Lower Egypt, such as the falcon headed Sokar who gave his name to the necropolis of Memphis at Saqqara, where he existed in a cavernous underworld. As a prehistoric king he also assimilated the similar god Andjeti of Busiris in the Delta, usurping his herdsman's crook and 'flail', and the two tall plumes of his headgear. Andjeti was evidently in origin a deified pastoral chieftain who had been ritually slain by drowning, and his dismembered corpse buried in various parts of the country for its greater fertility. By the middle of the Fifth Dynasty at least, a song sung by peasants as they drove their animals around the threshing floor refers to the Herdsman of the West drowned in the Nile flood and immanent also in the grain that is being trodden out, for Osiris was also a corn-god.

At Abydos, the nome-sign was a beehive-shaped object elevated upon a standard, probably representing the primeval mound that arose from the waters of Chaos in this place at the First Time. It was later reinterpreted as the bewigged reliquary that held the head of the dismembered Osiris, and was surmounted by the two plumes of Andjeti.

Abydos rapidly rose to fame in the Middle Kingdom as Osiris' principal cult-centre, and the place where his mythical tomb was located. The Egyptian antiquarians of the Thirteenth Dynasty, seeking for tangible proofs of the ancient myth, mistook the cenotaph of Djer, the third king of the united Egypt, for the tomb of the god, and so directed to it thereafter the votive offerings of generation after generation of pious pilgrims. The mounds of broken pots that bear witness to their faith have given the locality the modern name of 'Mother of Pots'.

This pilgrimage to the holy city of Abydos became an essential funerary ceremony and those who could not make their tombs near the burial-place of Osiris, had their mummies taken there by boat before entombment and participated in the water festivals that formed part of the Osirian mysteries; or made the journey by proxy. Other devotees contented themselves with

setting up memorial tablets or statuettes in the precincts of the temple of Osiris, thereby assisting in the rituals or religious dramas. Their very modesty has preserved many of these private monuments intact, though the crude methods of recovery practised by Mariette have deprived us of the details of how they were erected.

The royal monuments have suffered more severely, perhaps through iconoclasm in the region of Akhenaten. The best preserved is the celebrated temple of the Osirian triad and the state gods of Egypt built by Sethos I in **15** fine hard limestone which allowed the sculptors of the reliefs full scope for delicate and detailed work of great technical excellence. Its very perfection, however, tends to give an impression of little more than splendid nullity to the subject-matter of the reliefs which are largely concerned with repetitive scenes from the daily ritual, although the chapels of companion Memphite gods, such as Sokar and Nefertem, show some esoteric aspects of the Osirian mysteries in brilliant colour. The additions to the main structure made by Ramesses II in coarser sandstone are far less accomplished.

Immediately behind the rear wall of the temple was a curious sub- **16** terranean complex within a natural tree-girt mound, to which the name of the Osireion has been given in recent times. This construction has as its nucleus a central hall of massive granite monoliths on an island surrounded by a water channel, with emplacements for a sarcophagus and a canopic chest which were probably still lacking on the death of Sethos I. The Osireion is the cenotaph of the king at Abydos, and was evidently made in the form of the mythical tomb of Osiris, with whom he would have been identified on death. Although the completed monument is certainly the

15 (*left*) Relief of Sethos I showing the king on his throne at his coronation carrying the sceptres of a pastoral chieftain, wearing the Atef Crown and supported on one side by Edjo, the cobra goddess of Buto, and on the other by Nekhebet, the vulture goddess of Elkab, both in the guise of elegant queens.

16 The so-called Osireion behind the temple built at Abydos by Sethos I was evidently designed as the cenotaph of the king assimilated to Osiris. It comprises subterranean chambers, inscribed with funerary texts like a contemporary royal tomb, and a great central hall, its roof upheld by ten massive granite piers (cf. ill. 62), and surrounded by a channel filled with water from an underground conduit, so imitating the island on which the mythical tomb of the god was located. The hall was covered by a great mound around which were planted tamarisks in which the soul of Osiris-Sethos could repose.

work of Sethos and certain Nineteenth Dynasty successors, the resemblance of the basic structure to Old Kingdom work has been much remarked. Some scholars are now reverting to an old view that it was indeed an Old Kingdom foundation, rediscovered and rebuilt by Sethos I as his own. Sethos I promoted a restoration of ancient traditions after the collapse of Akhenaten's religious innovations, and associated with the god Osiris in the main temple a number of deified ancestors from Menes the first pharaoh onwards. Not the least valuable feature of these reliefs is the famous Abydos list of seventy-six predecessors whom Sethos considered important or legitimate enough to commemorate.

Middle Egypt and the Faiyum

There could be no greater contrast to this stronghold of orthodoxy than the next great site some 100 miles downstream, the modern Tell el Amarna, the ancient capital of heresy. At this point the flanking cliffs on the eastern bank recede to leave a semi-circular sandy plain about 8 miles in diameter. It was in this amphitheatre that one of the great dramas of ancient Egypt was played out when for scarcely more than a decade it became the residence of King Akhenaten (c. 1360–1343 BC), visionary and religious reformer. Here it was that he was directed by divine guidance in his fifth regnal year to found a great city to his sole god, Re-Herakhty, immanent in the sunlight that streamed from the Aten or disk of the sun. Akhetaten, or Horizon of the Aten, was built, occupied and dedicated to the Aten all within the space of the remaining twelve years of his reign. Here the palaces, temples and official buildings, the mansions of the wealthy and the hovels of the poor, were hastily constructed of mud brick, wood and stone, only to be abandoned by his successor, the young Tutankhamun. Half a century later, when Akhenaten and all his works were execrated as heretical by the kings of the next dynasty, iconoclasts were sent to the desolate site to smash statues of the king and his family, and to obliterate his features and names, and sometimes the name of his god on the temple and tomb reliefs. In the reign of Ramesses II demolition groups squatted among the ruins while they removed the stonework right down to its foundations for use elsewhere, and particularly for the new temples that were being built at Hermopolis across the river.

Despite this brutal destruction in antiquity and even more inexcusable vandalism in modern times, much of the township has survived, even to the ancient chariot roads and the paths tramped into the desert sands by long-dead feet in their walk between residence and place of work. But far less vestigial are the fourteen great stelae hewn into the cliffs that enclose the site on the east and west banks and define its boundaries. On them, beneath scenes of the king and queen worshipping the rayed symbol of the Aten, are carved

18 (right) A view taken soon after its excavation of the central hall in the house of the vizier Nakht at Tell el Amarna. A stone lustration-tank and splash-back can be seen in an inner reception room. The walls and floor were of mud-brick: the red-painted wooden columns that upheld the ceiling were supported on the bases in the foreground.

17 Family scene in a kiosk, showing Akhenaten and Nefertiti, with their three eldest daughters, rejuvenated by the rays of the Aten above them. This relief is in the extreme style of the earlier years of Akhenaten's reign; later work is rather more mature, although it retains the same fundamental principles.

texts, now much damaged and weathered, recounting how Akhenaten came to choose and demarcate the bounds of Akhetaten, and listing the various buildings that he proposed to erect there, such as palaces, temples, a family tomb in the eastern hills, and tombs nearby for his followers.

The other surface monuments at Akhetaten are these same tombs on the eastern bank. Their rock-hewn chapels with their scenes in relief are nearly all incomplete, but still give vivid pictures of the daily life of the royal family at Akhetaten, and are almost our only means of learning of events that happened at this critical and turbulent moment in Egyptian history. In them we catch glimpses of the passing royal pageant, the private and state functions within the palaces, the entertainments by night as well as by day, the reception of foreign embassies bearing rich gifts, the investiture of loyal courtiers

with orders, decorations and other rewards, the daily worship in the temples with lavish offerings made to the Aten under an open sky, and the royal family mourning the early death of an elder daughter.

The buried evidence has proved no less eloquent. Amarna built and abandoned to the desert after a mere twelve years is an archaeologist's paradise with its simple stratigraphy. The most dramatic discovery was made not by a professional excavator but, as is so often the case, by a casual cultivator. In 1887 a local peasant woman digging for *sebakh*, the nitrous fertilizer into which ancient mud brick so often decays, uncovered a cache of some 300 sun-dried clay tablets impressed with cuneiform signs. By the time they were accepted as genuine by the learned world, they had mostly been sold to the museums of Berlin, London and Paris. The hoard had evidently been hidden under the floor of the Bureau for the Correspondence of Pharaoh at the time of the abandoning of Akhetaten, and were part of the discarded despatches sent to the pharaoh from the great kings and vassal princes of Asia during the time the court was in residence at this place.

19

19 Letter from King Ashuruballit I of Assyria to the pharaoh asking that diplomatic relations should be established and reporting the despatch of a chariot and horses as a gift.

A most vivid and scarcely suspected picture has since emerged from the study of these sadly damaged lumps of clay. We see that in the civilized world of the 14th century BC privileged officials, part-couriers, part-legates and part-ambassadors, travelled from one court to another bearing despatches by which marriage treaties were arranged, trade-goods exchanged, extradition requested, diplomatic alliances negotiated, protests submitted, demands made, aid requested, warnings administered, in fact all the features of a sophisticated system of international relations, with its own protocol, which differs little in essence from that of Europe in modern times and suggests an already long development before we catch this fleeting glimpse of it in action.

The chance discovery of the Amarna Letters or Tablets, as they came to be known, brought other investigators to the scene. First Petrie, then the Germans, then the British again have dug over the site and laid a great part of it bare. In the process, much has been learnt about town-planning and domestic architecture in Egypt, but little definite about the course of events during the reign of Akhenaten. Since the 1970s, the Egypt Exploration Society has resumed its investigations on this site.

A most spectacular find was made by the Germans in 1911–12 when they excavated the ruins of sculptor's studios in the central city and found a number of statuettes, plaster casts, sketches and studies which have given us a new appreciation of the scope of Egyptian sculpture and its techniques. Among them was the painted bust of Queen Nefertiti which has since become the most publicized portrait from the ancient world, though not even the many copies and travesties of this masterpiece can lessen the impact that the original makes upon the visitor to Berlin.

Opposite Amarna, on the west bank, lie the remains of Khmunu ('Eight-Town'), a name which survives in the modern Ashmunein, so called from the eight primeval gods present in the waters of Chaos, and later understood as male and female aspects of the abstract qualities that make up the primordial void, namely, eternity, darkness, invisibility and endlessness. But by historic times their worship had been largely displaced by the cult of the moon god, Thoth, the inventor of the lunar calendars of Egypt, the god of learning, writing and calculation, and the divine messenger, whom the Greeks equated with their Hermes, hence the name of Hermopolis which they gave to the place. Ramesses II erected a temple here built of stone largely pillaged from Amarna, the remains of which were excavated by the Germans from 1929 to 1939. A British expedition has investigated earlier foundations in the area, including a shrine of Amenophis III which housed colossal quartzite statues of a squatting baboon, the familiar animal of Thoth.

Khnunu, however, is very much older. In the Middle Kingdom it was the capital city of the 'Hare' province, or *nome*, to use the later Greek word for a province, whose powerful princes held the balance between the Thebaid in the south and the metropolitan power in the north. They made their rock tombs at Deir el Bersha across the river on the east bank. A statue of one of them has been found as far afield as Megiddo in Palestine. The Bahr Yusuf ('the River of Joseph'), which is a branch of the Nile that leaves the main stream on the western bank near Asyut and flows northwest to drain into the lake district of the Faiyum, separates Ashmunein from its necropolis at Tuna el Gebel. This place is a veritable city of the dead dating from Ramesside times, but particularly notable for a free-standing tomb-chapel of 20 Petosiris, a much-travelled high priest of Thoth in the 4th century BC, who evidently called in a Greek to assist in the design of the reliefs on the exterior vestibule. His tomb shows the only notable example to have survived of an attempt to marry Greek and Egyptian conventions of drawing, with somewhat discordant results.

Nearby is a chapel built also as a house for visitors to the tomb of Isadora, a young woman who was drowned in the Nile in the reign of Antoninus Pius

20 The tomb-chapel of Petosiris, the high priest of the local god Thoth of Hermopolis in the 4th century BC. The cosmopolitan taste of Petosiris is seen not only in the design of the chapel as a miniature Egyptian temple (cf. ill. 11), its exterior reliefs revealing Greek influence, but also in the 'horned' Canaanite altar in the forecourt. The tomb of Isadora drowned in the Nile is visible behind, on the left.

in the 2nd century AD, and given a splendid burial at the expense of the local community in conformity with a very ancient tradition mentioned by Herodotus, and demonstrated also in the honours paid to Antinous by Hadrian in the preceding reign.

In following the Nile northwards from Hermopolis, the traveller also journeys back further in time as the predominantly New Kingdom sites of Upper Egypt give way to the Middle and Old Kingdom centres. This region was full of thriving provincial towns during the early Middle Kingdom until a decline following the reign of Sesostris III (c. 1881–1840 BC). At Deir Rifa, Asyut and Meir southwards, and at Beni Hasan northwards, are important quarries, rock tombs and cemeteries of the period which have contributed greatly to our knowledge of Middle Kingdom culture and politics. But a district closely associated with this particular period of Egyptian history lies farther downstream at the Faiyum depression, which is really the most easterly of the string of oases which extend as declivities in the Libyan tableland and are fed from the subterranean waters of the Nile basin. The Faiyum, with its lake, the Birket Qarun, now very much smaller than it was in ancient days, is irrigated by the Bahr Yusuf which enters the depression through a gap in the chain of Libyan hills at el Lahun and divides into innumerable channels to water the whole region.

The Faiyum has been noted from early days for its wonderful fertility and pleasant climate, its vines, olives, wheat and legumes. The earliest Neolithic settlements in Egypt have been found here. The vigorous kings of the Twelfth Dynasty increased its prosperity by improving its irrigation and colonizing the area with new settlements. They built their residences in the vicinity at el Lisht on the frontier between Upper and Lower Egypt. Here

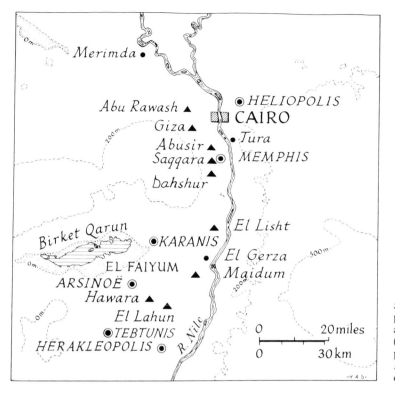

Sketch map of the main pyramid sites of the Old and Middle Kingdoms. (Greek place-names are printed in capitals, modern Arabic names in lower case.)

at el Lahun and Hawara in the Faiyum and further north at Dahshur, they erected their stone and rubble pyramids which have ill resisted the hand of time and the despoiler. Nevertheless, treasures belonging to royal ladies of this dynasty and the next have been recovered from these sites and have bequeathed us a most impressive testimony of the fine taste and superb technical skill of the ancient court jewellers. The Faiyum enjoyed a second period of prosperity during Ptolemaic and Roman times, when it was

22

22 This pectoral of the princess Sithathoryunet, made of gold chased and inlaid with polished carnelian, turquoise and lapis lazuli, is part of a hoard excavated by Petrie and Brunton in a rifled tomb near the pyramid of Sesostris II at Lahun. The design signifies that the divine power that came out of the waters of Chaos is incarnate in the pharaoh.

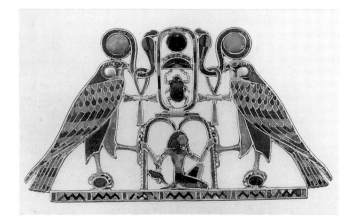

re-colonized by Greek settlers from the officials and soldiery of the Greek and Roman pharaohs. The rubbish mounds and cemeteries of their townships such as Arsinoë, Karanis, Bacchias, Dionysias, Tebtunis and Dime have yielded a great hoard of Greek literary works previously unknown or incomplete, as well as letters, historical and judicial documents and many other records. These discoveries have rejuvenated Classical studies and instituted the science of papyrology.

Near the pyramid of Sesostris II at el Lahun have been found the remains of the walled village that was built, largely of mud brick, for the workmen and officials servicing his pyramid-tomb. Its excavation by Petrie in 1889 brought to light a wealth of domestic equipment and household fittings of the workers and their families who lived there. Fragments of accounts, medical treatises, testaments, census returns and letters written on papyrus showed that it was occupied long after the reign of Sesostris II.

The migration of birds to the reed banks of the Faiyum in winter is still an impressive event, but in antiquity the wealth of pond fowl and fish in the area with its marshes and pools was even more prodigious. The sudden arrival of these creatures at similar times in the year and their migration

23 This is the most opulent version of the theme of the tomb-owner and his family fowling in the marshlands. Here, Nebamun stands in a papyrus skiff holding three egrets as decoys and hurls his unerring throw-stick into the flock of birds. The handsome cat, trained to retrieve the quarry, is also a part of this ideal world of richness and virtuosity.

seemed to the Egyptians miraculous events. Hunting birds with the throw-   23
stick and spearing fish with the bident were not only recreations but of religious significance – the sport of the marsh goddess. A royal palace for
recreation at Gurob in this region was prominent during the Eighteenth
Dynasty, and only declined in favour when roving bands of marauding
Libyans in Ramesside times made the entire district untenable for farmers.

Memphis

The ruined pyramids at the very lower margin of Middle Egypt form the
southernmost end of a chain of such monuments that lie on the west bank
of the Nile and mark the sites of the ancient residence-cities of the Pyramid
Age (c. 2663–2195 BC) all the way to Cairo, and north of it as far as Abu
Rawash. At Dahshur, near the crumbling mud-brick and rubble ruins of
pyramids of the Twelfth Dynasty, and to the south of it at Maidum, are the
earliest stone pyramids of the Old Kingdom. In the neighbourhood of each
pyramid are clustered the *mastaba* tombs of the relatives and officials of their
king (the mastaba being the bench-like superstructure built over the tombs),
though none of these subsidiary cemeteries rivals the city of the dead that
King Kheops laid out for his family and courtiers on the east and west envi-
rons of his Great Pyramid at Giza. The stone walls of the chapels or
offering-chambers of these private mastaba tombs were invariably sculptured in low relief and painted with scenes which are the chief source for our
knowledge of everyday life and funerary ritual and belief during the
Pyramid Age. In a *serdab* or separate chamber, usually sealed off but con-   24
nected by a spy-hole to the chapel, were stored statues of the owner and his
family in painted wood or limestone, rarely in granite. Some of these tombs
in their sculpture and statuary have preserved the artistic masterpieces of
their day, though hardly one is now in its pristine condition. The majority
of these mastabas lie buried in the sands at Saqqara, where kings of the
Third, Fifth and Sixth Dynasties built their funerary monuments, but
others are at Dahshur, and yet others are at Giza near the most celebrated of
all ancient tombs, the three stone-built pyramids of Kheops, Khephren and
Mykerinus of the Fourth Dynasty.

These various cemeteries were near the northern capital of Memphis of
which scarcely any other record survives. Memphis was the premier city of
Egypt, a vast metropolis, the 'white walls' of which were traditionally
thought to have been raised by Menes, the first pharaoh, on reclaimed
ground at the junction of Upper and Lower Egypt. It was a great religious
and administrative capital throughout its long history. As a trading-centre
all manner of crafts were carried on there, from shipbuilding to metalwork,
under the auspices of the city god, the artificer Ptah, whose high priest
proudly bore the title of 'Greatest of Craftsmen'. Even in Roman times it
was still prosperous and only suffered decline and extinction when the Arab
conquerors pillaged its stone for building Cairo 10 miles to the north on the

25 opposite bank of the Nile. The modern village of Mitrahina is the site of the temple of Ptah and near its palm groves the colossal statues which Ramesses II raised there have lain for centuries in fallen grandeur, though the smaller red granite specimen was re-erected outside the railway station in Cairo as a memorial to the new Egypt. Now, a victim of Cairo's polluted atmosphere, it is due to be moved again. Votive statues and other monuments from the temple site have come to light as a result of sporadic digging, but the greater part of Memphis lies under the Nile silt and must irretrievably have been lost. Various expeditions have dug selected portions of the vast site from time to time during the past century, but the high water-table has necessitated expensive pumping operations and specialized excavation skills. The Egypt Exploration Society has now begun explorations in the area on a regular basis with promising results. Most importantly, drill-core work has shown how the city moved eastwards over the millennia, as the Nile shifted its course in that direction. Until this capital city is properly excavated our knowledge of ancient Egypt cannot be but lop-sided.

24 Family group of Khaemheset, his wife Thenenet, and their son, from his mastaba tomb near the pyramid of King Teti at Saqqara. Khaemheset came from a family of king's architects and was clearly able to command superior craftsmen for his tomb statues, c. 2350 BC.

25 Detail of colossal crystalline limestone statue of Ramesses II, from the Great Temple of Ptah at Memphis. The king is shown wearing the *nemes* headdress, uraeus and royal beard.

Lower Egypt

A few miles below Memphis in ancient times the Nile divided into several branches as it wandered across the broad alluvium of its Delta, eventually entering the sea through seven principal and five secondary mouths. It was a region of potentially great fertility but in antiquity it was only very gradually developed, its pools and marshes being progressively drained, so eliminating their thickets of reeds and papyrus rush. It was flanked on its eastern and western borders by wide pastures where large herds of goats, sheep and cattle could be raised. The flowery meadows produced both milk and honey, and it was thither that the magnates sent their beasts to be fattened. Along the 'Western River', presumably the Canopic branch of the Nile, lay the large estates from which the pharaohs obtained their choicest wines. Wine labels in the form of dockets written in ink upon the jars themselves defined the particular *clos*, the vintage year, the name of the vintner, and the quality of the wine, suggesting that the pharaohs or their butlers enjoyed a cultivated palate. Surrounded by their domains among the watercourses stood the famous towns of Lower Egypt, Heliopolis, Sais, Buto, Mendes, Bubastis and Tanis, each centred around a shrine of ancient foundation, and some of them the objective of pilgrimages by both pharaohs and their subjects.

Heliopolis, the On of the Bible, was the centre of the influential sun cult. The temple of Re-Herakhty, the active form of the supreme god, was the largest outside Thebes and its high priests were the traditional wise men of Egypt, even in the Late Period when the solar faith was in eclipse. The preoccupation of these sages with the movement of the sun and other celestial bodies encouraged the development of astronomy and the mensuration of time as well as space. An early high priest of the sun god at Heliopolis was Imhotep, later deified as Imuthes, a god of healing and wisdom, who was celebrated throughout the history of Egypt as the virtual founder of its culture. One of the last of these intellectuals was Manetho.

The temple of Re-Herakhty has also vanished, but its appearance can be surmised from reconstructions of the sun temples that have been excavated near the pyramids of some kings of the Fifth Dynasty, and from a model of the *dromos* of the temple dedicated by King Sethos I at Tell el Yahudiya, not far from Heliopolis. Worship focused upon a cult object, the *ben–ben*, a stone of pyramidal or conical shape, probably a meteorite, elevated upon a podium or tall pillar (from which On gets its name) to form an obelisk. One such monument, the earliest now surviving from a pair erected by Sesostris I, still stands amid the fields, in a small park, surrounded by a suburb of modern Cairo, to mark the site of the vanished temple entrance. The pair raised here by Tuthmosis III now adorn London and New York under the incongruous name of Cleopatra's Needles.

The cattle economy of the Delta was evident in the cult of the sacred Mnevis bull at Heliopolis, as it was in the Apis bull of Memphis. A quarter of the Lower Egyptian nomes had images of cattle upon their standards, whereas Upper Egypt could not boast of even one, though a bull cult did exist at Armant, some 12 miles south of Luxor. A ram cult was observed at Mendes, the ruins of which at Tell el Qasr, near the northeast corner of the Delta, have been excavated by American and Canadian expeditions. Mendes was the seat of the fighting pharaohs of the Twenty-Ninth Dynasty, who with their Greek mercenaries successfully resisted the onslaughts of the Persians in the 4th century BC. The tomb of the first of them, Nepherites I, has now been identified there by the excavations of Donald Redford.

South of Mendes near modern Zagazig lie the ruins of Bubastis, the Pibeseth of Ezekiel, a city with an ancient foundation that goes back at least to the reign of Kheops and may well be earlier. It was, however, greatly developed during the 1st millennium BC when immigrant Libyans settled in

26

different areas of the Delta. Their kings, ruling as the Twenty-Second Dynasty, embellished Bubastis as their chief residence, enlarging its ancient tree-girt temple. The city deity was Bastet, an aspect of the universal mother goddess, incarnate in the Egyptian domestic cat. On the occasion of her joyous festivals, pilgrimages were made to her shrine by boat with fluting and castanet playing. Such fetes are well described by Herodotus, who was also impressed by the quantity of wine consumed on such occasions.

    To the northeast of Bubastis, near the shores of Lake Manzala, are the ruins of Tanis, the Biblical Zoan, which has been explored by Mariette, Petrie, and most recently by the French who are still investigating the place. Tanis was a prosperous entrepot for trade with the Levantine states during

27

26 (*above*) Granite obelisk at Matariya, the village in which the Virgin's Tree grows, near ancient Heliopolis. Of several original pairs, only this single example remains standing, on the site of the temple of the sun god. Some 20 m high, it was erected with its companion to celebrate the jubilee of Sesostris I, *c.* 1940 BC. This extract from a watercolour drawing painted about 1800 by Luigi Mayer, a German artist trained in Rome, shows the obelisk as it was before recent buildings obscured the view.

27 Bastet, the local goddess of Bubastis, was thought to be incarnate in the Egyptian domestic cat. She was identified with other feline deities but represented gentler passion, particularly of joy, sexual and maternal love. When the Suez Canal was dug, it cut through a number of extensive cat cemeteries and much of the spoil was imported to Europe as fertilizer. In this way many cat-mummy coffins in bronze and wood found their way into the art market.

the late New Kingdom. It grew to greater importance as the chief city of the kings of the Twenty-First and Twenty-Second Dynasties, who in their stirring times found it expedient to have their seat of power nearer to their Mediterranean frontier. They adorned it with the monuments of earlier kings moved from elsewhere and as far afield as the Faiyum which was then in the process of being abandoned. In 1939 the French Egyptologist, Pierre Montet, made a brilliant discovery within the temple precincts of a group of tombs containing the remains of six kings of this period and their relatives. Most of the burials had been violated at one time and rearranged, but despite certain depredations, Montet was able to recover an extremely rich funerary equipment containing much gold- and silver-work and throwing new light upon the history, art, beliefs and resources of an age which was contemporary with that of Solomon in all his glory. Tanis was not far from the great fortress of Tjel, the last outpost on the northeastern frontier, and was always

28, 29 Both Western Thebes and Delta sites have rendered up faience tiles of the Ramessides, made to be set into plastered mud-brick walls. Plain blue tiles containing the royal titularies in white glyphs were used for framing doorways and balconies. The examples here show (left) a traditional captive, an Asiatic in his gaudy robes; and (right) a Nubian depicted almost as a caricature.

subject to influences from Asia. In the vicinity is Tell ed Dab'a where the Austrians have uncovered the huge site, which was founded in the Middle Kingdom and rapidly became a centre of Palestinian immigrants into Egypt. A number of Canaanite temples and other material clearly deriving from eastern inhabitants shows without doubt that this was Avaris, the capital city of the Hyksos. Even more exciting have been the discoveries of the remains of Cretan Minoan frescoes, considerably earlier than those known on Crete itself. The paintings' significance, and their relationship to others found over recent years in the Levant, remain the subject of much debate.

A mile to the north at Qantir is the site of Pi-Ramesse, the great treasure-city and residence-town of the Ramesside kings, which a poet of the day describes as, 'beauteous with balconies and dazzling halls of lapis lazuli and turquoise, the place where the chariotry is marshalled and the infantry assembles and where the warships come to anchorage when tribute is brought.' The mooring posts for these ships have recently been found on a dried-up branch of the Pelusian arm of the Nile by an expedition from Hildesheim which is re-excavating this area. Pi-Ramesse was bereft of its statues and monuments to adorn Tanis, and the crumbling brick ruins of houses and a palace are all that are left of its glory, with the exception perhaps of a great number of blue and polychrome faience tiles dispersed 28, 29 among different collections and which are doubtless the (artificial) lapis lazuli and turquoise referred to by the poet.

Of Sais, the wealthy residence of the powerful kings of the Twenty-Sixth Dynasty, only 'inconsiderable' ruins exist near the modern Sa el Hagar. Herodotus visited it soon after its apogee and describes the remarkable temple of the presiding archer goddess Neith, with its gigantic monolithic shrines and obelisks and its sacred lakes. He speaks too of the tombs of the kings in chapels of the temples, evidently similar to the earlier royal sepul chres at Tanis. Of all this nothing now remains.

Sais shared with Buto the distinction of being a place of pilgrimage, particularly in the Old Kingdom, when the blessed dead were taken to these holy cities, if not for burial, then for consecration, at the shrines of ancient kings, a ritual later usurped for the cult of Osiris at Abydos. Buto was the Place of the Throne, the old capital of the prehistoric kings of the Western Delta, and the legendary birthplace of the demiurge who manifested himself here upon the primeval hill in the form of a heron just as a falcon had appeared at Hierakonpolis, the counterpart of Buto in Upper Egypt. Buto now survives only as a few mounds near Tell el Farain, which have been partly explored by the British in recent years with disappointing results. But in Herodotus' day it was a flourishing city with a noted oracle in the temple of Edjo, the cobra goddess of the city and the presiding genius of Lower Egypt. From the top of the temple pylon on a clear day it would have been possible to glimpse on the far horizon the flash of light upon what our Egyptian guide would have called the Great Green, and which we today call the Mediterranean.

3 · The natural resources

Foodstuffs

Within these boundaries ancient Egypt enjoyed many resources. When the inundation was neither too copious nor too meagre, the tremendous fertility of the soil, rich in phosphates, brought forth produce of all kinds. The main grain crops were summer and winter wheat and six-row barley, providing the staples of the national diet, bread and beer for both king and peasant. In the Late Period, the rations of the soldiery contained about 5 lb (2.25 kg) of bread per day for each man, a regimen that induced the Greeks to dub them *artophagoi*, 'the bread-eaters'.

This fare, however, was supplemented by such vegetables as leeks, onions, lettuces, melons, cucumbers, beans and other pulses. Vegetable oils used in cooking, lighting, cosmetics and medicine were expressed mostly from the fruits of the balanos and moringa trees and from sesame and the castor-oil plants. The olive was not extensively planted, but its oil was imported from Palestine in large quantities and probably also from Libya.

Fruits were provided by such trees as the jujube (*Zizyphus spina Christi*), sycamore fig and date palm. The *dom*-palm, with its nuts encased in a hard carapace resembling gingerbread, could be raised only in latitudes south of Asyut. The caprification of figs was practised, and doubtless also the hand pollination of date palms. Grapes in abundance were grown from predynastic times, and vineyards in historic times were planted in new ground in the Delta and the Oases. Pomegranates and possibly the carob, yielding the sweet fleshy bean, St John's bread, were not introduced until the New Kingdom. Apart from the groves of palm trees around villages, most fruit trees were cultivated in gardens, that characteristic Oriental pleasance with its pool of water open to the evening breeze.

Trees, in fact, were valued as much for their shade as their fruit and flowers. Several trees were regarded as sacred, such as the persea (*Mimusops schimperi*), the unidentified *ished* tree of Heliopolis, and the sycamore, inhabited by a goddess, sometimes Nut but usually Hathor, who is represented as leaning out of the trunk to pour a cooling draught of water for the deceased in paradise. Individual trees growing in isolation were often venerated as sacred, their shade sought by a particular god. Hathor was worshipped at Memphis as the 'Mistress of the Southern Sycamore'. At the site of Heliopolis today, both Moslems and Copts revere a centuries-old sycamore

30 A calf, which is part of a scene of offering-bearers bringing gifts to the tomb-owner. The animal is garlanded for sacrifice with a collar of lotus flowers and buds and mandrake fruits sewn onto a papyrus backing, and is led along on a coiled halter by its attendant.

as the Virgin's Tree, under which the Holy family is believed to have sheltered on the flight into Egypt. Nearby is a spring of sweet water originally called into being by the Christ child.

The papyrus plant abounded in the Delta and the undrained areas of Upper Egypt and supplied a host of needs, including a food prepared from its roasted rhizome. Herbs and aromatic plants provided flavourings, medicines and perfumes. Together with such plants as the woody nightshade, the mandrake and wild celery, and with the leaves of the olive and willow, with cornflowers and the petals of blue and white water-lilies, they could be made into formal bouquets or wreaths and garlands by sewing them onto sheets of papyrus or strips of palm fibre. Such gay and sweet-smelling but ephemeral decorations were lavishly used at feasts and religious festivals not only for adorning the person, but also for decking animals destined for sacrifice and for offerings to the gods.

In addition to its vegetable products, Egypt supported a vast population of domestic animals. The chief ceremonial meat offerings were usually beef   30 in the form of head, legs, ribs and offal. Religious tradition prescribed the creatures of the wild as the preferred victims for sacrifice; and domestic animals, apart from the ox, do not therefore appear among the offerings. Nevertheless, pigs, sheep, goats and asses were also raised. The pig was an important article of diet among the peasantry and lower orders, though representations of the animal, and references to it, are rare. Pig bones have been found in the middens of workmen's villages at Amarna and Deir el Medina. Dockets from jars which contained fat rendered down from goat, beef and mutton have been found in the ruins of a palace of Amenophis III. Even if fabrics made from goat's hair and sheep's wool have not been found until the Classical period, clips of sheep's wool have been excavated at Amarna. There is no doubt that certain garments, such as shawls, were woven from these animal fibres from earliest times, though evidently they were not deposited with the dead, probably because they were considered as ceremonially impure.

Cattle from Nubia, and hump-backed bulls introduced from Asia in the New Kingdom for breeding purposes, were imported to replace losses caused by the murrains which periodically have devastated herds in Egypt until very recent times. Milk was an important farm product and cheese and butter were prepared from it, though the evidence is scanty. The same flowery meadows that fattened the prize cattle, so that their legs became bowed under the weight of their bodies, also produced honey which was used, as in Europe until recent times, as a main source of sugar. Beehives were made of hollow cones of dried mud similar to those found in rural Egypt today. Clear honey was evidently obtained, probably by heating and straining the product, and removing the solidified wax. Another variety, red honey, presumably retained much of the comb. A jug of ancient honey in the Rhind Collection in Edinburgh plainly shows the hexagonal construction of the wax comb.

The Nile and its pools abounded in fish, and although fish, like pork, was regarded as ritually impure, it is shown among the water produce offered by the personified figures of the Nile. Fish was an important article of food for the working population; and the artisans concerned with hewing and decorating the royal tombs at Thebes were entitled to share in the 18 kg of fish provided every ten days by the fishermen attached to each gang.

The enormous flocks of migratory birds that visited Egypt in the winter could be trapped with the clap-net and supplemented the herds of geese and duck that were raised on the Egyptian farms, and supplied eggs, flesh and fat. The domestic barnyard fowl does not make its appearance until the reign of Tuthmosis III, and then only in isolated instances. Cranes caught in the 31 wild were artificially fattened with prepared pellets and are often depicted with geese among the heaps of offerings. Swans and pelicans also appear, but very rarely, and are not represented among the sacrifices. Pigeons are depicted at all periods, and with geese and ducks in feeding pens; but in the absence of representations of dovecotes, so characteristic of modern villages in Egypt, it is impossible to be sure that such fowl houses were used, though it is highly probable. The northern palace at Amarna had an extensive aviary with nesting boxes cut as niches into the walls, but the birds painted on its decorated dado are of different species. All such birds, like fish and various cuts of meat, could be preserved by jerking in the dry Egyptian climate and storing with salt in sealed pottery jars.

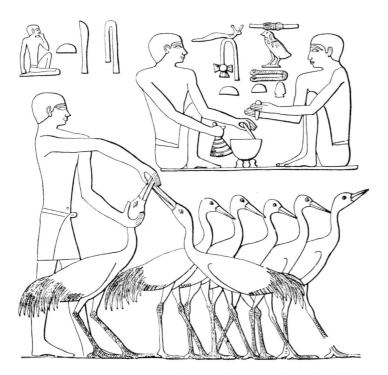

31 Scene from the tomb of Ti at Saqqara of men preparing and cooking dough-pellets as food for cranes captured in the wild and artificially fattened for sacrifice.

Besides Nile water, which was supposed to have special life-giving virtues, and could be kept cool in porous jars, beer was brewed; this used to be thought of as a thick substance not unlike modern Nubian *bouza*, but has now been shown to be a far more palatable brew, although rather unlike modern confections. A sweet sort of beverage called *seremt* was also prepared, but its composition is unknown though it could evidently be drunk or eaten. Wine made from palm sap was occasionally fermented. The annual grape harvest in various parts of the country, chiefly the border areas, and in the oases of the Libyan desert, was the most usual source of wine.

Except for certain interludes when the inundation failed, Egypt was a land of plenty, its surplus grain succouring the Hittites during a famine in the reign of Merenptah (*c*. 1211 BC), as well as the city mob at Rome well over a millennium later in the days of the emperors. The residence-city Pi-Ramesse, on the building of which the Israelites have been alleged to have toiled in the 13th century BC, is celebrated by the poet Paibes as being

> full of good things and provisions every day. Its channels abound in fish and its lakes in birds. Its fields are green with herbage and its banks bear dates. Its tall granaries are overflowing with barley and wheat. Garlic, leeks, lettuces and fruits are there for sustenance and wine surpassing

honey . . . He who dwells there is happy, for there the humble are like the mighty elsewhere. (After Erman 1966, p. 206.)

Well might the Israelites in the wilderness of Zin bewail the loss of the fleshpots which they enjoyed even as a subject people.

Vegetable products

Only in one thing was Egypt notably deficient, and that was good constructional timber which had to be imported from the Lebanon, a traffic which is probably as old as the sea-going ship. The native trees, mostly acacia, sycamore and tamarisk, were too knotty, contorted or unresilient to provide good quality timber, though they were used for simple domestic furniture, boxes and coffins, and were often veneered with ivory, ebony and other fine woods to make a better appearance. The palm tree, however, served a multitude of purposes: its trunk for ceiling rafters and staircase supports, the fronds for cladding brick piers and for roofing, its ribs for cages and frails for holding produce. The Egyptian from earliest days was skilful in using various rushes and reeds for making all sorts of articles in wickerwork, such as tables, stands, stools and boxes. Baskets of all sizes, with lids or without, were made of grasses in stitched coil-work similar to those in use in parts of East Africa until very recent times. Others of a coarser type were sewn from continuous plaits of palm leaf.

Above all, the remarkable Egyptian discovery of how to prepare a flexible paper from the pith of the papyrus rush, on which it was possible to write rapidly with a pen and ink, made the highly organized Egyptian state possible. Portable records of all kinds could be kept by this method. By the 1st millennium BC at the latest, Egypt was exporting rolls of papyrus to other civilized states in a trade which reveals that writing with pen and ink was ousting the old cumbersome system used in Asia of impressing lumps of clay with cuneiform signs.

Another valuable vegetable crop was flax which was grown during the winter. The bundles of stems were rippled through a large fixed comb to remove the bolls containing linseed from which the oil was extracted. The bast fibres were separated by retting the stems in convenient pools, and spun by the spindle-whorl into thread of all weights. Linen was woven on a simple horizontal loom in various grades. It formed the essential material for all clothing and bedding. On death, a person's sheets were torn into strips for use in bandaging his mummy. A fine material, royal linen, was evidently of a gossamer-like texture and was celebrated in erotic poetry as being semi-transparent. It was highly prized abroad. The thieves who plundered the royal tombs were in search of linen garments as much as gold and silver. Upper Egyptian line was also celebrated, and bolts and garments of this material were sent to the prince of Byblos by Smendes the governor of Lower Egypt in the 11th century BC to pay for supplies of high-quality timber.

Minerals

While the cultivation yielded produce in ample quantities, the deserts that bordered the Nile Valley were not totally sterile. The wadis had not yet been overgrazed by goats and camels, and they supported game, particularly various species of antelope, ibex, ostriches and hares, and their predators, the lion and his relations. Gazelle, oryx and hyaenas trapped by hunters were fattened in captivity by forcible feeding for eventual sacrifice.

Occasional native trees and low, thorny shrubs provided kindling and charcoal for fuel. The inhabitants of the oases in the Western Desert had carried on a trade with Egypt in such products as wine, aromatic woods, grain, fruits, hides, salt, natron and minerals since early times. Similarly the inhabitants of Nubia and the Lower Sudan exchanged their goods for the industrial products of Egypt – weapons, furniture, faience and textiles. By this commerce Egypt became the great entrepot for the export to the rest of the Eastern Mediterranean of the tropical products of Africa, ebony, ivory, ostrich feathers and eggs, gold, amethysts and other semi-precious stones, and exotic pelts.

The main products of the Eastern Desert, however, were minerals, gemstones such as carnelians, garnets, jaspers, rock crystal and amazonite, and metals, particularly gold and silver and their naturally occurring alloy, electrum. The mining of the gold-bearing rocks, and the transport of their crushed fragments by donkey-back to washing stations on the Nile, were energetically pursued during the New Kingdom when it became proverbial among the nations of Asia that gold was as dust in the land of Egypt. This desirable metal made Egypt wealthy and courted in a world which recognized a kind of gold standard in international trade.

For most of its ancient history Egypt lived in the Bronze Age, or rather the Copper Age, bronze not coming into use until the later Middle Kingdom. Copper ore was mined in Sinai and the Eastern Desert, and copper ingots were imported in later times from Cyprus and Syria. The smelting of iron, however, lagged behind the craft as practised in other countries of the Near East, such as Philistia. The introduction of copper tools did not replace flint implements overnight; and in many crafts, such as the working of hard stones, the techniques and equipment of the late Stone Age were retained to the end.

Other products of the deserts were the large deposits of sodium salts in the form of natron, brine and soda. These were necessary for all kinds of industries, providing the salt required for preserving, flavouring and tanning, as well as a host of medical uses. Natron was employed in the manufacture of faience and glass, and as a flux for the soldering of copper, gold and silver. It was also used with salt for preserving fish and fowl; and was essential in the similar mummifying processes. Used with oils it produced a kind of soap for cleansing; alone it acted as a mouth-wash to render the user ritually pure.

32 Near the southern end of the sandstone quarries on the west bank of the Nile at Gebel es Silsila. The two most prominent monuments have the appearance of doorways to rock shrines with their clustered columns, architraves and cavetto cornices. That on the left is dated to the first regnal year of Ramesses II, and that on the right to the same year of his son and successor Merenptah. They were erected by high officials, who came here at the beginning of the reigns of their kings to initiate work on extracting stone for the royal monuments. Both these shrines have hymns inscribed to the god of the Nile and a list of offerings to be made to him.

Quartz sand was an important ingredient in glass and faience-making; and when used with copper saws and drills enabled hard stones to be cut, perforated, worked and polished. The great industry of the desert regions, however, was the supplying of the various stones in which Egypt was remarkably abundant. Apart from its semi-precious stones, it had inexhaust- ible deposits of limestone and sandstone of varying qualities flanking both banks of the Nile. These were easily worked and transported, and provided the bulk of the materials for the monumental buildings. At the cataracts, chiefly the First, were vast intrusions of igneous rocks, granites, basalts, dio- rites and dolerites, which the Egyptians early learnt to work supremely well. Quartzite sandstone, greywacke, alabaster (calcite) and indurated limestone had to be sought out in desert places. In the case of the grey-green diorite, used particularly in the Fourth and Twelfth Dynasties for statuary and cos- metic vessels, a remote quarry in the Nubian desert some 40 miles west of Abu Simbel was the source of supply. Deposits of serpentine, steatite and similar rocks were also prospected and used for small and delicate articles from scarabs to statuettes.

The consummate skill of the Egyptians in the working of stone was rec- ognized widely abroad, and their stone-masons, for instance, were employed by Persian kings, not only to carve their granite statues but also to cut the reliefs on palace walls at Persepolis.

Human

The people of ancient Egypt were very much like those of today, ranging in skin tone from olive-skinned Mediterranean types, to the dark brown of the inhabitants of the south and Nubia. Movements within the country and immigration from abroad led to wide varieties being present in the major population centres, although in the more remote villages blood lines remained long intact.

These human resources, despite a steady infiltration of contiguous peoples, remained fairly constant throughout their ancient history and reveal an ability to assimilate the immigrant. This was doubtless because the vast majority of the ancient population was concerned with agriculture, and committed to the cultivation of the land as much by predilection as by necessity. The peasant was deeply attached to the soil and unhappy away from his valley. His successful methods in contending with the peculiar agrarian conditions in Egypt, doubtless the result of much trial and error, were more in the nature of gardening than farming. Nevertheless, his was a technique that was followed for many generations, like the mystique of other crafts. Even mercenaries, settled by the pharaohs on the land after their retirement from military service, had to learn the same native skills in dealing with such unique conditions. The racial type of the Egyptian peasant, like his physical environment, remained remarkably constant throughout historic times, and is still apparent in some of the more remote areas of Upper Egypt.

The ruling class which directed the toiling mass of peasants was often of foreign origin, but nationalistic ideas played a very subordinate role in the ancient world. It is not until the New Kingdom, when Theban princes challenged the northern Kingdom conscious of its Asiatic ties, that any awareness of a racial and national identity becomes dominant. Just as the peasantry assimilated other cultivators settled on the land, so the strong traditions of the divine kingship and its institutions ensured that the pharaoh and his entourage, whether native, Hyksos, Semitic, Libyan, Kushite, or Greek, would always act as the government of the Egyptian people.

The amalgam of Asiatic and African elements in the ancient population is reflected in the language they spoke which is related to the Semitic tongue in grammar and some of its vocabulary, and yet has affinities with Hamitic languages, particularly Berber dialects, suggesting a fusion of two tongues. The Egyptian language, however, has its own peculiarities, and if speech is but a natural expression of the genius of a people, we must remark that Egyptian is characterized by its conciseness, concrete realism, and keen observation. It has, as Sir Alan Gardiner pointed out, a preference for the static over dynamic expression and apart from some rare survivals has no genuine active tense.

Herodotus regarded the inhabitants of Upper Egypt in his day as among the healthiest in the world, and certainly the region with its sunshine and dry winter climate has always attracted invalids from the days of the Romans. In the last century Egypt became immensely popular as a sanatorium for Europeans seeking relief from the affliction of phthisis and respiratory diseases. But pathologists who have examined Egyptian mummies have claimed to identify some of the lesions of several ailments that trouble the modern fellahin, notably rheumatism and water-borne diseases. Moreover, owing to the Egyptians' practice of using fine quartz sand in the milling of grain, their bread contained enough grit to wear down to the pulp the grinding surfaces of their teeth over the years. Even the governing classes who enjoyed a more varied diet did not escape the scourge of chronic toothache in their later years. Both Amenophis III and his father-in-law Yuya, for instance, must have suffered miserably from alveolar abcesses in middle age.

Most Egyptians, however, escaped this fate, for while they prayed for a good old age and set the ideal lifespan at a hundred and ten years, the average expectation of life for the wealthier settlers in Graeco-Roman times has been estimated at about thirty-six years, and there is no reason to believe that it was any higher in pharaonic days. While the birthrate was doubtless high, the infant mortality rate was far from low, and it has been computed on somewhat insecure foundations that the population in the Eleventh Dynasty did not greatly exceed a million, though in a valley which still had vast undeveloped areas, this meant quite a concentration of human beings in scattered towns and villages.

In common with so many of the nations of antiquity in the Mediterranean, the Egyptians matured early, puberty being attained at the age of twelve and official manhood at not more than sixteen. Heavy responsibilities were undertaken by people whom we should now regard as children. A certain nomarch of Asyut relates how the king appointed him governor of a province when he was only a cubit high (the royal cubit was 52.3 cm), and made him learn swimming with the royal children. The high priest of Amun, Bakenkhons, who entered the priesthood on reaching the age of sixteen, had already spent some years as chief of the training stable of Sethos I. Of course such statistics can be as misleading as any average and the short and youthful reign of Tutankhamun or Siptah, for instance, can be offset by that of Pepy II who is generally believed to have had the longest recorded reign in history (ninety-four years), or Ramesses II who ruled for sixty-seven years, celebrated thirteen jubilees, and was succeeded by his thirteenth son. Nevertheless, there is sufficient evidence to show that much of the Egyptian achievement was secured by an extremely youthful population schooled by strong traditions rather than by personal experience.

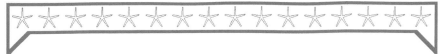

4 · The settlement of Egypt

From nomad to colonist

The first Egyptians to have bequeathed us some traces of their physical presence in the Nile Valley have left a few of their fossilized bones at Qaw el Kebir, 30 miles south of Asyut. Experts who have examined these late Palaeolithic relics have pronounced that they resemble similar remains of predynastic date. Palaeolithic humans of earlier epochs have left their characteristic flint handaxes on the four lower terraces that flank the Valley and were formed as a result of the retreat of the vast gulf in the Mediterranean during Pleistocene times. A few camp sites have also been uncovered near prehistoric branches of the main Nile channel, and additional evidence is coming to light at Sebil near Kom Ombo and other places in Upper Egypt as more expert investigations into these remote periods are being made, though the most recent Palaeolithic and early Neolithic sites must remain buried under the Nile silt. Such studies tend to show that the end of the fourth interglacial period in Europe, *c.* 30,000 BC, coincides with the last of the pluvial epochs in North Africa which then alternated rainy interludes with drier conditions down to the end of the Neolithic wet phase *c.* 2350 BC. During the earlier part of this epoch a warm and humid climate favoured the growth of lush savannahs and forests in what are now the desert regions of North Africa and made it possible for early Palaeolithic people to lead a hunting and food-gathering existence, living in the open under light shelters, probably of reed and thatch.

In the Nile Valley, when the river was cutting its channel deeper and narrower into the accumulations of gravels and other water-borne detritus, the floodplain was covered in winter and spring with luxuriant herbage that provided rich grazing for such large game as elephant, rhinoceros, wild cattle and asses. The wadi beds were also carpeted with vegetation that supported a population of antelope, gazelle, ibex and barbary sheep, while the Nile and its creeks teemed with fish, hippopotamus and the ever-lurking crocodile. The reedy swamps gave cover to resident and migratory birds in profusion. This favourable environment allowed humans to find ample sustenance while staying in one tribal settlement, by fishing, trapping, hunting and gathering seasonal foods such as the wild banana, the papyrus rhizome and wild grasses, perhaps a form of primitive barley. The hunting part of this economy persisted with diminishing importance well into historic times,

33

33 Drawing of the later Palaeolithic period on a rock in the Wadi es Sebua, now submerged beneath Lake Nasser. The animals of the desert wadis are shown, mostly onager and gazelle.

though by then it had become more of a recreation than a way of life. Thus the appearance of a herd of 170 wild cattle in the Wadi Qena as late as the second regnal year of Amenophis III (c. 1387 BC) caused great excitement, and the operation that resulted in the rounding up of 96 of them was commemorated in a special issue of large scarabs.

The Palaeolithic world left its faint imprint upon the later civilization of Egypt in other ways. That empathy that develops between the hunter and his quarry ensured that the Egyptian never lost his awe of the animals of the wild as repositories of numinous force. Their periodic migrations, particularly of birds and fish, seemed to him divinely inspired, purposeful and effective. The magic-working rock drawings of Palaeolithic times near the ancient water-holes in what is now desert are early examples of that veneration shown to certain animals in historic times which never wholly lost its power. Similarly the keen observation of animal forms evident in the ivory carvings of predynastic times anticipates the precision of the later hieroglyphic designs of mammals, birds and reptiles.

The nomad camping out under clear night skies is especially conscious of the brilliance and proximity of the moon and stars. Apart from the polar stars, like him they were wanderers, traversing celestial tracts, but returning after due season to former starting points. He imagined a destiny among the stars, or a future existence as a star, beliefs which survive in the later eschatology of the historic Egyptians, especially during the Old Kingdom.

The later phases of the Palaeolithic age (*c.* 15,000–10,000 BC) were characterized by erratic climatic conditions as the ice-cap over Europe retreated. Increased rainfall allowed vegetation to revive in parched savannah-lands in North Africa, while intervals of drought encouraged migrations of man and animals to more fertile tracts. With a general aridity creeping over the upland plains, the wandering tribes became ever more dependent upon their rain-makers, who like their equivalents in the Sudan in recent times, were believed to exercise a magic control over the weather. Presumably like their Sudanese counterparts, too, they might be ritually slain when their powers began to wane or failed altogether. Increasing desiccation steadily drove men and animals into the more fertile regions of the oases in the Libyan desert and the verges of the Nile itself, where they found themselves in competition for food resources with earlier groups of squatters.

As the Nile Valley was gradually settled, the first colonists encountered an entirely new set of conditions which obliged them to modify their beliefs and practices even if they did not entirely discard them. For the land of Egypt exhibited an environment absolutely unique in the ancient world. It was not dependent upon the caprices of the local weather for its prosperity, but straggled, a long oasis, in the increasing wastes of North Africa, favoured by a circumstance that rendered it potentially the most fertile of all the countries of the Near East. The inundation of the Nile, which began to rise each year in July, submerged the entire alluvial plain beneath its flood until September, when the waters receded to the proximity of their former channel, leaving behind a deposit of rich silt in which new crops could flourish under the beneficent rays of the winter and spring suns. The inundation was predictable in its yearly appearance, soon after the heliacal rising of the bright star Sirius, only its volume was uncertain. While a succession of low Niles could spell privation, even disaster, pharaonic Egypt remained for most of its existence an agricultural paradise to which its less privileged neighbours migrated in times of famine like Abraham and Joseph's brethren.

This sanctuary, however, was a later development. While early squatters near the Nile in Palaeolithic times may have found an environment extremely congenial to their hunting and fishing way of life, later immigrants experienced difficulty in adapting the conditions to a farming economy. The annual inundation reduced the entire area to a long narrow lake which, while it may have flushed rubbish and vermin into the Mediterranean, also swept away dwellings and landmarks, and made use of the land impossible for several months. But this destructive flood also deposited the heavier sands and gravels into turtle-back mounds, or levees, along the verges of the river, eventually building them up into banks that only an exceptional rise of the Nile could cover. Such hillocks formed suitable sites for settlements; and in their lee, flooded land could be developed into basin cultivation. From these physical features, the characteristic husbandry of Egypt developed; for the natural gaps between the levees could be filled by raising dykes, and the water trapped in the basins beyond could be slowly released by breaching embankments as the Nile began to fall. Growth was rapid and lush in the well-soaked virgin soil left behind.

These natural conditions, however, were not extensively exploited until grain crops were introduced, from southwest Asia in Neolithic times. Wheat and barley could be grown in basins on an ever-increasing scale and harvested rapidly in the summer heat. The grain could be stored on the dry desert margins to provide seed for next season's crops and a surplus for unproductive workers who rose to importance as the agrarian revolution gathered momentum, and the features of urban culture began to assert themselves.

The organization of the land of Egypt as a rich agricultural state was, however, a gradual process and was still incomplete by the end of the pharaonic period. New land was won from the deserts and swamps in most years of prosperity, and brought into the fiscal system. While the wayward force of the inundation could level, irrigate and fertilize tracts of sterile land, it could also shift the cultivation by altering to a minor extent the former course of the river. Land could also go out of production some years through excessive flood, or drought, or fallowing, or neglect in times of political upheaval. The chief concern, however, of good government was to maintain agricultural prosperity.

The Nile and the Cosmos

The change from hunting and food-gathering to crop cultivation affected profoundly the outlook of the dwellers on the banks of the Nile, and their view of their universe and how it functioned. The exploitation of the land to sustain a farming economy was wholly dependent upon hydraulic engineering, on the raising of dykes and embankments, the draining of swamps, the cutting of channels and sluices and the transporting of water. Furthermore most of this work had to be done rapidly. In the absence of any machinery, apart from primitive picks, hoes, baskets and water-jars carried in pairs on yokes, such projects required the conscription of labour under skilled organizers, and inevitably involved the peasantry thrown out of work by the drowning of their fields annually under the flood.

The Egyptian thus early became inured to a disciplined way of life in which he docilely accepted direction from a corps of specialists, the ancestors of the hydraulic and civil engineers of pharaonic days. Above all, such irrigation works could not be confined to narrow sectors of the river banks, but inevitably spread ever further involving neighbouring tracts, together with their denizens and governors. The outcome was a political system to ensure the success and persistence of the methods of controlling and exploiting the Nile flood. Since in order to do this, decisions had often to be taken at short notice and in conditions of stress, it was inevitable that the form of government would be authoritarian.

The magic powers of the rain-maker were irrelevant in the Nile Valley, where the life-giving water came from the inundation and not from the heavens. Nevertheless, it is almost certain that magic was still exercised by the tribal leaders to ensure that the Nile flood would arise at the proper time and in sufficient quantity. Eventually such power was vested in the national leader, the pharaoh who was thought to have command over the Nile in a virtually rainless land. Each year he performed ceremonies which were designed to bring about the rise of the Nile at the proper season with a bountiful flood. Thus the advent of King Merenptah (c. 1212 BC) is hailed as a cause for rejoicing since 'the water stays and fails not, and the Nile carries a high flood'. Even the sun-worshipping Akhenaten is greeted by his followers as 'a Nile which flows daily, giving life to Egypt'.

We are poorly informed about the rites which the pharaoh observed at the time of inundation, though the myth of Osiris suggests a sacrifice of some sort, perhaps in primitive times the ritual drowning of a suitable victim. There is, however, rather more evidence for the ceremony of Opening the Dykes, performed at another critical time when the inundation had reached its limit and the new land was about to emerge. This rite was still observed by the Copts up to the end of the last century; but the best known reference to it in pharaonic times is on the large commemorative scarabs which 34

34 The reign of Amenophis III was exceptional for the five large scarabs that he issued in his first eleven years on the throne to commemorate important events. The last in the series are the scarabs of year 11 which describe how the king brought new agricultural land into production for his chief queen, Tiye.

Amenophis III issued in his eleventh regnal year (*c.* 1377 BC). The text relates how on the first day of the third month of the inundation, the king decreed that a basin should be made for Queen Tiye in her township near modern Tahta. It was to be 3700 cubits long and 700 cubits wide. The king celebrated the feast of the Opening of the Basins (or Dykes) fifteen days later, when the ground had been thoroughly soaked and silt deposited, by sailing in his state barge through a breach in the dykes into the new basin. As a result of her husband's edict, Tiye enjoyed the revenues of a tract of new cornland over a mile long and a quarter of a mile wide.

35   A much earlier celebration of the same rite is seen in the votive macehead of the predynastic king, Scorpion (*c.* 3060 BC), found at Hierakonpolis. Here the first sod is cut by the king wielding a pick, and is received in a basket held by a high official. Scorpion's barge is moored nearby for his entry into the basin he is inaugurating. In both examples the king plays the central role as the controller of Nile water.

Of even more importance, however, than these magico-political implications was the effect of this oasis culture upon the beliefs and speculative thought of the ancient Egyptians. Looking across the Nile, for most of its length they could see the boundaries of their world in the rich red-brown mud that was deposited each year. Beyond this narrow fertile belt was tawny desert, mostly sterile, inhospitable and dangerous. The division between cultivation and wilderness, fecundity and barrenness, life and death, good and evil, was therefore clear and complete, and gave the Egyptian his characteristic awareness of the essential duality of his universe.

The phenomenon of the yearly rising of the waters, with its cycle of destruction and rebirth, entered deeply into the consciousness of the Egyptian and determined his ideas of the world, his cosmology as much as his system of agriculture and his political institutions. Each year he saw his world dissolve into a waste of water, followed by its reappearance, first as a narrow spit or mound of new land as the flood subsided. Perversely, he interpreted this emergence as caused not by the subsidence of the waters but by the raising of the land. It was on these mounds of sand and alluvium that seeds and bits of vegetation carried on the flood found a resting place and began to germinate. In a short time what had been a barren hillock showing above the watery waste was a flourishing thicket of plants with its attendant insect and bird life. The Egyptian came to believe that this was a model of how the world began. Out of the waters of Chaos, containing all the germs of things in inchoate form, had arisen a primeval mound on which the work of creation began in the First Time, as he phrased it. This miracle was repeated every year when the waters that are under the earth welled up and reproduced the primordial Nun or Chaos from which the new land in due course emerged.

This idea of Creation is fundamental to a number of different beliefs which existed in Egypt and make up the fabric of the ancient religion. In the course of its prehistory, the Egyptian state was slowly formed from various

35 The relief on this votive macehead shows the predynastic king Scorpion opening a breach in a dyke that will allow floodwater to flow into an irrigation basin. A high official bends to receive the first sod in a basket. Fan-bearers, standard-bearers and a priest take part in the ceremony. Below, the prow of the state barge may be seen that will carry the king into the new basin he is inaugurating.

human settlers, pastoralists and hunters from the savannahs and deserts, herdsmen of the marshlands and coastal pastures, primitive farmers, fowlers and fishermen from the creeks and marshes. As these people were obliged to cultivate the Nile Valley, they brought their different beliefs and myths with them, which were modified by the gradual welding of these isolated groups into larger communities until by the end of the 4th millennium BC, a unified state had been created. Throughout Egyptian history attempts were made at different religious centres, and particularly at Heliopolis and Memphis, to reflect a unity in theological thought that had been achieved in the sphere of politics, and to reconcile the various regional beliefs without entirely discarding any of them. All had in common the concept of the primeval mound on which the Creator first appeared to fashion the universe out of elemental chaos. We shall find that this idea influences profoundly many of the institutions of Egypt, its ideas of kingship, of death and burial, even of its architecture.

5 · Predynastic Egypt

The earlier phases, *c.* 5000–3500 BC

Some recent stages in the long march of the Egyptians from the savagery of food gathering and hunting to the civilization of King Scorpion have been recognized as a result of excavations on various sites; but the earlier horizons still lie hidden under the Nile silt. Five blank millennia separate the Sebilian remains of the most recent Palaeolithic hunters at Kom Ombo from the earliest traces of Neolithic farmers in the Faiyum. During this interlude a momentous revolution occurred in the production of food. Meat ceased to be the chief article of diet and was replaced by plants grown intensively as crops and not gathered at random in the wild. Superior strains of wheat, barley and flax, were introduced into the Nile Valley and there became the lifetime concern of countless generations of Egyptians to cultivate for food and clothing. The cereals required special processes in their preparation and cooking to make them palatable and digestible; and with their introduction came also the widespread adoption not only of milling stones, but also that other index of a sedentary culture, receptacles of baked clay that could hold liquids as well as solids and withstand the heat of fire. Thereafter man's progress during several millennia is mapped in the infinite forms and differing qualities of his almost indestructible pottery.

In step with his cultivation of selected plants came his domestication and breeding of certain animals, notably sheep, goats and pigs, which were also developed in southwest Asia. Later with increasing experience, cattle were raised on the pastures of the Nile Delta, and the wild asses of the wadis were tamed and bent to man's will. By the time the Neolithic age begins to reveal its vestiges in Egypt the agrarian revolution is gathering momentum.

The later prehistoric age, or Predynastic Period, as Egyptologists are apt to term it, is most conveniently divided into two broad phases, the earlier, from *c.* 5000 to *c.* 3500 BC, and the later, from *c.* 3500 to *c.* 3050 BC. The first has been identified on Neolithic sites at Merimda on the southwest verges of the Delta, in the Faiyum depression (the Faiyum A culture) and at Deir Tasa in Upper Egypt. It extends through the distinctive Chalcolithic cultures of el Badari, and el Amra near Abydos in Upper Egypt. The later manifestations of this earlier phase are referred to by continental prehistorians as the Naqada I culture from the extensive sites at Naqada and Ballas near Koptos.

From a survey of the material remains found on these sites, it is evident that the early Egyptians gradually adapted themselves to a farming economy which by the end of the period differed little from that surviving among the tribes of the Upper Nile in recent times. Both wheat and barley were grown and stored in pits lined with mats. Basketry was practised and the techniques of weaving linen improved steadily. Garments were also made of animal skins which could be tanned and softened. Needles were of bone. Bracelets of shell and ivory, and perforated stone beads and disks made from shell, are common as personal ornaments. Eye-paint ground from green malachite on schist palettes, and cleansing oils expressed from the wild castor plant, show that the cosmetic arts, always important in the hot, dry, fly-bitten Egyptian summer, with its eye and skin disorders, were surely developing. Combs made from bone or ivory are decorated with figures of animals in Amratian times. Tools and weapons were almost exclusively of stone or flint, arrows being tipped with chert points or bone barbs. The throw-stick, probably used in fowling, was known in a form that differed little from that used in pharaonic times. A mace with a pear-shaped stone head replaces earlier disk and bi-conal patterns by the end of the Amratian Period, but the narrow per-foration suggests that the haft was still of some resilient material such as horn or hippopotamus hide.

During this early phase, food was apparently plentiful. Dogs, goats, sheep, cattle, pigs and geese had been domesticated and wild game still abounded. Grain was probably boiled for porridge as well as ground for bread. Cooking and storage vessels were of pottery made by the coiling method; and the ceramic arts show a steady advance from the coarse clay cups and bowls of Faiyum A, through the Badarian thin black-topped red ware, often with a combed as well as a polished surface, to the fine red-burnished pottery of the Amratians, with its fanciful shapes and linear decoration in white slip. Vases   36
hollowed out of stone also appear near the end of the phase, the precursors of one of the most characteristic and cherished products of ancient Egypt.

The earlier cultures of Faiyum A, Merimda and Deir Tasa reveal no evi-dence of the use of metals. Copper appears a little later among the Upper Egyptian sites of Badari, as at Mostagedda and Matmar, in the form of pins, ornaments and a few modest tools. This suggests that the first employment of the metal was in the form of native copper found at sites in the Eastern Desert. The technique of smelting copper from its ores, however, must also have been developed during this period, as the cognate craft of covering soapstone beads with a green alkaline copper glaze was certainly practised.

The true nature of the spiritual life of these early Nile dwellers in the period before the invention of writing can never be known to us. They evi-dently believed in a hereafter for some members of the community at least, since in the burials of this period in Upper Egypt, the body is usually crouched on its left side as though awaiting re-birth, wrapped in skins or matting, and is accompanied by a garniture of pots, cosmetic palettes, weapons and personal ornaments. Sometimes rudimentary clay or bone

37 figurines of women are found in the later examples, and these tend to resemble the so-called concubine figures of historic times, though their exact purpose is somewhat obscure. A statuette, usually in bone, and often reduced to a simple plaque, in the form of a cloaked and bearded figure, also appears occasionally in these deposits; and it has been hazarded that this object may represent a local chieftain worn as a protective amulet.

At the Faiyum A site no traces of any dwellings were found, but at Merimda and on Amratian sites post-holes have been found and remains of hearths; but it is disputed whether these indicate the presence of true houses or mere shelters. At Merimda the dead were buried usually in a crouching pose within the village area and even within the house precincts, a distinctly Lower Egyptian custom which has parallels with similar practices found on Neolithic sites in Western Asia. The graves were often elaborately lined with reed-work. By contrast, at Badari and other Upper Egyptian sites, the dead

36 (*above*) Group of artifacts from the Amratian culture (Naqada I): beaker and bottle in black-topped red ware, red bowl with white cross-lined decoration and red jar with white plant motif; two basalt jars with perforated lug handles; rhomboidal slate palette with pebble muller, and another in the form of a fish; red breccia biconal macehead, black breccia disk-shaped macehead; flint lancehead: ivory amulet surmounted by a bearded head and suspension lug.

37 (*left*) Terracotta statuette of a bird-headed steatopygous woman wearing a long white skirt and evidently performing a dance, perhaps inspired by a bird-mating dance. The figurine may therefore have magic fertility functions. Late Amratian (Naqada I) Period.

were interred in cemeteries on the desert borders, separated from the settlements where they dwelt.

The political system under which these people lived is quite obscure. Probably communities were small, self-supporting and relatively isolated around village centres. They doubtless combined in larger units under the direction of one of their more charismatic leaders to meet a challenge from nature or from rival groups.

The later phases, *c.* 3500–3050 BC

Further cultural developments have in the past often been attributed to direct influences from Western Asia, and it is certain that Delta sites show evidence of close links with contemporary Palestinian culture. However, the transitions in Upper Egypt certainly do not require direct intervention; the processes leading from the earlier Predynastic phases to the Archaic Period are best explained with reference to the infiltration of concepts from, for instance, Mesopotamia. Good examples of the latter are the imprinting of clay with cylinder seals, and certain artistic motifs, such as confronted figures and intertwined motifs; also derived from Mesopotamia may have been the idea of writing, a pictographic system being in place in the Jemdat Nasr culture by the end of the 4th millennium BC.

Important sites for the study of the later phases of Egyptian prehistory have been identified at el Gerza, Haraga and elsewhere in Middle Egypt. The first was nominated by Petrie as proving the type-specimen for the entire period; he therefore called it Gerzean. Nowadays, it is generally referred to as Naqada II, after the distinctive cemeteries on the extensive sites at Naqada in Upper Egypt, where it succeeds the Amratian cultures (Naqada I). The sequence of grave goods shows clear advances in technology and increases in population.

Copper working is more widespread and developed. The ceramics reveal better design and finish with the introduction of a characteristic pottery coated with a fine pinkish buff slip, and painted with designs in red of animals, ships, plants, human beings and religious emblems. Some pots are shaped and decorated to simulate the stone vases that now become common, probably because of the widespread use of a cranked borer fitted with a flint bit, the wobbly drill. The working of flint itself achieves an unrivalled perfection, knives of thin section with regularly rippled blades being produced by pressure flaking. In this mastery over material the Egyptians were already displaying that superb technical skill that distinguishes their best work from that of other nations of antiquity.

The same skill is evident in the cosmetic palettes which are a development of the greenish slate slabs and rhombs of the earlier Badarian and Amratian deposits, and become more common in the Gerzean burials. They are thinner, more finely worked, and often take the shape of animals, birds and fish. One of flat ovoid design is carved in relief with the head of the celestial

cow, having stars at her vertex and the tips of her horns and ears, a forerunner of those large scutiform palettes at the very end of the period, and at
the beginning of the Dynastic age.

In the second half of the Late Gerzean Period (Naqada III) there is
evidence of increased political activity, and the general opinion is that a
struggle for predominance developed between Upper and Lower Egypt. In
both regions the basic unit was now the local community clustered around
a town or group of villages, under the protection of a local variant of one of
the universal deities, and looking for leadership to some powerful chieftain.
These districts, or nomes, were the smallest fragments into which the
country naturally splintered in times of anarchy. There has been much
debate over the development and form of the earliest proto-states in Egypt.
On the basis of later myth and legend, there is the implication that there was
an Upper Egyptian confederation, centred at first on Naqada, presided over
by the storm-god Seth, incarnate in a long-snouted animal, perhaps a wild
pig. This was paralleled by a Lower Egyptian group, which looked to Behdet
as its leader, with the falcon-god Horus as its lord. Both these deities were
looked upon in historic times as personifications of the Two Lands.
However, it is wholly unclear whether such northern and southern polities
actually existed in the form apparently envisaged in later times. All that one
can say is that during the latter part of the Predynastic Period there was an
increased clustering of villages into larger territories under the leadership of
notables who we may see as proto-pharaohs. One of these men built a

38 The Battlefield Palette, front face with design of a
lion probably representing the victorious king savaging
a foeman, while vultures and crows attack the fallen.
On the left of the central depression, the standards of a
district in the Eastern Delta arrest pinioned captives;
on the right, a cloaked figure drives another captive
region before him. The palette has been interpreted as
the record of a Libyan victory over other Delta states,
but until the rest of the palette is found this must
remain a doubtful conjecture.

39 (*left*) The Bull Palette, fragment only, showing the king as a powerful bull goring a foreign foeman who wears a beard and penis-sheath. The nome-standards terminating in hands hold a rope doubtless binding captives and signifying the allies of the king who share in the victory. The other side bears two crenellated town-signs similar to those on one side of the Libya Palette.

40 (*above*) The Libya Palette, lower fragment, with on one side the tribute exacted from a conquered region, with cattle, asses, rams and incense trees (?). On the right of the lower register are two conjoined glyphs which read, 'land of the throw-stick', i.e. Libya.

painted tomb at Hierakonpolis – the first of its kind – and others founded what was to become the national royal cemetery at Abydos.

In Naqada III times, one may trace the first emergence of a pattern that occurs again and again in Egyptian history – it is from the south that an ambitious prince arises who puts an end to a period of anarchy by combining the districts of Upper Egypt under his sway and swallowing piecemeal the local rulers of the north, so creating one state out of a congeries of rival powers. The character of the unification of Egypt in the Eleventh, Eighteenth and Twenty-Fifth Dynasties may perhaps indicate how unity was achieved for the first time at the dawn of history.

The evidence for the political ferment which produced Dynastic Egypt is contained in a number of votive objects, chiefly palettes and maceheads, some of which have been excavated at Hierakonpolis, while others come from Abydos or sites not specified. The palettes are concerned with the all-conquering might of the supreme ruler, who is shown on these greatly damaged monuments as a lion, wild bull, or jackal triumphing over foes who appear to be of northern type, wearing the penis-sheath, the characteristic male garb of Libyan tribes in historic times, and of Egyptians themselves in hunting rig.

The Battlefield Palette, shared between collections in London, Oxford 38 and Lucerne, shows corpses on a battlefield being savaged by the lion-king,

41 Votive palette (reverse) carved
with a relief of King Narmer
accompanied by an attendant
sacrificing a submissive foe before
a symbol of Horus triumphant
over the Delta. Below, two Asiatics
lie fallen.

and attacked by crows and vultures, while an incomplete cloaked figure
drives a personified captive district before him, and the standards of the
Third Nome of the Delta similarly have other captives in their power.
Another fragment, the Bull Palette in Paris, shows the presence of a confederacy of symbolic nomes from Upper and Lower Egypt, assisting to hold
captive by a rope the Libyan foeman (?) that the bull-king has subdued. On
the reverse side, two symbols of townships are shown presumably captured
by the triumphant bull above them. A third fragmentary palette from this
group, now in Cairo, evidently represents operations in Libya. The high
relief on one side shows tribute or booty marshalled in rows of cattle, asses,

42 Votive palette (obverse) carved with a relief of King Narmer and his retinue inspecting a battlefield with rows of victims. Below, as a strong bull he breaks down a fortified town and tramples an Asiatic underfoot. Around the central depression attendants hold long-necked felines in leash.

rams and probably incense trees, together with two glyphs which later become important in the hieroglyphic group for 'Libya'. On the other side, beleaguered walled towns, similar to the pair shown on the Bull Palette, are being demolished by symbols of the king, or his confederates, wielding picks.

These last two palettes have the picture-space organized by division into registers with straight baselines, a more sophisticated system of representation, suggesting that they are less ancient than the others, a conclusion that is reinforced by the appearance of hieroglyphs of somewhat ambiguous import. Together with the damaged votive macehead of Scorpion from

Hierakonpolis, they acquaint us with the figure of this early king or paramount chief, nowadays classified as part of 'Dynasty o', associated with the latter part of the final Predynastic cultural grouping, Naqada III.

Hierakonpolis (Nekhen) is proving to be a pivotal site for the study of the earliest Upper Egyptian monarchy, finds there including the earliest decorated tomb and the earliest cult sanctuary, apart from later caches in the temple that preserved such items as the Scorpion macehead and other commemorative items from the dawn of Egyptian history.

The most spectacular of all of these is the great shield-shaped palette of King Narmer, which has often been interpreted as recording the very unification of Egypt. In any case it can easily be regarded as the first complete antiquity of 'pharaonic' Egypt to have survived, and in its almost immaculate condition, fine detail and clear design, it worthily inaugurates three millennia of Egyptian art-works of all kinds.

Its reverse shows Narmer wearing the White Crown which is thereafter to become the emblematic headgear of the king as ruler of Upper Egypt. He is accompanied by his foot-washer and sandal-bearer, and stands before a falcon with a human arm perched upon a symbolic tract of papyrus-land which the falcon holds by a leading-string, a rebus with the significance, 'the god Horus offers the captive Delta to the King'. Narmer raises his club to dispatch a foeman of Northern appearance: below lie two fallen men of Asiatic type doubtless symbolizing fortified villages and kite-shaped gazelle traps characteristic of the Sinai peninsula. On the obverse, Narmer, now wearing the Red Crown of Sais and Buto, soon to distinguish the king as ruler of Lower Egypt, and accompanied by his retinue, inspects a battlefield evidently near Buto the northern capital. Around the circular grinding depression are arranged two lionesses with serpentine necks in the charge of attendants, perhaps symbolizing the idea of union. Below them Narmer as a wild bull breaks into a fortified place and tramples upon its fallen chieftain, probably an Asiatic.

The palette commemorates a series of victories by Narmer, evidently in Lower Egypt and on its Eastern and Western borders. Its virtually perfect condition shows how carefully it had been prized over the centuries, despite the destruction of the temple in which it was found. Several features distinguish the design of the reliefs. The name of the king appears in a representation of his palace at the top of each scene, between the cow's head of the deity for whose shrine this votive was presumably destined. This is the first appearance of the *serekh*, or rectangular frame, in which one of the names of the pharaoh as the incarnation of Horus was subsequently to be inscribed. Moreover, each figure is accompanied by hieroglyphs, which though for the most part were to remain in the repertory of such signs, are here difficult to interpret, but seem to be the personal names of the protagonists in the scene. We have thus to do with the writing of a civilized state and the record of a historical event.

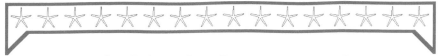

6 · The Archaic Period

Menes and the pharaonic state

According to Manetho and other Classical writers, seconded by some of the extant pharaonic lists, the first unification of Upper and Lower Egypt was achieved by Menes. However, his name has not yet been found securely on contemporary documents, although two occurrences may associate it either with Aha, second king of the First Dynasty, or his predecessor. That the latter was the Horus Narmer is likely, but unproven. Some scholars equate Narmer and Menes, while others make the latter Aha, or a conflation of Scorpion and Narmer. Narmer was, however, the first of the 'historic' kings to build his tomb at Abydos, although a number of generations of earlier monarchs built their tombs near the site chosen for his. Only discovered in the 1990s, the latter may provide us with the names of some of the last pre-historic kings of this part of Egypt.

It is from the plundered royal tombs at Abydos, and the less desecrated sepulchres of the senior nobility at Saqqara in the north, that the archaeological evidence has been recovered from which a tenuous history of the Archaic Period has been reconstructed. The kings mentioned in these tombs were identified by their Horus names (i.e. their names as incarnations of the god Horus), which differ from their personal names recorded in the king-lists; but no scholar believes that these kings are not the rulers of the first two dynasties, nor that acceptable equations between the two sets of names cannot be established. There is ample evidence that the Union of the Two Lands (c. 3050 BC) by Menes, whoever he may have been, was regarded as the most important event in Egyptian history, a 'First Time', similar to the establishing of the universe by the Creator. By uniting two opposed forces, Horus and Seth, the gods of Lower and Upper Egypt, in his own person, Menes set a precedent for every pharaoh who followed him.

He did more, he created a new fulcrum between the two regions by building a residence-city on neutral ground that belonged neither to Upper nor Lower Egypt. Tradition ascribed the founding of 'White Walls', later to be called Memphis, to Menes; and this capital was built on ground recovered from the Nile by diverting its course, perhaps by the huge dyke that formerly existed near modern el Wasta. Memphis was thereafter to be intimately associated with the pharaoh and the union for as long as the kingship lasted, being the primal place of the king's coronation and his jubilees.

The new land that was reclaimed by Menes also probably gave form to the concept of the demiurge Ptah, the god of the new town of Memphis. Ptah caused the primeval mound to arise from the waters of Chaos, in which he existed before the First Time, by taking thought and uttering a word. In the beginning was the Word. To the primitive mind, to name a thing is to create it from nothingness. So important was this utterance that in time it came to be represented as a separate deity, together with the magic thought that had created it. Thereafter the pharaoh, the incarnation of the Creator, was believed to rule by the same divine attributes of creative thought and authoritative utterance.

Ptah as the new-risen earth-mound contained within himself all the seeds of vegetation, as well as the clay, earth, stones, metals and minerals from which the works of men as well as nature were formed. As such, and with his intangible means of procreation through utterance, he represented a more sophisticated concept than earlier deities such as Atum (see below p. 99). His late arrival in the pantheon is suggested by his human aspect as a man, closely shrouded and inert upon his mound, carrying a sceptre which incorporated the attributes of divine kingship – stability, power and the ability to confer life. He has the mark of an intellectualized concept like the later universal god, Serapis, of the Ptolemaic Dynasty; but also like Serapis he made a wider, more popular, appeal by his identification with an ancient seminal bull-cult of the locality, that of Apis.

The invention of Ptah as the god of the new land upon which White Walls was built thus reflected the same independence that had been secured by Menes in the political sphere. Thereafter Ptah remained exclusively the god of Memphis. The later temples to him at Thebes and in Nubia were built at a time when the pharaohs were anxious to stress the universality of the gods of Upper and Lower Egypt. A popular cult of Ptah-of-Menes in Ramesside times perpetuated the connection of the first pharaoh with the god he had promoted.

The successors of Menes

The pattern of kingship set by Menes was followed by his successors as a divine formula for success. Each king in turn was crowned at Memphis, when he made a circuit of the (white) walls in a ceremony which signified his taking formal direction of his kingdom. He continued the policy of extending irrigation works and land reclamation as much by the power he was supposed to exercise over the flood as by the demands of a growing population. A steadily expanding prosperity is to be inferred from the progressive increase in the size of the tombs of the dynasty and in the magnificence of their furnishings, though all that remains of them is now mostly in random fragments. The large timber joists, roofing beams and linings used in these constructions suggest that trade with Lebanon flourished. Articles in ivory, ebony and lapis lazuli show that trading contacts had been

43 Djet, the fourth king of the First
Dynasty, like other rulers of the Archaic
Period, had his tomb at Abydos marked
by two stelae bearing his name. This was
'Serpent' (*djet*) written within a *serekh*,
a representation of his palace both in plan
and elevation and surmounted by the falcon
Horus of whom he was an incarnation.

made with tropical Africa and Hither Asia. Menes evidently engaged in
operations against tribes in the Western Desert and in Sinai. His successor,
Aha, was active in Nubia. Djer, the third king, is commemorated in a relief
on the rocks near the former second cataract showing Nubian foes fallen in
battle, others taken prisoner and townships captured. The fifth king, Den,
is shown on an ivory label from his tomb smiting the bedouin of the Eastern
Desert or Sinai.

The monuments of the Second Dynasty (*c.* 2813–2663 BC) are even scant-
ier than those of their predecessors. The substructures of two of their kings'
tombs have been found at Abydos, while two more lie at Saqqara. Fire
damage to tombs of the First Dynasty has been attributed to hostility on the
part of the new line, but remains unproven.

Hotepsekhemwy, the name of the first king of the Second Dynasty, means
'The Two Powers are at Peace'. However, the second part of the dynasty
seems to have been riven with conflict. This may have begun when King
Peribsen seems to have overturned the tradition that the pharaoh was the
incarnation of the falcon-god Horus by surmounting his name in his *serekh* 43, 44
by the Seth-animal. King Khasekhem seems to have been forced to retreat
to Hierakonpolis in the south, before being finally victorious under the name

44 The *serekh* traditionally enclosed the Horus-name of the pharaoh, and was accordingly surmounted by that deity's falcon. However, Peribsen (far left) adopted one topped by the animal of Horus' opposite number, Seth. The location of both gods atop the *serekh* of Khasekhemwy (left) was clearly meant to symbolize his reconciliation of the factions that had disturbed the latter part of the Second Dynasty.

Khasekhemwy – 'Appearance of Two Powers'. As self-proclaimed reconciliator, he prepares the way for the emergence of a new dynasty, the Third, from the mists of the Archaic Period.

The culture of the Archaic Period

Despite the evidence of religious contention, the achievement of the first two dynasties was considerable and resulted in the establishment of many of the institutions and traditions of the pharaonic state. In particular, the office of kingship gradually evolved. From the first the pharaoh wore the trappings of a pastoral chief, as is seen on the Narmer palette, his loins protected by a *shemset* apron, his back guarded by a bull's tail hanging from his belt, the goat beard of his flocks attached to his chin, and carrying the crook and incense-gum collecting flail of a Mediterranean shepherd. When he officiated as King of Upper Egypt, he wore the tall conical White Crown. As King of Lower Egypt he wore the Red Crown; but in the reign of Den a combination of both crowns appeared in a new headgear, the Double Crown. At the same time a new title, He-who-belongs-to-the-Sedge-and-the-Bee (usually translated as 'the King of Upper and Lower Egypt'), and an additional name to accompany it, were added to the name he had adopted as an incarnation of the god Horus. As early as the reign of Menes, the king had assumed a name in his capacity as the ruler of Upper and Lower Egypt, and with it the title of The-Two-Ladies, signifying the sponsorship of the goddess-representatives of the two halves of the country. Alongside this 'conventional' interpretation of these two sets of insignia, however, it is also now argued that a more complex duality was involved, and that the concepts usually translated as King of Upper Egypt and King of Lower Egypt might rather mean kingship *per se* and its earthly manifestation respectively.

The pharaoh also inherited all the magic virtue of a primitive medicine man. His power over the Nile and its life-giving waters accredited him with seminal influences, keeping drought and sterility from his peoples. He contended with Evil which manifested itself in the form of human predators on the cultivators of the Valley, or in the wild animals and birds that preyed

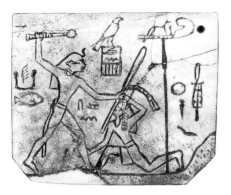

45 Ivory label for tying to sandals, incised with a scene of King Den smiting an Asiatic, and the text, 'First Time of Smiting the East', a means of dating a certain year in the king's reign.

upon the domestic flocks and the ripening crops. So he is represented not only as smiting the Asiatic bedouin of Sinai and the Eastern Desert, or the 45 Libyans of the Northwest and the Nubians of the South, but also as the intrepid hunter of the lion and wild cattle. In his guise as Horus, the harpooner of the hippopotamus foe into which Seth has transformed himself, he seeks his enemy among the marshlands. On death he is assimilated to the Creator of whom he is an incarnation, and his tomb becomes holy ground, while his cult is observed as that of a great god.

A concomitant of such beliefs was the practice of sacrificing subsidiary wives and servants with their equipment to accompany the king into the next world, and so achieve immortality, by ministering to him in the hereafter. Around the tombs of the kings, queens and certain nobles of the First 46 Dynasty are ranged the pit burials of their women and retainers, dwarf attendants, even pet dogs. The custom reached its peak in the reign of Djer. Thereafter it declined and ceased at Saqqara by the end of the Dynasty. It lingered on at Abydos into the Second Dynasty, when a solitary pair of servants was buried with Khasekhemwy. It was, however, the custom at all periods for some high officials to be buried in large tombs, as distinct from mere pits, near the kings they had served in life, but it is probable that they were also related to them and chose to rest in the family burying-ground.

46 Mastaba of a First Dynasty official at Saqqara. The mud-brick walls are panelled in the so-called 'palace-façade' pattern, actually a repeated set of doors set between twin towers. The small tombs surrounding the mastaba are those of servants.

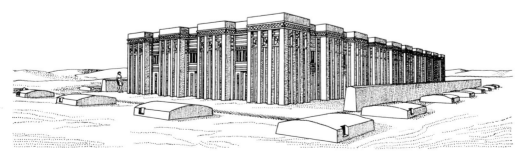

The civil service

The presence of the tombs of high officials in close proximity to those of their kings emphasizes the importance of such men in the life and government of Egypt. Land in Egypt was made suitable for cultivation as much by seasonal organized human effort on a large scale as by natural conditions. This circumstance favoured the emergence of technocrats who directed labour, determined the right moment for raising dams and piercing dykes, cutting canals and re-defining boundaries. They organized the collection and storage of harvests, and decided how much of it was to be allocated to imposts and to the next season's seed. Apart from the companions of the king, who assisted him in his administrative duties and in the affairs of his household, there were the two chancellors in charge of the Red and White Treasuries, as the store-houses of Lower and Upper Egypt were designated from their national colours. The collection and distribution of supplies of all kinds from wine and oil to corn and honey were under their direction and that of the two Controllers of the Granaries. The distribution of supplies to the temples, and to a privileged elite of courtiers and officials, was administered from the Office of the Overseer of the King's Bounty.

This centralized administration was probably duplicated on a minor scale in the provincial centres of Upper Egypt, but the exact situation at this period is obscure and little is known beyond the titles of some of the officials. The administration in Lower Egypt, however, with its large centres of population clustered around thriving towns, probably differed markedly from the government of the more rustic population scattered the length of Upper Egypt. It was not until the last reigns of the Sixth Dynasty that Upper Egypt was to exert any influence upon the central government despite the pre-eminence of the South over the North. This is in fact a pattern that occurs again in all subsequent unifications of the Two Lands after periods of political upheaval.

The development of Egypt as a powerful political entity under a divine king would not have been possible, however, even with a dedicated bureaucracy of competent officials, in the absence of another element – a staff of learned scribes, skilled in the magic arts of reading, writing and mathematics. It is the ubiquitous scribe with his writing-palette and papyrus roll that obtrudes himself upon the notice at most periods of the Egyptian past. Papyrus paper had already been invented by the beginning of the First Dynasty: two rolls of blank papyrus were found in a store-chamber of the tomb of Hemaka at Saqqara. A rapid and cursive system of writing adapted to the use of pen and ink upon papyrus was soon evolved from the hesitant glyphs carved on the Narmer Palette. Writing, as elsewhere, was developed in Egypt not for the purpose of enshrining great thoughts in a memorable literary form, but for the utilitarian purpose of recording the minutiae of state business in a portable and durable form, and not entrusting it to fallible human memory. Precise instructions could be issued at a distance and

47

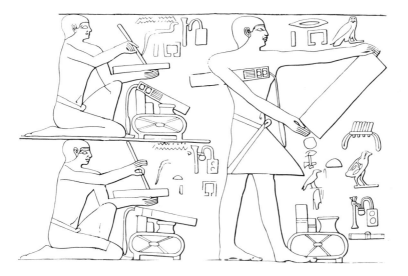

47 The steward Khai reads out an inventory from a papyrus which the funerary scribes with their palettes, pointed erasers on cords, water-pots, pens and papyrus rolls in corded portfolios have prepared.

reports received from afar. The classic example of the system in action during the Old Kingdom is the correspondence between the young king Pepy II and the explorer Harkhuf (c. 2280 BC), who on his return to Aswan from his fourth trading expedition into the Sudan, had written to the king reporting that he had acquired a dancing pygmy similar to one brought back by a certain Bawerdjed a century earlier. The king replied to Harkhuf giving detailed instructions for him to come immediately to the court at Memphis, bringing the remarkable creature with him in the care of reliable attendants; and promising him greater rewards than Bawerdjed had received, if the pygmy arrived in good health and spirits.

The early use of data preserved by such a system is evident in entries on the Palermo Stone where the heights of the inundation and the periodical censuses of men and animals are noted over a period of some five centuries. Without the medium of writing, the highly centralized administration of the Egyptian state could never have been devised: in fact, the creation of a unified government may well have had to await the invention and spread of writing.

With the art of writing there was a parallel development in the science of calculation. A decimal system had existed in predynastic times, and it is possible that during the Archaic Period nearly all the edifice of later Egyptian mathematics was raised on this foundation, but since most scribal learning was transmitted verbally from one adept to his pupil as a mystery, we have no means of assessing the full extent of their theoretical knowledge. The incentives were also probably utilitarian, the need for solving the many problems that faced a centralizing state dependent for its wealth upon a scheme of taxation that was ultimately determined from measurements and calculations of possible and actual yields. The bureaucrat would also be required to solve problems connected with such matters as the distribution of rations or seed-corn, the number of bricks required to build a given structure, and the number of men necessary to perform different kinds of labouring work. The **48** Rhind Mathematical Papyrus in the British Museum, written about 1600 BC, and other similar texts, reveal that by the end of the 3rd millennium BC the Egyptians had developed a system of numeration with which they could make arithmetical calculations involving complicated fractions with comparative ease and accuracy. They could solve problems involving two unknown quantities and had simple notions of geometrical and arithmetical progression using fractions. They were also familiar with elementary solid geometry and the properties of circles, cylinders, triangles and pyramids. Since they could find the area of a circle with tolerable accuracy, they could also calculate the volume of a cylinder. They could also determine the volume of a pyramid or truncated pyramid.

The inundations of the Nile often swept away old landmarks and an accurate survey had periodically to be made to re-establish former boundaries according to the written records. While linear measure, like that of Europe before the introduction of the metric system, was based upon the dimensions of the human body, the finger, palm, forearm, and so forth, measure**49** ments of capacity also existed for assessing the corn, oil and wine harvests. In the important tomb of the high official Hesire, of the early Third Dynasty (*c.* 2640 BC), two elaborate sets of fourteen wooden and leather tubs with strikers for measuring his taxes in corn are included among other essential equipment painted on the chapel wall.

The science of computing time did not lag behind that of measuring space. The prosperity of Egypt depended upon forecasting the annual rise

48 A section of the Rhind Mathematical Papyrus written in hieratic, *c.* 1600 BC, dealing with problems concerning triangles.

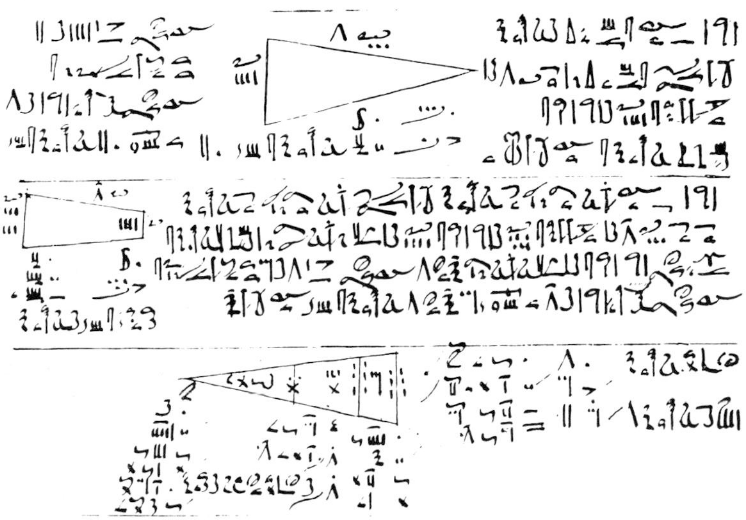

49 A farmer among the standing grain swearing an oath that the boundary stone at his feet is in its proper location. The assessors' chariots, one pulled by mules, wait with their drivers in the shade of a sycamore.

of the Nile and its probable volume, and what in a pre-scientific society was just as important, the auspicious moment for a feast or religious ceremony to ensure the success of an undertaking. The prehistoric Egyptian could hardly fail to observe recurring celestial phenomena such as the rising and setting of stars on the horizon as a means of dividing time into sequences. Astronomy was studied with particular attention at the temple of the sun-god at Heliopolis where the ritual was closely concerned with time-measurement and the movement of heavenly bodies. Architects and engineers of Heliopolitan origin seem to have been responsible for the accurate orientation of pyramids and their geometrical perfection during the early Old Kingdom.

It was observed at an early date that the dog-star Sirius, regarded as the goddess Sopdet (Greek, Sothis), vanished from sight for a period of seventy days in midsummer and then rose on the eastern horizon for the first time before dawn, and this appearance foretold the rising of the Egyptian Nile in inundation a few days later. This annual heliacal rising of Sothis was regarded as a prime event, the beginning of a new year and the means of fixing the first of the month of the old Egyptian calendar.

Like many other primitive peoples and the nations of antiquity, the Egyptians had an original lunar calendar determined by the phases of the moon during the cycle of growing, fruiting and resting that made up the agricultural year. They early realized that four lunar months went to the season of inundation (*akhet*), another four to the season of planting and growth (*peret*), and a further four to the season of harvest and low water (*shomu*). Since, however, twelve lunar months average a total of 354 days, they added an additional month of twenty-nine or thirty days every three, or less often, two years. A lunar calendar, kept in place by oscillating around the heliacal rising of Sothis, was quite adequate for the ordinary purposes of the Egyptian farmer; but when Egypt became a highly organized state such a variable calendar must have been felt as a great inconvenience. It was some unknown genius during the Archaic Period who devised a schematic lunar year of 365 days and fixed its inception upon the rising of Sirius. The new calendar, called by modern scholars the civil calendar, had a year consisting of twelve months of thirty days each, with five extra days at the end regarded as the birthdays of the gods of the Osiris cycle. Each month of thirty days was divided into three ten-day weeks, an arrangement which involved a day of twenty-four hours. The resulting calendar has been described as 'the only intelligent calendar which has ever existed in human history'.

It was some time before the Egyptians realized that their civil calendar was lagging behind the astronomical year. They never corrected this discrepancy by intercalating an additional day every four years, but allowed the civil year to get out of phase until in 4 × 365 years it came into conjunction again. This occurred at the end of the Eighteenth Dynasty, *c.* 1317 BC. Instead of a leap year, the Egyptians introduced *c.* 2500 BC a second lunar calendar tied not to Sothis, but the civil year. For most of its existence therefore the pharaonic state had three calendars, the civil year and its lunar counterpart for administrative and fiscal purposes, and the original lunar year to fix the dates of religious festivals and temple services.

50 (*left*) Restored statue of King Khasekhem wearing a festal robe and the crown of Upper Egypt, over which he may have ruled only in the earlier part of his reign. The base is inscribed with contorted figures of slain northerners, numbered as 47,209, doubtless an exaggeration.

51 (*right*) Spouted libation bowl carved in the form of a pair of arms reading 'Ka', embracing an 'ankh' sign, thus ensuring that water poured from it would be magically imbued with 'life'. It may also have belonged to an official of King Den of the First Dynasty, named Ankhka.

The immense stimulus given to cultural enterprise by the first unification of the Two Lands was to be repeated in all subsequent reunions. In the Archaic Period it is evident in all departments of human activity. Despite the absence of texts, it is possible to detect in embryo many of the features that characterize the fully developed pharaonic state.

The struggles that preceded the Union and which are reflected in the design of the votive palettes from Abydos and Hierakonpolis, show the importance of the nomes as the allies of the king; but thereafter their influence wanes, except as representatives of the various districts of the land at the coronation, and at its repetition during the jubilees of the pharaoh. In their place, the figure of the king towers over all, just as his tomb out-rivals those of any others, apart perhaps from one or two belonging to chief queens or queen mothers. The presence of the large mastabas of such women, bearing names compounded with Neith, the great goddess of Sais in Lower Egypt, is redolent of the importance assumed by royal women at all subsequent periods in Egypt. It also suggests that political conquest was consolidated by marriage treaties between rival powers.

The age was one of ferment in the theological field, too, evident in the dispute between the cults of Horus and Seth with its effect upon the politics of the kingship. Elsewhere the Palermo Stone speaks of the 'birth' of various gods during the early reigns, by which we are to understand that the iconography of the pantheon was being settled by devising the image of individual deities, installing them in shrines built for their cult and endowing them with a priesthood and revenues.

Little of the art of the age has survived intact, but the two statues of King Khasekhem (*c.* 2680 BC) show a progressive mastery in carving soft limestone and hard schist. The great glory of the two dynasties is their wealth of fine stone vessels cut from selected boulders in breccia, rock crystal, diorite, slate, alabaster and other hard stones. Some show a virtuosity in the carving of intractable materials which borders on the contemptuous. The introduction of the potter's wheel and the consequent production of fine pottery in the Second Dynasty reduced the quantity and quality of later stone vessels. 50 51

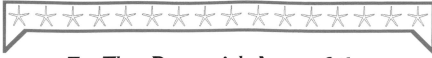

7 · The Pyramid Age of the Old Kingdom I

Imhotep and Egyptian culture

With the Third Dynasty, Egypt entered fully and gloriously into those five centuries of high culture to which modern historians have given the name of the Old Kingdom. Khasekhemwy was followed on the throne by Sanakht and Djoser; although apparently Khasekhemwy's sons by Queen Nimaethap, they were regarded by posterity as beginning a new dynasty. Reliefs on the rocks near the turquoise and copper-ore mines in Sinai show these kings, and their successor Sekhemkhet, in the now classic pose of keeping evil from their borders by smiting the local bedouin. All the figures reveal the dour, heavy portraits of the Third Dynasty kings and their followers.

It is, however, more in the arts of peace than in war that they are now celebrated, and here the chief actor is not a king but a king's man, the chancellor Imhotep, pre-eminent in his time, and renowned in later ages as an astronomer, architect, writer, sage and physician, being eventually deified. As a heroic instigator of Egyptian culture, his reputation never lost its lustre

52 Rock carving in the Wadi Maghara in Sinai showing King Sekhemkhet, probably the successor of Djoser in the Third Dynasty, smiting an Asiatic of the region.

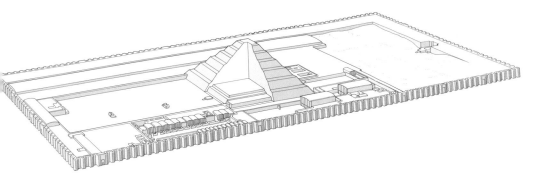

53 The Saqqara funerary complex of King Djoser was modelled on the brick enclosures of earlier kings, and incorporated a whole series of ritual buildings. The pyramid began life as a low square massif, but was extended into the first pyramid – the Step Pyramid.

until in Ptolemaic times, as Manetho records, he was famed for the invention of building in dressed stone in the reign of Djoser. The truth of this traditional association was vindicated when excavations at the Step Pyramid at Saqqara brought to light a statue base of Djoser on which the name and titles of Imhotep are given equal pride of place with those of the king. As the architect of the Step Pyramid, Imhotep in point of fact did not invent building in stone. Stone flooring and walling, lintels and jambs, had appeared sporadically during the Archaic Period: but a great building made entirely of cut stone appeared first in the world during the reign of Djoser to remain for ever the wonder of its age.

The tombs of the kings and nobles of the Archaic Period show a steady evolution in size and design. The burial chambers were soon located below ground while the magazines for grave goods were built into the mass of the superstructure, the rectangular mound, or mastaba of mud brick which surmounted the private tombs. The faces of such mastabas were built in a panelled design similar to the façades of great houses, and the presumption is that in their complete state each would have represented a great mansion in which the dead eternally rested. What sort of superstructure overlaid the ruined Abydos royal tombs is uncertain, but it may also have been a rectangular mound surrounded by trees.

The funerary enclosures which complemented them were the truly monumental elements, paralleling the private mastabas in having their enclosure walls bearing the panelling represented, for instance, on the stela of King Djet. These brick walls enclosed a large open area that seems to have 43 contained a variety of buildings constructed in wood and reeds. The latest of these structures added inside it a brick-skinned mound, perhaps paralleling that long placed over the actual royal sepulchre. It was the genius of Imhotep to take the basic plane of the funerary monuments of the kings of the Second Dynasty, and by introducing new elements to develop it into a funerary complex of great originality. He chose a site at Saqqara, opposite 53 the capital at Memphis, where its position on an escarpment on the Western

Desert verges would ensure that it would dominate the skyline. Furthermore, he eventually developed the mound of the superstructure into a stepped construction rising in six diminishing tiers to a height of over 60 m, like a giant double staircase reaching into the sky, each face orientated to a cardinal point. The various buildings associated with this central feature were enclosed by a wall of palace-façade pattern over a mile in its perimeter and covering a rectangular area more than sixty times the extent of Khasekhemwy's tomb at Abydos.

Of the fourteen great portals that interrupt the pattern of the panelled walls, only one is a true entrance, its doors represented as though folded back, giving access to a vast dromos through an impressive colonnade of engaged piers. The mortuary temple adjoining the pyramid on its northern side is an elaboration of a similar structure in the brick mastaba tomb of Merka, dating to the end of the First Dynasty. There are other familiar features, such as the magazines housing provisions and furnishings on the north side, and (in galleries and chambers) beneath the pyramid. But there are also a number of elements that appear for the first time, such as a jubilee court, containing the two rows of shrines of the nome gods of Upper and Lower Egypt, with the attendant throne-podium and vestries. On the south side of the pyramid was an extensive dromos with its hoof-shaped markers for defining the course that the king would encircle in a running ceremony at his coronation when he took possession of the land. He repeated this rite

55

54 Relief, framed in faience tiles imitating rush matting, in a chamber of the South Tomb at the Step Pyramid. Djoser, holding a 'flail' and a 'portfolio' containing his title-deeds (?), runs over a course between hoof-shaped markers, a ceremony that was performed at his coronation, and repeated at intervals, symbolizing his taking possession of the land.

55 The Step Pyramid, panelled wall of the chapel adjacent to the South Tomb, its cornice decorated with a frieze of cobras, the first appearance in stone of this protective device.

at his jubilees. A remarkable feature was a large mastaba-type tomb on the southern boundary (nearest to Abydos) with its adjacent chapel and subterranean apartments that duplicated the funerary chambers beneath the pyramid itself. In addition, there was a wealth of precious objects and furnishings, such as the panels of blue glazed tiles that decorated some of the subterranean rooms in imitation of rush-mat hangings. Statues of gods and of the king, either alone or with members of his family, in standing and seated poses, were installed, including a life-sized statue of Djoser upon his throne. This particular statue has survived undamaged, apart from the loss of the inlaid eyes, through being enclosed in a special limestone chamber, or *serdab* next to the mortuary temple. There were also delicate low-relief panels of the king performing his running ceremony. In various chambers were stored over 40,000 stone vessels, evidently royal heirlooms of the Archaic Period. In addition to all this, of course, was the more costly treasure which has doubtless been pillaged from it long ago.

54

In his great design, it is evident that Imhotep incorporated and expanded the elements previously separately provided at Abydos within the same complex, and included also such traditional features as subsidiary tombs for members of the royal family. The monument, in fact, was a vast city of the dead, enclosed within a temenos, the walls of which imitated the white walls which Menes had built around his Residence four centuries earlier. But the various components were buildings by magic only. They were mere dummies, façades behind which lay rubble fillings. Imitation doors, with their cross-battens, hinges and bolts, stand open where approach is permitted. Stake fences carved in high relief on blocking walls bar access where entry is forbidden.

56   The truly novel aspect of the Step Pyramid complex, however, marking a turning-point in the development of architecture, was that there sprung complete from the mind of Imhotep a system of building entirely in quarried stone, in local limestone for the mass of the various structures, and fine limestone from Tura across the river for the casings and claddings. The burial chambers were constructed of pink granite from distant Aswan; and black granite from the same quarries was used for such features as corbels carved as the heads of foreign foemen. The handling of the building stone betrays the pioneer nature of the craft in which the masons were feeling their way. The outer facings are in blocks of fine limestone no bigger than their mud-brick archetypes. It is only towards the end of the reign that the architect and workmen became sufficiently confident and skilled to handle the large masses of limestone that are characteristic of the megalithic construction of the ensuing dynasty.

The Step Pyramid of Djoser was a translation into stone of a technique of building in wood and vegetable products, such as bundles of reeds, stalks of papyrus rush and palm fronds stripped of all but their uppermost leaves, coated with argillaceous mud. It is doubtful, however, whether the domestic architecture which Imhotep immortalized in stone reproduced contemporary buildings, except perhaps in the more secluded and primitive areas of the marshlands. Houses had been made of mud brick from Amratian times; and the royal mastabas from the time of the First Dynasty show that the palaces of the kings were built on strictly architectonic principles, based upon rectangular units. The design of the structures that Imhotep raised for Djoser at Saqqara seems to hark back to a very remote past, deliberately recalling the occasion of the First Time, when creation arose in the primeval marsh, to which Djoser would return on death. This was a style of architecture that would never be seen again in Egypt, a giant stage-set for the enactment of a miracle-play of the king's resurrection as a great god in the hereafter. Only in one feature did subsequent architecture preserve the same principles of design: the holy-of-holies of the Egyptian temple is a rendering in stone of the primitive rush-work cabin that arose on the primeval mound at the First Time to shelter the Creator at his work.

56 (*right, above*) The Step Pyramid at Saqqara, the first of such monuments of the Third Dynasty, showing part of the reconstructed enclosure wall of fine Tura limestone, with the entrance portal admitting to a colonnade of engaged columns leading to the great central courtyard.

57 (*right, below*) The strange form of the pyramid of Maidum is the result of the stone-robbing and possible structural failure of a monument that began life as a step pyramid, was enlarged, and then converted to a geometrically true pyramid. It appears to have been built by Snoferu, although it has often been suggested that it was begun by his predecessor, Huni.

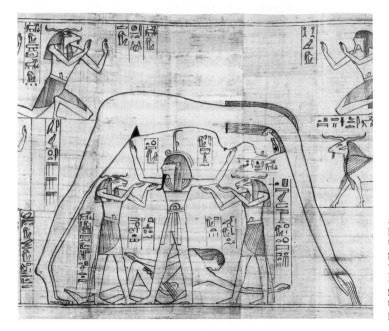

58 Drawing from a funerary papyrus of the procreation of the third generation of the gods of Heliopolis. Shu, the void, lifting and lowering Nut, the sky, upon the earth god, Geb. Ram-headed manifestations of the magic power of the demiurge assist.

The rise of Heliopolis

There is, however, another and scarcely less important aspect of the entry upon the scene of Imhotep, the architect. He was also the high priest of the sun god in Heliopolis where Djoser also built a temple decorated with elegant stone reliefs. We are now confronted with the clear emergence of the powerful and widespread influence of the solar cult which was to dominate Egyptian civilization thereafter. The priesthood of Heliopolis served the office of an intelligentsia, fulfilling a role which the scholars of Alexandria were to play much later in the Hellenistic world. It was from their study of the heavens in which their god was lord that they derived their knowledge of the movement of celestial bodies, the calculation of time-spans from the rising and setting of stars, the geometry of angles, the measurement of space and similar studies. Such science was jealously preserved as the mysteries of their religion and handed down from one adept to another, like the secrets of writing, reading, mathematics and any other craft. Such knowledge too conferred power, and ensured that in the developing technology of the Egyptian state the wise men of On would be paramount.

The learning of such pundits had its effect upon the politics of the kingship from an early date. Nebre, a king of the Second Dynasty, incorporated the name of the sun god in his own. The doctrines of Ptah were greatly influenced by the teaching of Heliopolis, 20 miles to the north of Memphis. Above all, the fusion of the sun religion with the cult of the pharaoh is shown in the design of a comb of Djet, incised with a design of Horus in the barque of the sun-god sailing across the heavens in the form of the outspread wings of the sky goddess Nut. The king is an incarnation of Horus; and thus arises the idea of the sun god as a heavenly king, Re-Herakhty (i.e. Re-the-Horus-of-the-two-horizons, or the sun god in his active aspect, ruling the day-sky from dawn to sunset). The pharaoh rules on earth as his representative.

The sun cult of Heliopolis taught that out of the waters of Chaos arose the primeval mound in the shape of the pyramidal stone, the *ben-ben*, or High Sand, in the sanctuary at Heliopolis. It was on the *ben-ben* that the Creator first manifested himself, either in the form of a heron-like phoenix (the bird of light which dispelled the darkness over the waters) or as Atum, the demiurge in human form. Atum immediately created from himself by masturbation two other deities, Shu and Tefnut, to form a trinity. Shu, the   58
god of Air or the Void, and Tefnut, the goddess of Moisture, created by their coupling another pair, Geb the earth, and Nut, the heavens. In these primordial gods appear personifications of the elements later recognized by Empedocles as constituting all matter. Four others were added to these quintessential gods to form the great ennead, or group of the nine gods of Heliopolis. Shu by interposing himself between Geb and Nut separated the heavens from the recumbent earth, which was regarded as male in Egypt against the universal concept elsewhere of mother earth. By lowering the goddess every evening on to the earth, Shu brought about the procreation of two pairs of other deities, the gods Osiris and Seth, and the goddesses Isis and Nephthys.

These legends reveal a very early syncretization between different sets of beliefs, in which the divinities of the Osiris cycle of Abydos and Busiris were

59 The night-boat of the inert sun god towed by the people of the underworld through the fourth division of *The Book of Gates*, bringing light and life to its denizens. The ram-headed sun god stands in the cabin protected by a great serpent. He is accompanied by the gods of authoritative utterance and magic understanding.

assimilated into the Heliopolitan pantheon, this process doubtless reflecting the political unions of city states that preceded the consolidation of the country under one ruler. By historic times the sun god was generally represented in his active role as a heavenly king Re, or Re-Herakhty, and usually appears in the form of a king with the head of the falcon Horus bearing on his vertex the solar disk.

Djoser in one inscription is hailed as the sun god himself, but by the Fourth Dynasty it was established that the pharaoh was the son of Re, who would on death journey to the horizon where he would be assimilated to the god who had begotten him. Re-Herakhty sailed over the waters of heaven in a day-barque bringing light and life to a sleeping world that imitated that moribund state that existed before there was light at the First Time. At sunset he stepped into the night-barque and continued his circuit over the waters that are under the earth in the form of Flesh, an inert ram-headed manifestation of the Creator, undergoing various transformations like the phases of a long dream, that ensured that he would awake in the redness of dawn as a child-king within the uterine sun-disk, or as the young god Khepri who alights as a scarab on the day-barque and begins another daily cycle of Creation.

The influence of Heliopolitan theology can be seen in the conversion of the superstructure of the royal tomb from a palace to the High Sand of the sun cult. The design did not develop without several changes of plan, and the Step Pyramid eventually appeared as a staircase whereby the dead king could mount up into the sky to join the crew of the solar barque as it sailed across the heavens from the moment that the rising sun lit up its topmost stage. Subsequent kings of the Third Dynasty adopted the same pattern of superstructure for their tomb complexes, though none of them succeeded in completing his monument. Most remarkable of these structures is the Brick Pyramid at Abu Rowash, which on the grounds of its substructure design must date to this period, but which was built of mud brick, a material not used again for pyramid building for eight centuries. Now almost destroyed, it may well have been a step pyramid.

The last step pyramid to be built lay at Maidum, and marks the transition between the Third and Fourth Dynasties. Only its core now survives as a tower-like structure, thrusting out of a mound of rubble which comprises, and covers, the remainder of the mantle which was added by Snoferu to convert it into a straight-sided true pyramid.

Snoferu, first king of the Fourth Dynasty, was also responsible for erecting the first true pyramids, at Dahshur. The earlier of these, the Bent Pyramid, changes its angle half way up; the later, the Red Pyramid, is the

60 (right) The pyramids of Giza, from the south. In the foreground are three small pyramids, two intended for wives of Mykerinus, and one as a ritual annex to the king's own pyramid. Beyond lie the much larger monuments of Khephren and Kheops.

earliest structure with an uninterrupted slope. The building of two such monuments by one king (three if the original step pyramid at Maidum was his as well) was the result of structural failure at the Bent Pyramid; Snoferu was interred in the Red Pyramid, where some of his body was found.

61 With his son and successor, Kheops, the Pyramid Age fairly gets into its stride. Kheops built at Giza the Great Pyramid; and this, together with its two companions on the same site, was considered one of the wonders of the
60 ancient world. It is still able to stun the spectator into silence despite all its ruin, its casing-stones having been stripped off to build medieval Cairo. It contained well over 2,000,000 blocks of limestone, some of them weighing 15 tons apiece. The core blocks were quarried on the spot – the actual quarries have now been located on the plateau by Mark Lehner and his colleagues – but the finer casing blocks were cut at Tura and ferried to the site during the times of high flood. In addition granite boulders were hewn as jambs and relieving beams; and basalt blocks were used to floor the mortuary temple where the cloister was supported by granite piers. The quarrying of such hard stones had become sufficiently expert by the end of the dynasty for plans to be laid for encasing the lower third of the pyramid of Mykerinus, the smallest of the Giza group, in red granite; the work was never finished.

Internally, the Great Pyramid is the most elaborate of its period. This seems to have been the result of a series of changes of plan, which the late

61 The necropolis of Giza, looking westwards from the central field to the pyramid of Khephren left, and that of Kheops right. In the foreground is a ruined mastaba cemetery of the Old Kingdom.

I. E. S. Edwards convincingly argued was the result of a decision to employ a stone sarcophagus for the first time in a royal tomb since the early Third Dynasty. The original burial chamber was deep underground, reached by a passage far too narrow to allow the passage of such an item. A new chamber was thus constructed in the superstructure, through whose roof the sarcophagus could be introduced (this room is now known erroneously as the 'Queen's Chamber'); in the event this was abandoned in favour of a further, much grander, new chamber, in which the king was ultimately buried (the 'King's Chamber').

From these rooms lead apparently unique 'air shafts', although traces of beginnings were found in Khephren's pyramid. They are generally assumed to have had some astronomical significance; when investigated using a robot in 1990, one of the small channels in the Queen's Chamber, 20 cm square, was found to be blocked with a piece of stone to which two copper items were attached. This led to much ridiculous media speculation about a 'secret door'; investigation of the blocking has yet to take place. Another discovery made during the same decade was that of the foundations of the lost subsidiary pyramid of Kheops by the Director of the Giza Plateau, Zahi Hawass. All pyramids of the Old Kingdom have small pyramids on their south/south-east sides, which should not be confused with those built for queens, some of which have subsidiaries of their own. The meaning of these subsidiary monuments remains wholly obscure, none having revealed any material that might provide a proper explanation.

Each pyramid had its ancillary buildings within its complex. Nearby, in the royal tradition, the mastaba tombs of relatives and high court officials clustered around their kings in death as they had attended them in life. Two such cemeteries that Kheops built to the east and west of the Great Pyramid were particularly grand in their design and use of rich materials. The dilapidated condition in which many of these monuments have come down to us, however, gives an impression of cold austerity, though in their original state it is now clear that the mortuary temples and causeways were decorated with the most delicate low reliefs, brilliantly coloured, of which only small, scattered fragments remain. The Valley Temple of Khephren, the best preserved of the subsidiary buildings at Giza, is indeed impressive in its stark simplicity with severe granite piers upholding equally massive architraves, and with the cyclopean limestone walls clad inside and out with large granite ashlars, unrelieved by any ornamentation, apart from a hieroglyphic inscription deeply incised around each entrance doorway. In its original condition, however, it must have been tremendously impressive with the sunlight streaming through louvers cut at ceiling level and falling upon the polished alabaster floor and scattering a diffused glow upon the twenty-three statues of the king carved from alabaster, greywacke and green diorite from the Nubian desert, that stood before the piers in the interior hall. In the uncompromising severity and nicely calculated effects of this, the most complete realization of the mortuary concept in Egyptian architecture, we are aware

62 The interior of the Valley Temple of Khephren at Giza, built of red granite from Aswan, with a floor of alabaster laid with emplacements for the statues that stood in the T-shaped hall.

63 Upper part of a dark green diorite statue of Khephren, a little over life-size, seated upon his lion throne and protected by the falcon of Horus who perches upon the backrest. Found in the well of the Valley Temple by Mariette in 1853.

64 Limestone statue of the Prince and Vizier, Hemon, from the serdab of his large mastaba tomb on the west of the pyramid of Kheops at Giza. He served as the Overseer of Works of the King and was therefore probably responsible for the building of the Great Pyramid to an astonishing degree of accuracy. The inlaid eyes of the statue were prised out by robbers in antiquity for superstitious reasons.

of the same intelligence at work that raised the pyramids at Giza in all their accuracy, and orientated them with great precision. In the impressive portrait statue of Kheops' cousin, the Vizier Hemon, who was evidently responsible for the building of the Great Pyramid, there is more than a hint of that supreme assurance and intellectual ruthlessness which these early engineers must have possessed to plan, organize and complete such mighty works. 64

The Giza monuments, of course, were also repositories of statuary, reliefs, furniture, vessels and other funerary equipment upon which the best artists of the day were encouraged to lavish their talents. Most of it has been destroyed without trace, but we are fortunate that some samples have survived of the brilliant art of this classic period of Egypt's past. In particular, the painstaking work of the Boston–Harvard Expedition has succeeded in accurately reconstructing the magnificent gold-covered furniture of Queen 65

65 Bedroom furniture of Queen Hetepheres, the mother of Kheops, consisting of a canopy for supporting mosquito curtains, chair, bed with footboard and headrest and a box for holding graduated silver bracelets, all of wood overlaid with chased gold foil and inlaid with carnelian and faience: excavated at Giza in 1923.

Hetepheres, the mother of Kheops, from her greatly decayed secondary burial. The superb design, proportions and workmanship of her boxes, chairs, bed and canopy, with their fine work in carved ebony and cedar-woods, their overlays of cast, chased and tooled gold, and their inlays of blue and black faience and red carnelian, display a taste that is both opulent yet under perfect restraint.

The immense necropolis of the Giza plateau, a veritable city of the dead élite of their time, was protected by a guardian colossus, the Great Sphinx. This huge statue of a recumbent lion with the head of a king, in this example, Khephren, is hewn out of a knoll of rock left after the extraction of stone from a local quarry. It is the first known version, and the largest, of a type of representation that haunted the imagination of the ancients, and attracted legends around it in Egypt, before the days of Oedipus. According to Egyptian belief, the lion and its derivative, the sphinx, were the protectors of thresholds and would seize any intruder who violated sacred precincts. By the New Kingdom at the latest, however, the Great Sphinx was regarded as a manifestation of Re-Herakhty, the sponsor of the ruling king, and its connection with Khephren had been almost entirely lost.

The heavy drain upon human and material resources that the building of the Giza pyramids evidently imposed, was not demanded of their subjects by later pharaohs. Even before the end of the Fourth Dynasty, a decline in the royal pretensions is discernible. The courtiers of Khephren and Mykerinus are buried in modest rock-hewn tombs, and the pyramid of the latter king is a third of the size of either of its giant companions. Shepseskaf, the last king of the Dynasty, rejected the pyramid design for the super-structure of his tomb and was buried beneath a monument in the form of a massive sarcophagus resting upon a podium. Mud brick was also substituted for stone in some of his funerary works.

66 (right) The head of the Great Sphinx, against the backdrop of Khephren's Second Pyramid at Giza. The sphinx appears to have been cut as part of Khephren's funerary complex, possibly to make use of a rock outcrop left behind after quarrying stone for pyramid core masonry.

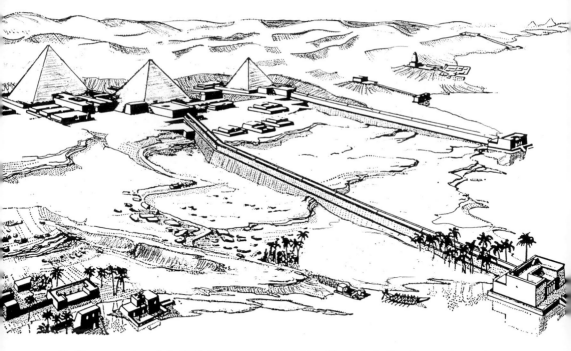

67 Reconstruction of the Fifth Dynasty pyramid field at Abusir, including the complexes of Neferirkare, Niuserre, and Sahure with causeways and valley temples. The causeway of Neferirkare was incomplete at his death and was later adapted for Niuserre. In the far distance are the sun temples of Userkaf and Niuserre.

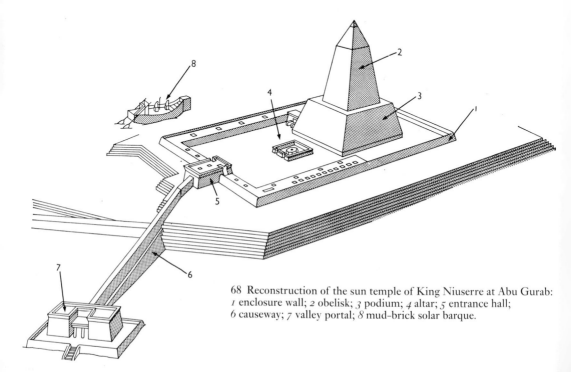

68 Reconstruction of the sun temple of King Niuserre at Abu Gurab: *1* enclosure wall; *2* obelisk; *3* podium; *4* altar; *5* entrance hall; *6* causeway; *7* valley portal; *8* mud-brick solar barque.

8 · The Pyramid Age of the Old Kingdom II

The triumph of Heliopolis

The influence of the sun cult, increasing throughout the Fourth Dynasty, as may be seen in the names compounded with Re of some of its kings, makes a full impact in the Fifth with the appearance of the myth of the theogamous birth of the pharaoh. According to the folk story recounted in the Westcar Papyrus, the first three kings of this dynasty were the offspring of the wife of a priest of Re, by the sun god himself, and were destined to rule in turn after the eldest had become High Priest in Heliopolis. The sun kings of this dynasty returned to the tradition of building pyramid tombs, though on a more modest scale and to a lower constructional standard, which is why their monuments exist today as mere mounds of rubble after the loss of their casing-stones.

Although the dynastic founder, Userkaf, built his pyramid at Saqqara, close to the Step Pyramid, at least four of his successors erected their monuments at Abusir. Since 1976, excavations by a Czech expedition have revealed much new information about the royal necropolis, in particular through the clearance of the mortuary temple of Neferefre. Back in 1893 and 1903, important fragments of temple papyri had been found in the Abusir 67 temple of Neferirkare; in the 1980s, yet more came to light in that of Neferefre. The latter, although of mud brick and attached to a pyramid that had been hurriedly finished off as a mastaba, was exceptionally well-preserved, and also contained a cache of exceptional statuary, a pair of ritual boats, and various other elements of the temple furnishings.

Besides their pyramids, at least six Fifth Dynasty kings also built special temples to the sun god, of which two have been found in the Abusir area. The construction of such buildings ceased from the reign of Isesi onwards, perhaps for the reason that they diverted resources away from the building of the royal pyramids.

Despite their ruinous condition, it is clear from their shattered fragments that the monuments of this dynasty must be numbered among the architectural gems of ancient Egypt. The reliefs of Userkaf and Sahure are drawn by gifted artists with complete assurance and carved in low relief with great sensitivity. The beauty of the materials also continues the best traditions of earlier works. With pavements and dadoes of black basalt, monolithic chambers hewn out of banded alabaster, red granite columns imitating palm trees or bundles of papyrus rush, architraves also of red granite, painted reliefs of Tura limestone, and ceilings, vaulted or flat, coloured blue and sown with yellow five-pointed stars, they must have presented an appearance at once rich and harmonious. Names and titles were elegantly spaced and carved, and inlaid with coloured paste. Of all this glory, little now remains among the sand-engulfed ruins.

68 The great innovations of the age are the sun temples, of which the badly dilapidated example built by Niuserre at Abu Gurab near Abusir remains the most complete. They are presumed to be based upon the design of the temple of Re at Heliopolis. The main feature of these temples was a court open to the sky with a colonnade around two of the walls, sheltering reliefs and giving access to a large courtyard with a great altar positioned in front of an abstract symbol of the cult – the gilded *ben-ben* elevated upon a podium like a squat obelisk. The most striking feature of the complex, however, was a long narrow chamber, now known as the 'Room of the Seasons' from the subject of its reliefs which portray all the activities during the Egyptian agricultural year as a kind of visual hymn of praise to the sun god for all his bounty. Only disjointed fragments of these scenes have survived, but they can be supplemented by versions in contemporary mastaba tombs of the kings' courtiers.

A somewhat bizarre element in Niuserre's temple was a brick-built version of the boat of the sun god. The imagery of the cult envisaged the journey of the gods across the waters of heaven by boat, the natural form of

69 Causeway leading from the valley building to the mortuary temple of the pyramid of King Unas, showing a restored portion of the rebuilt walls, and the roof with its ceiling slot for casting sunlight upon the interior walls which were carved in low relief (see ill. 78).

70 Burial chamber in the pyramid of King Unas with the alabaster niche at the far end containing the plain black basalt sarcophagus. The niche is painted to represent the walls of an early Egyptian house or tent. The saddle-back roof is carved with yellow five-pointed stars on a blue ground and the Pyramid Texts are continued upon the gables and walls of the chamber.

transport in Egypt on the Nile waterway. From prehistoric times, models and pictures of boats for the use of the dead had been included in the grave goods. The royal tombs included two or more great boats, representing not only the day and night barque of the sun god, but also actual examples used in life, as for instance the dismantled state barge of Kheops, over 43 m long, discovered in a sealed pit adjacent to the Great Pyramid in 1954. Those who 71 could not afford such expensive items made do with models, including those of the two simple reed floats that according to the sacred texts the deceased would need when he struck out upon the waters for the Field of Reeds where the gods dwelt.

The two boat-pits near the pyramid of Unas (c. 2385–2355 BC), the last king of the Fifth Dynasty, may not be enclosures for actual wooden boats, but giant models in stone. The pyramid of Unas at Saqqara, in fact, shows all the features of the royal tomb in a greatly developed form despite its ruinous state. The Subsidiary Pyramid, employed for still-obscure ritual purposes, is on its southern side. The Valley Temple was built with granite columns in the form of palm trees, similar to those used in the Mortuary Temple and which are pictured being shipped to the site in a relief on the

69 Causeway. This latter adjunct, greatly dilapidated though it may be, is the best preserved of such structures. Over 700 m long, it changes direction twice. Its walls were embellished with reliefs on the interior which appear to be inspired by scenes from the Room of the Seasons, though there are also subjects representing the procuring and manufacture of all the goods used in the building, furnishing and functioning of the temple, and the services associated with it. The mortuary temple follows what is now a fairly standard pattern of being located on the east side of the pyramid, with the colonnaded court surrounding an altar open to the sky, and separated from the inner chambers by a corridor, all embellished with reliefs. These inner chambers include store-rooms, a hall for housing five statues of the king, and an offering-place in front of the focal point of the entire complex, the stela or false door.

The entrance to the burial chamber was on the north side of the pyramid facing the circumpolar stars, which according to some beliefs, the soul of the king would eventually join. A subterranean corridor, blocked by three granite portcullises, led to an offering chamber adjoining the burial chamber, and here in 1881, Maspero found its most impressive feature, columns of elegantly drawn and spaced hieroglyphs cut into the white limestone walls and gables and coloured blue. These inscriptions are the earliest and the best preserved of a corpus of magic spells and prayers which were henceforth to be carved in the burial chambers of subsequent kings and queens and some high officials. These writings, to which the name of the Pyramid Texts has

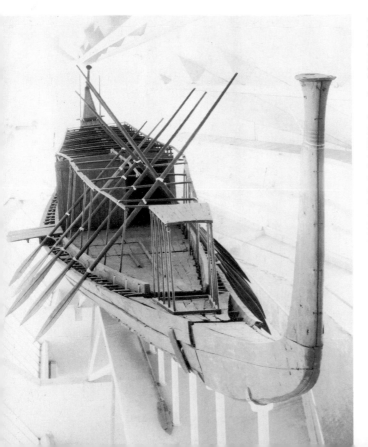

71 Of the five boat-pits around the pyramid of Kheops, two retain their original contents intact, and of this pair, only one has so far been emptied – the other remains sealed. The great flat-bottomed boat found dismantled in the pit uncovered in 1954 is made from over 1200 pieces of timber, mostly cedarwood, pegged, or sewn together with halfa-grass ropes. Reconstructed it is 43.4 m long and 5.9 m in the beam and displaces about 40 tons. The cabin is of wood, with a canopy supported on tent-poles and beams stretched over its roof and extending forwards. Six pairs of huge sweeps were used for steering the ship which would have been towed by smaller vessels.

been given, show the preponderant influence of Heliopolitan theology, although some of them hark back to primitive beliefs of a very remote past. Generally, the texts are selected and positioned on the tomb walls to ensure that the *Ba* or spirit of the dead king shall mount to heaven by various means, shall join the entourage of the sun god and eventually become absorbed by the Lord of All, or the demiurge. But there is also another deity whose influence is beginning to obtrude in some of the texts and that is Osiris, the god of Abydos whose cult will have to be discussed later.

While the soul of the king was aloft in the heavenly circuit, his body remained on earth, and the persistence of the Lower Egyptian belief that some aspect of the deceased could live on in his mansion of eternity is evident in the design of the sarcophagus of wood or stone as a house. Unas was buried in a severely plain sarcophagus of polished black basalt, but this was housed in a part of the burial chamber walled with alabaster and painted 70 to resemble the mat-hung chamber of a palace.

The pyramids of the Sixth Dynasty followed much the same pattern until the last of the series, the complex of Pepy II. In after years, this seems to have been especially hallowed as the last classic utterance of the Old Kingdom. Its reliefs were copied both in style and substance by pharaohs of the Middle and New Kingdoms, eager to return to the traditions of what seemed in ret rospect to have been a veritable Golden Age.

Country life during the Old Kingdom

While the kings were provided for so handsomely, their relatives and officials were buried in mastaba tombs or rock-hewn hypogea in the vicinity. The superstructure of such private tombs usually preserved the rectangular bench-like form, at first in mud brick but later in stone, with two dummy doorways on the eastern façade. The southernmost doorway soon became a niche where prayers and offerings could be made by pious relatives or priests endowed for the purpose. As the idea of the afterlife became more spiritual-ized there was a tendency for the tomb stela to be carved in relief with a like-ness of the deceased seated at a table on which the staples of bread and beer 72 were represented. The spirit (*ka*) of the owner received its sustenance by magic invocation, and once this idea took root, by the Second Dynasty other items were added to the bread and beer in quantity such as flesh, fowl, wine, milk, vegetables, even sacramental oils and linen, and eventually 'everything good and pure on which immortals live'. A list of such offerings was added when there was space enough, but the essential prayer for funerary offerings existed in its canonical form almost to the end of pagan Egypt.

The offering niche with stela was gradually expanded to a small cruciform chapel, and by the Fourth Dynasty into a simple chamber with the stela filling the upper part of a false door on the rear wall, with reliefs of the de-ceased on the jambs as though coming forth from the tomb to partake of the offerings. The walls of this chamber were carved with scenes of the children

72 The 'False Door' from the mastaba chapel of the palace official Iteti, shown stepping forth to receive the offerings. A detailed list of such provisions is given on the jambs of the doorway. In the 'window' above is the stela with the owner seated before an altar having stylized slices of bread upon it, libation ewers and bowls below it, and the thousand good things which Iteti will enjoy by the mere recitation of the list, inscribed above it.

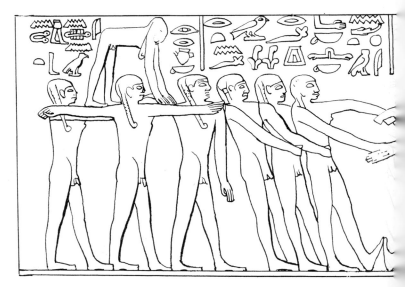

73 In the upper register goldsmiths are weighing out gold under the eye of a scribe, heating the crucibles with blow-pipes, pouring out the molten metal and beating it out. Below, dwarfs assemble a collar and a choker and chase a pectoral.

74 Two butchers are cutting up the sacrificial ox by removing a foreleg: another sharpens his knife on the bone hanging from his belt, a fourth bears away a portion of ribs.

75 (*below*) Children playing at pick-a-back, tug-of-war, and a kind of leapfrog known as *khazza lawizza* in modern Arab countries.

and servants of the owner bearing offerings towards his stela. This basic idea is the motive for the decoration of the innermost chamber of the chapel, whether in the mastaba tomb or hypogeum of the private person, or in the mortuary temple of the pharaoh. But in the Fifth Dynasty such tomb decoration was greatly extended under the influence of Heliopolitan doctrines. The size and number of rooms in the superstructure increased until by the Sixth Dynasty, the mastabas of the great officials, who were often near-relatives of the pharaoh, contained suites of rooms, some of them large enough to have their ceilings upheld by piers. The figure of the owner too in the stela-cum-false-door became a life-sized statue almost in the round.

The walls of these chapels were lined with fine limestone from Tura, and the reliefs that were carved on them are among the glories of the Pyramid Age. They vary in style from the precise drawing and delicate carving of the Fifth Dynasty, to the bolder, more lively, if often less elegant, work of the Sixth Dynasty. The subject matter is largely inspired by scenes in the Room of the Seasons, with its pictures of the cycle of work throughout the agricultural year. But the various activities represented, such as the sowing and harvesting of grain, the baking of bread, the brewing of beer, the raising and butchering of cattle, the trapping and fattening of birds and poultry, are dynamic elaborations of the idea of materializing a funerary meal by a magic invocation. Similarly shipwrights are shown building the boats for the pilgrimage to Buto, or for the last journey across the Nile to the West. Other craftsmen make the furniture, jewels, clothes and similar wordly goods that may accompany the owner to the tomb. All the components for a full life in the hereafter, like that passed on earth, are provided in a magic sublimation.

The main participant in all these activities is of course the owner, supporting the slighter figure of his wife. But his role is strictly passive, he merely 'inspects' with a benevolent eye all the work done on his country estates. Only in the royal sports of harpooning the hippopotamus, spearing fish in the pools, or fowling with the throw-stick in the reed thickets, does he find an active role worthy of his dignity, and his postures are copied from designs in the royal mortuary temples.

Apart from such borrowings, the events depicted show nothing of the owner's relations with royalty, even though his wife may be the daughter of the king. The life of the pharaoh and his entourage remains a closed book. By contrast the activities of the peasantry and the lower orders are recorded, as nowhere else, with a sardonic humour. Their toil-worn physiques, their ill-shaven jowls, their bald heads, their trouble with the refractory ass or the no less stubborn tax collector, their cheerful banter, their work songs, are faithfully reported. Such characterizations are not confined to the wall reliefs. Lively figurines of servants at their various duties in all their homeliness often accompany the handsome painted wood or limestone statues of their masters and mistresses in the serdabs of the great mastabas.

In addition, such themes as the entertainment of the owner with music and dancing may be illustrated; also the cult of the dead with the funerary

76 Inscribed statue of Iti, the servant of the Chancellor Werirni, grinding corn on a saddle-stone, her head bound with a cloth to keep chaff out of her hair. She has achieved immortality as her master's retainer (cf. ill. 46).

cortège and bands of mourners may be represented. Throughout all these scenes, there runs the connective thread of the private life of the owner, from the nursing at his mother's breast, through the games of his childhood, the pride of his vigorous youth, the corpulence of his prosperity, and the final farewell at the tomb door. 75

The intention of all these scenes was not only to recreate the past by magic. The tomb chapels were the resort of relatives and descendants of the deceased, who were accustomed to visit the necropolis on feast days, as is often the practice in Egypt today, and there partake of a meal in memory of their ancestor. This ceremony was a two-way affair, as much for the benefit of the living as for the dead. In antiquity, when premature death could suddenly arrive, the continuance of the family was a prime concern, and its fertility was thought to reside with the ancestral spirit. By this communion with the ancestor in a sepulchral meal the family's future could be assured.

External affairs

While thus our picture of life in Egypt on the great country estates seems sharply in focus, our knowledge of affairs elsewhere is nebulous indeed. Some control was evidently exercised over Nubia and the Lower Sudan, largely for trading purposes and for the recruitment of fighting men like the Medjay folk (later synonymous with police), and other renowned bowmen; but it is doubtful whether the Egyptians were able to subdue for long the warlike, though more primitive tribes of the region, who had the advantage of inhabiting difficult terrain through which progress even by boat was hazardous. By the Fourth Dynasty, a town had been established at Buhen near the head of the Second Cataract and included a copper-smelting works among its industries. This seems to have been under control of Egyptian officials until the reign of Isesi (c. 2413–2385 BC) when it was abandoned. By that time, Nubia was under the suzerainty of the agents of pharaoh, the

Keepers of the Gateway of the South, the local barons at Elephantine, whose forays into Africa were chiefly concerned with trade and maintaining peace among the rival tribes of the region, as much by diplomacy as by police action.

Trading ventures by sea to the mysterious spice land of Punt, thought to lie on the Somali coast or opposite it, were undertaken for the sake of the incense gums and resins demanded by temple ritual and the belief that the aromatic smoke of such a sacrifice would put the worshipper *en rapport* with the heavenly power. These expeditions included the transport in sections of sea-going ships across the Eastern Desert, their reassembly on the coast of the Red Sea, and a reversal of this onerous procedure on the return journey. As we have noted, the great ship of Kheops was found carefully dismantled in its boat-pit at Giza and reveals how such operations were made in the absence of a canal from the Nile to the Red Sea, for which there is no evidence before Ptolemaic times.

Mining operations in Sinai for turquoise and copper, and for copper only in the Eastern Desert, were probably in the hands of the indigenous Asiatic bedouin under Egyptian direction. When the less settled bedouin raided Egyptian settlements in times of drought and privation, punitive expeditions had to be dispatched against them. It is doubtful, however, whether the pharaoh took any personal part in these campaigns, though on the monuments he accepts the sole credit for the victorious outcome. Scenes of pharaohs smiting the bedouin are found in Sinai, particularly at Serabit el Khadim where fortified camps of local and Egyptian labourers worked under Egyptian foremen in extracting turquoise from seams in the local sandstone.

The Libyans on the opposite borders of the Delta were also persistent infiltrators into Egypt, and had to be repulsed from time to time – although it is almost certain that scenes in the funerary temples of Sahure, Unas and Pepy II, showing the king plundering them, are purely symbolic and refer to events dating back to the dawn of history. All give the same names for the conquered foe, the artificiality of the depiction being shown by its appearance, complete with the same names, under Taharqa – two thousand years later!

There is a little more evidence for Egyptian penetration in Palestine. Two representations have survived in different tombs of the Sixth Dynasty, 77 showing the storming of Asiatic fortresses, with scaling ladders and sappers undermining the walls, though such scenes could refer to events no further afield than Sinai. The autobiography which Weni inscribed in his tomb-chapel at Abydos describes more ambitious campaigns, including the conscription of men from Egypt and Nubia in a combined operation which he directed as far north in Palestine as Mount Carmel, during the reign of Pepy I. The most impressive testimony for Egyptian activity in Asia, however, comes from the great timber exporting region around Byblos, where objects bearing the names of pharaohs from Khasekhemwy to Pepy

77 Egyptian soldiers storm a fortified township with a scaling ladder: others undermine the foundations and lead off captives: within the walls women grapple with invaders while their ruler tears his hair in despair.

II have been brought to light suggesting a long and continuous association between Lebanon and Egypt. This was doubtless the result of close trading relations rather than colonization, though it may be that there was an influential Egyptian settlement in Byblos where a temple existed to Hathor, the equivalent of the local goddess Anath.

The rise of feudalism

From the time of the first kings of the unified Egypt, it would seem that the pharaoh ruled over the whole of Egypt as his demesne, and this system reached its greatest development in the Fourth Dynasty when Snoferu appears to have initiated the policy of administering the country directly through members of his immediate family. The office of vizier from his reign onwards became the most important office under the crown in this central-izing process. At the same time the kingship appears to have become more remote and hedged around with divinity, a difference well illustrated by the towering bulk of the royal pyramid over the neighbouring mastabas of the king's relatives. These were also his officials whom he had brought up and educated, maintained during their lifetimes, and granted decent burial on death. The king may be traditionally pictured as the Protector of Egypt, smiting the forces of evil, or as a sphinx or griffin treading down the national foes, but there is little evidence that any pharaohs of the Old Kingdom led any expeditions into the field. Such enterprises were the concern either of accomplished administrators, such as Weni, who was a mere magistrate before he was appointed Governor of Upper Egypt, or experienced agents such as the half-Nubian border barons of Elephantine. The picture received from such vestiges that have survived from the Old Kingdom is one of an Egypt enjoying security, prosperity and internal peace under the rule of the pharaoh. The change of dynasties appears to have occurred not as the result of strife, but through the extinction of the male line, a later legend recalling a Queen Nitokris, who had succeeded a murdered brother.

The arrival of the Fifth Dynasty, however, marks a distinct diminution in the power and prestige of the pharaoh. The great officials were no longer princes of the blood royal, or other near relatives, but claim a greater familiarity with the god-king by boasting of their privilege in being allowed to kiss the royal foot, rather than the ground on which it trod, and similar favours. The inscriptions in the private tombs which become progressively larger as the age advances now expand from a laconic list of titles and honorifics, to more revelatory statements, and even as in the case of Weni, a modest autobiography.

With the rise in the importance of the nobility there was a diminution in the stature of the pharaoh. Favoured courtiers were rewarded with gifts of land as endowments for the upkeep of their tombs and funerary services. Such gifts were often exempted from taxation in perpetuity, and the silent cities of the dead received large shares of the national resources at the expense of the Royal Treasury, when there were not lapses and defalcations. Much of this expenditure was upon activities such as the chanting of funerary prayers, which only encouraged economic stagnation.

While the kings became the poorer by these donations, their subjects reaped the benefits. The district governors, once they felt themselves secure in posts that became hereditary, handed on their offices to their children, according to the Egyptian ideal of appointing the son to the place of his father, in the belief that they owed their appointments by right of birth and not by royal favour. They no longer sought burial near the king's pyramid, but cut their own rock tombs at the provincial capital, importing craftsmen where necessary from Memphis.

From the middle of the Fifth Dynasty, the beginnings of a feudal state may be traced with an increase in the power and status of these provincial lords, particularly in Upper Egypt. The possibility of rivalry between them cannot be ignored, nor an attempt on the part of the Crown, evidently under Isesi, to come to terms with them by appointing one of their number to a new post, Governor of Upper Egypt. This office exercised a check upon them by conferring upon the holder the duty of collecting their taxes; but it was not long before it, too, became hereditary. The chasm that separated the pharaoh from such magnates was spanned when Pepy I late in his reign married two sisters, the daughters of a mere governor of the Thinite nome, who became in turn the mothers of his successors, Nemtyemsaf I (Merenre) and Pepy II. Their brother was appointed to the vizierate, and other members of the family held high office in Thinis, near Abydos. Thus by the middle of the Sixth Dynasty, the foundations of a feudal state had already been laid. Following Pepy II's death, a series of obscure kings held the Memphite throne, outshone by the provincial nobles of Middle and Upper Egypt. Only one pyramid of a Seventh/Eighth Dynasty king is known, a structure no larger than the one of the modest funerary monuments built for the queens of the late King Pepy.

Egypt during the Old Kingdom enjoyed a virile and self-assured culture which is the most characteristic expression of the national ethos. The calm faces that gaze out from so many statues and reliefs are untroubled by doubts; and the voices that speak from the scanty writings of the period, the books of precepts and etiquette, and the complacent autobiographies, are unfaltering in their belief that the good life consisted in being discreet, modest, honest and patient; prudent in friendship, not covetous, nor envious, nor violent, but respectful to superiors and inferiors alike; in short, keeping one's proper station and exercising moderation in all things. Such an ideal of the golden mean was essentially aristocratic. The king and his court, mostly his relatives and high officials who proclaimed their kinship with him, and inherited therefore in some degree his divine right to rule, were the educated élite for whom the economic and artistic enterprises of the state were created. But while forming a privileged class they were no idle *noblesse de la cour*. They comprised the architects, engineers, writers, theologians, administrators, all the men of action and intelligence of their day.

9 · The First Intermediate Period

Collapse

At this distance of time, the disintegration of the Old Kingdom at the end of the Sixth Dynasty has all the appearance of being sudden and complete. Egyptologists had attributed this downfall to the decline in the sole authority of the pharaoh after the Fourth Dynasty, when the rise of provincial governors resulted in the emergence of a hereditary caste of feudal potentates seeking an ever-growing independence from central control.

More recent research, however, has attributed the abrupt nature of the collapse to contemporary changes in the climate of Africa and the Near East. With the cessation of the Neolithic Wet Phase about 2350 BC, the spectre of famine begins to haunt the region. An isolated block from the Unas Causeway, and an earlier example from that of Sahure at Abusir showing piteously emaciated people weakened by famine and dying of hunger, might be an early portent of the evils to come. Egypt was protected from the worst of such irregular calamities by its unique irrigation system and the central control it could exercise over its granaries and supplies of corn. It is fairly evident, however, that a change in the pattern of monsoon rains falling on

78 Block from the Unas Causeway (see ill. 69) carved in relief with a scene of men, women and children suffering from the effects of severe famine. The significance of this, and similar scenes, is uncertain.

the Abyssinian plateau could lead to a series of low Niles which the basin system of cultivation in Egypt could do nothing to counteract; and the results would have been disastrous for the entire population. Hot winds from the south, similar to the stifling *khamsin* which today blows for two or three days at a time in the Spring, apparently accompanied this climatic aberration. There are veiled references to the sun being obscured by dust storms: 'the sun is occluded and will not shine that men may see . . . none may know that it is midday, and the sun will cast no shadow.' The high winds assisted the denudation by creating dust bowls and shifting sand dunes on to the cultivation. The whole political and economic system of Egypt, developed over the centuries, whereby a god incarnate was believed to control the Nile flood by his magic powers for the benefit of the nation, would have been discredited in a very short time. As we have remarked, the king-lists refer to many pharaohs during the three decades of the Seventh and Eighth Dynasties, each ruling for a year or two before presumably paying the penalty of being unable to make the Nile flow copiously, and disappearing without trace.

In these conditions, 'when the Nile was empty and men crossed over it on foot', Egypt splintered into a number of feudal states under the purely nominal suzerainty of the pharaoh, each governed by a petty ruler who tried to promote the welfare of his own principality without much concern for that of his neighbours. There are cryptic references in the meagre records that have survived to marauding bands of starving people searching for food in more favoured localities, and in at least one instance there is an account of cannibalism. This dismal phase in the fortunes of Egypt in fact seems to have been the first recorded instance of one of those periods of drought which have ravaged the land from time to time, as in AD 502, and especially in AD 1085, when the Nile inundation failed for seven years and brought dire famine and pestilence to the population.

In the 20th century BC the local governors took what measures were open to them to succour their own districts, by conserving water supplies, and reducing the number of hungry mouths by driving out famine-stricken invaders, whether natives, Libyans or Asiatics, from their provinces. The internecine strife further restricted the areas of cultivation; and the perils of these times are reflected in the boasts of the local rulers on their crude tomb 79 stelae that only by their organizing abilities and their strong right arms had they been able to preserve their people, their crops and their herds alive. The cataclysm is plain for all to see. The monuments of the period are very sparse and mere feeble copies of the Memphite style of the past. The materials are of poor quality, pottery for instance replacing stone, faience and metal in the manufacture of vessels. The widespread civil disorder is evident in the decoration of the crude model funerary boats, hacked out of the local wood, with their cabin roofs protected by large ox-hide shields. A ruler in Asyut 80 was buried with a painted wooden model of a company of Egyptian spear- men and another of Nubian bowmen to render him service in some troubled

79 A crude relief in the style of the Old Kingdom of a local administrator of all livestock at Dendera, Mery (?) and his wife Baba seated side by side and receiving offerings from their sons and daughters. A prayer to Osiris for funerary offerings is followed by a boast that by his own might he made men, oxen, goats, asses, wheat and barley to flourish, and planted sycamore figs on the river bank and trees in the fields.

80 Model of a company of forty Nubian archers found with a companion group of Egyptian spearmen from the tomb of Mesehti at Asyut. The darker-skinned Nubians wear a thick shock of hair as a protective helmet, and dyed leather garments.

afterlife. Another nomarch of this same region reports how the land was in terror before his soldiers, and how all were afraid when they beheld smoke arising in the south. Macabre reminders of the civil strife of these days are the bodies of some sixty shock troops who were accorded an honoured mass-burial at Thebes. Their wounds showed that they had fallen in the desperate storming of some key fortress.

With Egypt divided against itself, there was the inevitable immigration of foreigners into the pastures of the Delta. Famine in their own lands always drove Libyans and the bedouin of Sinai and the Negeb to graze their flocks on the borders of the Delta in the manner of Abraham and Jacob, and now with organized policing suspended, advantage was taken of the tradition of hospitality to add to the general tale of rapine and usurpation. The evils caused by famine, poverty, social upheaval and anarchy brought others in their train such as plague and sterility. A deep and lasting impression was left on the ancient Egyptians by the trauma of these times, so that in later literary works, such as *The Prophecy of Neferti* and *The Admonitions of Ipuwer*, when the writer wished to depict mankind tormented by intolerable miseries, it was most probably the sufferings of this period that he recalled.

Recovery

The history of the First Intermediate Period is concerned with the painful struggle by successive strong men to restore the divine power of the pharaoh which had been so effective for centuries in the past. The most notable of these efforts was made by a powerful family living at Herakleopolis near the Faiyum who regarded themselves as the legitimate successors of Pepy II, judging from his prenomen which two of their number adopted as their own. They appear to have united all Egypt under their sway for a brief interlude. Upper Egypt, however, from a little south of Abydos to the border at Elephantine, seems to have preserved some kind of nominal independence under princes ruling at Thebes.

The Herakleopolitans form the Ninth and Tenth Dynasties (*c.* 2160–2040 BC) and, according to Manetho, the founder of their line, Akhthoes, achieved supreme power 'by great cruelty which wrought woes for Egypt'. His name has survived on a number of small monuments; but there is a significant reference to a book of instruction in statecraft which he wrote for his descendants, though it has not so far come to light. It must however be the forerunner of two such works which we shall shortly have to consider. After a century in which the Herakleopolitans appear to have consolidated their power by expelling the Asiatic immigrants in the Delta, fortifying the eastern borders, re-establishing the importance of Memphis, improving irrigation works, and reopening trade with Byblos, the rising pretensions of the aggressive Thebans constituted a threat which could not be ignored, and sporadic fighting broke out between the rival powers with varying fortunes until the Theban prince Mentuhotep II (Nebhepetre) decisively defeated the Herakleopolitans and reunited Egypt under the rule of one pharaoh.

The interludes between the great epochs of civilization in Egypt had their birth-pangs as well as their death-agonies. Out of the social revolution of the time, which cast aside the old accepted forms of expression, and out of the acute suffering, which moved men to cry out with a new voice, there was born a secular literature quite different from what had preceded it, a literature, moreover, which continued to inspire Egyptian writers for centuries afterwards and helped to sustain an accepted style. At a time when men were no longer ordered by the divine sanctions of pharaonic authority, an appeal was made through the emotions by artistic processes; and the pessimistic literature that now flowered is cast in a poetic and elegant form. The ability of writing to influence men's minds is shrewdly recognized by a

Herakleopolitan king who exhorts his son to be a craftsman in speech so that he might prevail, 'for power is in the tongue; and speech is mightier than fighting'.

Such feelings fathered a genre of pessimistic writing which was to prevail even when it no longer reflected external circumstances in the high noon of the Middle Kingdom.

In this category is *An Argument between a Man Contemplating Suicide and his Soul*, and *The Complaints of the Peasant*, a series of rather turgid but doubtless elegant speeches by an Egyptian 'original' who is humanely tormented for the sake of his eloquent protests. These writings appear to have emanated from the court of the Herakleopolitans, and it is one of these kings, probably Wahkare, who has left us another work in this group of Egyptian literary classics, *The Instruction for King Merykare*. In this work, ideas appear which are different from the recipes for worldly success compiled by the Old Kingdom sages. There is, for instance, a confession of wrongdoing and repentance for past misdeeds. A warning is also given of retribution on the Day of Judgment when even the king will have to account for his deeds on earth. 'He that cometh before [the judges] without having done wrong, he shall continue like a god'. This is a distinct change from the assertions in the Pyramid Texts that the dead king will not be tried before any tribunal. While much of the 'instruction' takes the form of practical advice from a ruler who has few illusions about the frailty and treachery of the human species, there is a distinct preoccupation with a code of conduct determined by abstract moral factors:

> Do right as long as you are on earth. Calm the afflicted, oppress no widow, expel no man from his father's possessions . . . Do not kill; but punish with beatings or imprisonment. Then shall this land be well established. Leave vengeance to God . . . More acceptable to Him is the virtue of one who is upright of heart than the ox of the wrong-doer. (After Erman 1966, p. 77.)

This last extract refers to another transformation that was taking place in the social and religious heritage of the past. The promise of immortality in the Old Kingdom was greatly restricted; and it is doubtful whether in origin it extended beyond the divine king. He became a greater god upon death, entering the cosmic circuit, and certain ceremonies were observed at his demise to make the transfiguration perfect; but what kind of afterlife was enjoyed by his subjects is less clear – probably no more than a ghostly existence within the tomb was thought to be the lot of his more privileged entourage, subsisting on the funerary offerings provided by their pious descendants. The queens and members of the royal family were naturally interred in tombs near the mastaba or pyramid of the king they had served in life and to whom they expected to stand in the same relationship after death. Such tombs and the immortality they assured were in the gift of the king; but when local governors began to make tombs in their own districts they inevitably took over something of the divine privileges of the pharaoh himself. The history of burial customs thereafter, from the end of the Old Kingdom onwards, is the gradual arrogation by private persons of all the rights and appurtenances of royal burial, and the process was greatly accelerated during the First Intermediate Period when so many minor lords regarded themselves as little inferior to kings. At the same time the general poverty made it necessary to find substitutes for all the lavish furnishings of the royal burials. Thus instead of painted reliefs in fine limestone showing the procession of estates bringing their produce to the deceased, or the brewers, bakers and butchers preparing the funerary meal, a few servant-statues, often crudely hacked out of wood, were provided to perform their offices by magic. Rectangular wooden coffins, decorated externally in a manner reminiscent of houses, were painted internally with pictures of equipment which had formerly been the exclusive trappings of royalty – crowns, headdresses, staves, sceptres, kilts, girdles, aprons and tails. Even the uraeus-cobra, the essential symbol of royalty, which the pharaoh wore on his brow so that it might spit fire in the eyes of his enemies, was faithfully represented. 81

This wholesale usurpation did not stop at forms and emblems. The liturgy of the Pyramid Texts was altered to make it suitable for use by private

81 Painted wooden model of bakers and brewers at work. In spite of their crudity, these come from the tomb of King Mentuhotep II himself. The female servants kneel to grind barley on saddle-stones; the males stand to brew the beer in tall vats. An overseer, holding his baton of office, superintends the work.

82 In the upper register is part of a painted hieroglyphic inscription with a prayer to Anubis, the god of embalming, asking for a goodly burial for the chief physician Seni. Below it is a frieze of pictures of the equipment that the deceased desired in the afterlife, in default of actual examples, with their names written above them in hieratic script. Included in this section are such toilet (or medical) implements as razors, knives, whetstones and pouches for holding them. In the lowermost columns are spells written in hieratic from the Coffin Texts.

persons, to protect them from the hazards and terrors of the underworld, and to endue them with special influence and potency. New spells referring to contemporary conditions were added, and archaic utterances that could no longer be understood were omitted. In the impoverished burials of the period, in which the offering-chamber is often very modest or non-existent, the practice arose of writing these texts in cursive hieroglyphs upon the interior of the coffins below the painted frieze of accoutrements, and the name of the Coffin Texts is given by Egyptologists to this new group of religious writings. The custom appears to have arisen in Herakleopolis and was continued throughout the ensuing Middle Kingdom for some royal as well as private burials, although several of the more opulent tombs had their chapel walls inscribed with the old Pyramid Texts, in this probably aping royal burials in which, however, funerary inscriptions have not survived.

It seems clear, therefore, that whatever impediments there were to achieving the supreme office of pharaoh in life, few of the new governors and officials had any doubt about their becoming as kings at death.

82

10 · The Middle Kingdom

The feudal rivalry

Throughout the Herakleopolitan period, the princes of Thebes had been able to exercise an uneasy suzerainty over the five southernmost districts of Upper Egypt, enclosing their names in cartouches like any pharaoh. Their border with the northern powers was at the city of Abydos, now coming into even greater importance as the principal holy seat of the god Osiris (see below, p. 137). In sporadic fighting this town changed hands several times and it was not until their prince, Mentuhotep II (Nebhepetre), came to power that the Thebans began to prevail over the loyalist powers. After several years of hard fighting, however, Mentuhotep found himself the first effective pharaoh of a united Egypt since the reign of Pepy II.

His gradual advance from a provincial kinglet to the 'Lord of the Two Lands' is reflected in the funerary monument he built at Deir el Bahri with its early reliefs carved in a primly rustic yet curiously attractive style, and the later work done under the more sophisticated influence of Memphis. His activities are recorded in many parts of the country, in the region of the First Cataract, the Wadi Hammamat, and the quarries of Hatnub among other places, but he remained a devotee of southern culture, making his residence at Thebes and building largely in Upper Egypt. There is more than a flavour of Nubian culture in his entourage, with his dark-skinned womenfolk tattooed on their bodies, and in some of the artifacts that were buried with them. Mentuhotep II celebrated a jubilee in his thirty-ninth regnal year and died after a long reign of fifty-one years during which he had a good opportunity of pacifying the land and guiding it back to some of its former prosperity. His eldest surviving son Mentuhotep III (S'ankhkare) inherited a united and tranquil state populated by a new generation to whom civil war was only a legend and devoted his short reign of twelve years to the arts of peace. A trading expedition was sent to Punt, a voyage which involved the conscription of an expeditionary force of 3,000 men, the digging of wells and the cutting of stone in the Wadi Hammamat, the rounding up of hostile bedouin en route and the building of a ship on the Red Sea coast for the transport of the myrrh resins from Punt. The blocks of cut stone were for the sanctuaries in temples which Mentuhotep III built at Elephantine, Abydos and hamlets near Thebes. Some of the reliefs with which they were adorned have survived and show that the refined carving and drawing

83

84

83 The scene shows Queen Kawit, mirror in hand, having her hair dressed by a maid, while her steward encourages her to refresh herself with a cup of milk drawn from her cows in an adjacent relief.

characteristic of the last years of Mentuhotep II continued to be followed, but with even greater skill and subtlety, and were not surpassed even by the sculptors of the Twelfth Dynasty, though they too worked in the same tradition, but with rather deeper relief.

As with the long reign of Pepy II, the fifty-one-year rule of Mentuhotep II seemingly created confusion in the dynastic succession. After the death of Mentuhotep III we catch a brief glimpse of a fourth Mentuhotep, and find that during his short reign another expedition, this time of 10,000 men under the command of the Vizier and Governor of the South, Amenemhet, is in the Wadi Hammamat quarrying hard stone for the king's sarcophagus and its lid; then the mists of history come down again. When the scene clears, it is presumably the Vizier who is now on the throne ruling as Ammenemes I, the first pharaoh of the powerful Twelfth Dynasty.

The new king found the wearing of the crowns of Upper and Lower Egypt an uneasy privilege. Mentuhotep II had evidently curbed the claims of his fellow nomarchs in climbing to supreme power, but Ammenemes may have had to come to terms with them in order to obtain the throne. Under the early rulers of the new dynasty, the feudal structures of the First Intermediate Period remained in place, the nomarchs of Hermopolis arrogantly dating events to their own years, like kings. Some provincial governors maintained their own armed forces and fleets of ships, quarrying stone for their own monuments, some of which were of considerable size. For example, an alabaster colossus over 6 m high was erected by Djehutihotep of Hermopolis in the reign of Sesostris II. The difficulties that confronted Ammenemes I are sufficiently underlined by the co-opting of his eldest son Sesostris to act as his co-regent in his twentieth regnal year,

84 The deities of Upper and Lower Egypt, in the guise of two queens (one missing), crown King Mentuhotep III, who wears a broad collar and corselet decorated with the falcons of Horus.

a practice in which he was followed by the subsequent kings of the dynasty. Ammenemes died suddenly in his jubilee year, and according to Manetho he was murdered by his own chamberlains. There is further evidence for his violent end in a political testament, *The Teaching of King Ammenemes*, and in a fictionalized autobiography, *The Story of Sinuhe*, which have survived as literary classics. The policies that he inaugurated, however, were carried out by his successors. While a southerner, hailing from the Theban region to judge from his name, he abandoned the attempt to govern all Egypt from Thebes and moved his capital to the fulcrum of Upper and Lower Egypt some 30 miles south of Memphis, to Itj-tawi ('Seizing the Two Lands') near the modern el Lisht. Here he revived the Old Kingdom form of a pyramid for his tomb.

Ammenemes made a determined attempt to subjugate Upper Nubia and the Sudan by building a string of fortified townships in the region all the way to Semna, and planting trading posts in the lands beyond, as at Kerma above the Third Cataract. The climax of this development was reached with Sesostris III who rebuilt most of the forts and was so intimately associated with the region that in afteryears he was worshipped there as the local god. While the southern border was pushed farther upstream by a deliberate policy of expansion, the northeastern frontier of Egypt, which had so frequently been penetrated by Asiatics, was consolidated by means of a fortified barrier known as 'The Walls of the Prince', doubtless a series of strongholds set up at strategic points to command all the usual routes in and out of Egypt. During the last year of the co-regency, Sesostris I seems to have fought a campaign in Libya to repress raids on the western borders of the Delta, evidently with complete success since the later resettlement and development of the Faiyum would only have been possible in the absence of Libyan incursions into the western oases.

Political activity to protect the frontiers is matched by greatly increased intercourse with Palestine and Syria, where objects bearing the names of different kings of the Twelfth and Thirteenth Dynasties have been found at Gaza, Byblos, Ras Shamra (Ugarit), Megiddo and elsewhere. *The Story of Sinuhe* (see below p. 139) acquaints us with the fact that regular journeys by king's envoys were made to Syria by the beginning of the dynasty, and a deposit of Asiatic treasure in a temple near Thebes shows that the trade was not all in one direction. We also have a reference to a war against the Asiatics in the reign of Ammenemes I and a more ambitious campaign under Sesostris III, when Shechem was taken. Generally speaking, however, relations with Asia during this period seem to have been peaceful and largely concerned with trade. It was doubtless from Byblos or some such entrepôt that Aegean products reached Egypt and have left their trace in deposits of characteristic pottery at Abydos and elsewhere. Conversely, Egyptian objects of Middle Kingdom date have been excavated in Crete. The mining centres in Sinai also show evidence of the tremendous vigour with which the kings of this period increased the supplies of copper ores and turquoise from this source. The extent of this foreign trade is an index of the prosperity in Egypt itself. The capital at Lisht was near the Faiyum and kings of the Twelfth Dynasty devoted much attention to land settlement and improved irrigation in this region, turning it into one of the most fertile districts of Egypt.

85 This kiosk is hypethral with a ramp at opposite ends. A pedestal in the atrium probably supported two statues of Sesostris I, seated back to back and wearing jubilee costume and different crowns (cf. ill. 88), but was adapted in the reign of Ammenemes III as a way-station for the perambulation of the barque of Amun.

86 The dour features of the
Middle Kingdom rulers have
been softened in this portrait
of Ammenemes III to represent
the funerary concept of an
immortal.

Sesostris I proved to be a most energetic builder, founding a great new
temple at Heliopolis, where to commemorate his jubilee obelisks were
erected, one of which still stands. He built or rebuilt on sites all over Egypt,
not neglecting the family seat at Thebes whose obscure god, Amun, now
begins to come to the fore, as the name of several kings of the dynasty
proudly proclaims. The Theban buildings of the Middle Kingdom were
used as quarries by later pharaohs and it is out of the foundations of the
Third Pylon at Karnak that there has been reconstructed a white limestone   85
kiosk which Sesostris I built at Thebes for a symbolic re-enactment of his
main jubilee ceremonies at Memphis. The vitality shown by the architects
of Sesostris I was shared in differing measure by their successors and
reached its apogee during the reign of Ammenemes III (c. 1842–1794 BC),   86
for whom building and sculpture on a truly colossal scale was created. By
that time, however, the pharaoh had once more gained a lonely and unchal-
lenged pre-eminence thanks to the policies pursued by his predecessors,
particularly his father Sesostris III, under whom a restructuring of national
administration had diminished the power of the nomarchs in favour of more
centralized departments of state. In place of the former grandees, we find
crown officials bearing their titles but governing mere townships as local
mayors. It is during Sesostris III's reign that the great series of provincial
tombs at Beni Hasan and Deir el Bersha come to a sudden end, as those at
Asyut and Meir had ceased a generation earlier.

The half-century-long reign of Ammenemes III, the last great king of the Twelfth Dynasty, stored up troubles for the succession soon after, and the following dynasty ruled for a confused century during which we have scant details of too many kings to suggest that it was either prosperous or tranquil. Fluctuating climatic conditions seem to have returned to Egypt and caused irregularities in the flow of the Nile. High floods, slow to fall and allow seed to be sown at the proper time, were as disastrous in their effects as feeble inundations. The manifest inability of the pharaoh to control the Nile may have been the chief reason for another slump in the prestige of the kingship, which is apparent throughout the Thirteenth Dynasty, with a host of pharaohs each ruling in obscurity for a short time and leaving few memorials behind him. During interludes when more stable conditions prevailed, some kings were able to erect monuments including large statues and even a small pyramid tomb, but the general picture is one of slow decline. Unlike the similar crisis at the end of the Old Kingdom, however, the climatic changes were not so severe or protracted; and the bureaucracy established by the last two kings of the Twelfth Dynasty was able to carry on the government of the country under the direction of powerful viziers and chancellors who enjoyed a long continuity of office over several reigns. The capital remained at Lisht despite the Theban names of many of these rulers. At times some kind of control seems to have been exercised by more vigorous kings or co-regents. Building operations went on at the old centres, and trade continued with Byblos, but a steady decline in artistic and technical standards, and a gradual poverty in ideas and materials, tell their own story. A significant portent is the appearance of several Asiatic names in the king-lists of this period, and under a certain Dudumose an event occurred which receives special mention by Josephus who quotes Manetho at length:

> Tutimaeus. In his reign, for what cause I know not, a blast of God smote us; and unexpectedly, from the regions of the East, invaders of obscure race marched in confidence of victory against our land. By main force they easily seized it without striking a blow; and having overpowered the rulers of the land, they then burned our cities ruthlessly, razed to the ground the temples of the gods, and treated all the natives with a cruel hostility . . . (W. G. Waddell, *Manetho* (Loeb Classical Library), London and Cambridge, Mass., 1940, p. 79.)

Thus ended ingloriously, according to the official accounts, the second great period in the history of Egyptian culture destroyed by the Hyksos invaders (see, however, p. 142 below).

Funerary beliefs and practices

While the nomarchs of the First Intermediate Period had taken over most of the style and ritual of royal burial, they were still interred in rock-cut tombs, a practice which continued for wealthy private burials with a few

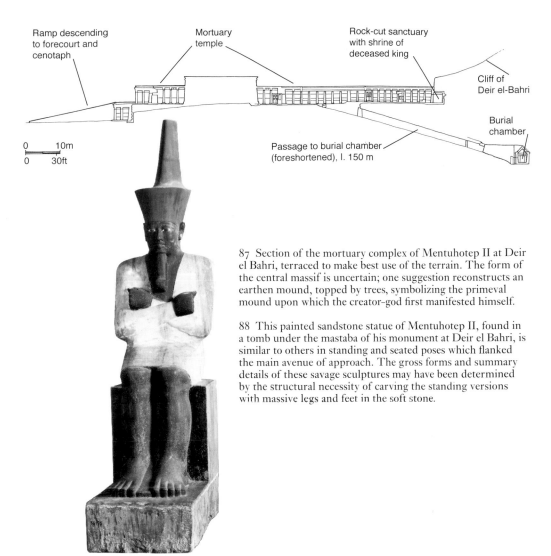

Ramp descending to forecourt and cenotaph

Mortuary temple

Rock-cut sanctuary with shrine of deceased king

Cliff of Deir el-Bahri

Burial chamber

0   10m
0   30ft

Passage to burial chamber (foreshortened), l. 150 m

87 Section of the mortuary complex of Mentuhotep II at Deir el Bahri, terraced to make best use of the terrain. The form of the central massif is uncertain; one suggestion reconstructs an earthen mound, topped by trees, symbolizing the primeval mound upon which the creator-god first manifested himself.

88 This painted sandstone statue of Mentuhotep II, found in a tomb under the mastaba of his monument at Deir el Bahri, is similar to others in standing and seated poses which flanked the main avenue of approach. The gross forms and summary details of these savage sculptures may have been determined by the structural necessity of carving the standing versions with massive legs and feet in the soft stone.

exceptions throughout the Middle Kingdom. The princes of Thebes followed general custom, having tombs cut in the desert surface of the west bank opposite Karnak. They took the form of great colonnaded courtyards, 87 the tombs of the nobility occupying the flanks, with the chapel and burial chambers of the king to the rear.

Mentuhotep II adapted such a conception to fill the whole valley of Deir 88 el Bahri: nobles' tombs occupied the cliffs at the north and south margins, while the king erected a temple-tomb at the western end, under the cliffs. This comprised a porticoed structure rising in three tiers, the uppermost comprising a massif that may be interpreted as a square mastaba, or the base for a mound, topped by trees. Its unknown architect showed a remarkable eye for the picturesque exploitation of a site with his use of terraces and colonnades. A curious feature of the monument was a dummy tomb with an entrance in the dromos of the temple leading by way of a long corridor to a burial chamber under the mastaba containing a statue of the king in jubilee costume wrapped in linen like a mummy. The statue, with its flesh painted black, the crown red and the jubilee-cloak white, is well calculated to give a savage force to what has been regarded as a substitute for the corpse of the divine king. In the precincts and vicinity of this temple were cut the rock-tombs of several relatives and officials, including the pit-tombs and adjacent shrines of six of the royal women, some of whose funerary equipment has survived, while that of Mentuhotep himself has been robbed and destroyed. Also near at hand was the famous chapel of his half-sister, Queen Neferu, with its painted limestone reliefs, and the walls of the burial chamber decorated with offerings, friezes of objects, and versions of the Coffin Texts, like the interior of a huge contemporary coffin. The chapel was a tourist attraction for sightseers in the New Kingdom who showed their appreciation by scribbling on the walls after the manner of their kind.

With the transfer of the capital from Thebes to Itj-tawi in the Twelfth Dynasty, there came a return to the Memphite form of a royal tomb, particularly under Sesostris I who followed the example of his father by erecting a pyramid at Lisht which shows the direct inspiration of the funerary monument of Pepy II, not only in its size, plan and scheme of decoration but also in the very style of the reliefs. While the monolithic sarcophagi, canopic chests and tomb chambers made of granite or quartzite are often of superb workmanship, the pyramids themselves are of an inferior standard of construction. They were usually built on knolls of rock with radiating interior walls to form compartments filled with rubble and, from the time of Sesostris II, mud brick. The mass was kept stable by the casing-stones which in some examples were pillaged from earlier monuments. These pyramids in their turn have ill-resisted the hand of the stone-robber and with the loss of their casings have collapsed into eroded black mounds. Apart from Lisht,

89 The pyramid of Sesostris II at Lahun has lost its casing, thus exposing the interior stone walls which formed compartments filled with mud-brick. Below this point in the surrounding platform, on the south side, were shaft tombs of members of his family including that of Sithathoryunet (see ill. 22).

90 A vignette from the so-called *Book of the Dead* made for the scribe Hunefer in the reign of Sethos I. It shows the weighing of the heart of the deceased against the feather symbolizing truth in the Hall of the Two Truths before the tribunal presided over by Osiris. Osiris is seated on a throne under a baldachin and supported by Isis and Nephthys. Hunefer is introduced by Anubis, left, who also reports the result of the weighing to the ibis-headed Thoth for an official record in writing. The verdict having proved favourable, and the composite monster Ammut the 'Eater of the Dead' having been frustrated, Hunefer is introduced to Osiris by Re-Herakhty. Above, Hunefer supplicates some of the assessors in the Judgment Hall.

el Lahun and Dahshur were also chosen as the location for the royal tomb. The last-named site was dominated by the pyramids of Snoferu, who was particularly honoured by the kings of the Twelfth Dynasty, perhaps because they traced their descent from him. Two other kings of this dynasty built pyramids at Lahun and Hawara at the entrance to the Faiyum, a district par-   89 ticularly associated with them. The pharaohs of the dynasty also renewed the old practice of building the mastabas of their high officials and mortu- ary priests around their own pyramids but on a reduced scale, for the truth was that burial near the king had now become something of an anachronism with the rise to importance of the cult of the god Osiris.

We have already referred to the nature of Osiris, and the spread of his influence (p. 39ff). He had become prominent in the Delta town of Busiris and was also adopted into the solar cult of Heliopolis, his companion deities Seth, Isis and Nephthys becoming the third generation of gods. By the end of the Fifth Dynasty he was prominently identified with the dead king in the Pyramid Texts, but Abydos was his probable place of origin and had become a town of political importance as well as religious significance under the pharaohs of the Sixth Dynasty. With the increase in the power of the Thebans in the later years of the First Intermediate Period and their capture of Abydos, the claims of Osiris were greatly extended. From being a chthonic god of agriculture and of the Nile, Osiris in the Middle Kingdom became the god of the dead *par excellence*, and every deceased person who in hopes of immortality had usurped all the trappings and prerogatives of royal burial was represented as the dead king, Osiris, even adopting the epithet of 'The Osiris (so-and-so)'. The increase in the pretensions of Abydos is seen in the great wealth of remains there, dating from the early Middle Kingdom onwards, from the hundreds of round-topped stelae and votive statues of private persons to the monuments of the Thirteenth Dynasty pharaoh Neferhotep I, all anxious to have some station near the 'staircase of the Great God', even if burial in the holy ground itself was not possible. While the cult of Osiris was concerned entirely with the life after death, and did not challenge that of other deities, a certain amount of encroachment was inevitable as Osiris took over the judicial powers which the sun god Re, for instance, had exercised over the Heliopolitan tribunal, and became the supreme judge of the dead, before whom all wandering souls after death had to account for their deeds on earth. The prestige of the pharaoh as a divinity, already sadly eroded from the last years of the Old Kingdom, suffered further decay with the ascendancy of Osiris as the deification of the idea of kingship. From now on, all men who were worthy had the promise of immortality in the realms ruled over by the kingly divinity Osiris, not merely those who had known the pharaoh in life. There was of course no revolutionary cleavage of thought since the pharaoh, on death, was assimilated to Osiris.

90

The cultural achievement

The decline which this religious development and the new political circumstances wrought in the kingship during the First Intermediate Period was arrested and reversed during the Twelfth Dynasty when a series of remarkable literary works were written in praise of various kings. It has become the custom in recent years to regard these writings as deliberate attempts at propaganda on behalf of the pharaohs who are the protagonists in these works. The first of them is a sort of *post-hoc* prophecy, known to Egyptologists as *The Prophecy of Neferti*, and describes how in the spacious days of King Snoferu of the Fourth Dynasty, a great prophet, Neferti, is called to the court to divert the king with 'choice speeches'. He describes what is to happen in the land in the distant future:

> I show thee the land wailing and weeping . . . a man's spirit will be concerned with his own welfare . . . Every mouth is full of, 'Pity me!' All good things have departed. The land is destroyed.

The Prophecy, however, ends on a more cheerful note:

> A king shall come from Upper Egypt called Ameni, the son of a woman of the south . . . He shall receive the White Crown and wear the Red Crown . . . Be glad, ye people of his time! The son of a high-born man

will make his name for all eternity. They who would make mischief and devise enmity have suppressed their mutterings through fear of him . . . There shall be built the 'Walls of the Prince' and the Asiatics shall not again be suffered to go down to Egypt. They shall beg again for water for their cattle after their custom . . . And Right [Ma'et] shall come into its own again and Wrong shall be cast out. (After Erman 1966, pp. 112–15.)

The Ameni of the prophecy is undoubtedly Ammenemes I, and his Upper Egyptian parentage, which was noble, is stressed as an apologia for his seizure of supreme power to end the miseries of anarchy at the close of the Eleventh Dynasty.

The second work, *The Teaching of King Ammenemes*, already mentioned, is concerned with events at the end of the reign of the same king, who was apparently murdered or ritually killed by his chamberlains. In *The Teaching* the dead king is made to appear in a dream to his son Sesostris I in order to give him some sage advice in the manner of the earlier *Instruction for King Merykare* (see p. 126):

Be on thy guard against subordinates . . . Trust not a brother, know not a friend and make not for thyself intimates . . . (After Erman 1966, p. 72.)

But *The Teaching* then goes on to justify this scepticism on the strength of the experiences of the king himself who had received nothing but ingratitude from those he had promoted. The major part of the work is, in fact, not a 'teaching' at all, but a testament and an apologia for the king's life and a eulogy of his achievements. It could also be in the nature of an official explanation and excuse for any extreme measures that the young co-regent may have had to take on the sudden and violent death of his father.

The third of these works of propaganda, *The Story of Sinuhe*, is cast in a typically Egyptian literary form, the novel, and is a simple success story told with an elegance, dramatic conciseness and humour that we can still appreciate. The scene opens in the camp of the co-regent Sesostris I who is returning from a successful campaign in Libya when the news of his father's death is brought to him. Sinuhe, an official in the service of the Queen, overhears the dire report, and flees from the camp in panic, so beginning his odyssey. The justification he gives for this flight is that 'it was like the dispensation of God . . . after the manner of a dream', and it is as a god-struck man that he continues his adventures. Fate takes him to the Lebanon where he prospers. But as a good Egyptian he is sick for home and eventually returns to the court where he is received by a gracious king.

The Story of Sinuhe is remarkable for the semblance of actuality that is given to all the incidents in the tale, suggesting a real tomb-autobiography rather than a work of the imagination. Apart from the divine impulsion that sets Sinuhe on his wanderings, the tale is free from the supernatural interventions of later Egyptian stories. Although the setting is fairyland – to the court Egyptian of the Twelfth Dynasty Asia was *terra incognita* where all

91 (*left*) Statue of Sesostris I, second king of the Twelfth
Dynasty. The massive handling and firm, uncompromising
expression are not in the idealistic tradition of some
statues of this monarch.

92 (*above*) A life-sized statue-head of King Sesostris III is
carved with the consistently brooding features of the
formidable ruler who suppressed the power of the feudal
nobility, and so attached Nubia to the Egyptian crown that
he was long worshipped there as a patron god.

things were possible – all the dramatis personae behave in a completely
rational manner. But there are two heroes in the story, Sinuhe and, no less,
Sesostris I, who remains prominent in the background, from the opening
paragraphs dealing with his victorious return from war, through the apos-
trophe to him in the body of the work, and the elegant letter inviting Sinuhe
to return, to his kindly reception of the fugitive and the honours he heaps
upon him. Sesostris is shown first as the dutiful son and valiant warrior
conquering through love as much as might, and finally as the god–like ruler,
forgiving and generous.

These and some minor works, hymns in praise of the kings and so forth,
form the classical literature of Egypt, and helped to enhance the prestige of
the pharaoh during the Middle Kingdom. They were painfully learnt by
schoolboys even half a millennium later, and quotations from them are to be
found unexpectedly in solemn monumental inscriptions during the New
Kingdom. That the kings of the Twelfth Dynasty should accept the services
of skilful writers to sustain their power and glamour may seem startling, and

probably it was no explicit directive that brought such literature into being; but the plastic arts reveal the same subconscious desire to show the king as a superman. The royal statues of this reign are remarkable for their forceful portrayal of the king either as the ruthless or regal overlord of the nation, or later as the world-weary 'Good Shepherd' of his people. Most of this sculpture in hard stones, such as obsidian, granites, quartzites and basalts, is of magnificent workmanship, both technically and artistically, with a haunting inner power.

91, 92

While royal statuary is differentiated by individual portraiture, private sculpture merely follows the fashion of a particular reign. Much of it was shop-work and on a small scale made for sale to modest patrons like the pilgrims to Abydos, and varies from the competent to the frankly inept. The chasm between the superb creations of the court sculptors and this mediocre hack-work only emphasizes the gulf which had opened again by the end of the Twelfth Dynasty between the king, aloof at the head of affairs, and the mass of the people.

It was only in the early Thirteenth Dynasty, when royal commissions were once more in decline, that superior statuary for private owners reappears. At the same time, the great number of votive stelae and statuettes suggests that the little man had increased his prosperity at the expense of the great feudal lords.

93

93 Few patrons outside the kings and nomarchs in the Middle Kingdom were able to command the services of first-class sculptors until the beginning of the Thirteenth Dynasty. At this particular period, for instance, the steward Sikahika was fortunate in finding a superior artist who was able to portray in this statue the ageing features of his sitter with remarkable realism.

11 · The Second Intermediate Period

The immigrations

Manetho's account of the appearance of the Hyksos on the Egyptian scene as the irruption of a conquering horde spreading fire and destruction, was coloured by memories of more recent Assyrian and Persian invasions in his own time, and has had to be discounted. As early as the First Intermediate Period, Western Semites from Palestine, driven from their own pastures by famine to seek sanctuary elsewhere, had infiltrated the Delta. The Egyptians referred to the tribal chiefs of these peoples as *Hikau khasut* or 'Princes of Desert Uplands', a term which Manetho by false etymology translated as *Hyksos* or Shepherd Kings, a name which has clung tenaciously ever since to the entire people rather than its rulers. At Beni Hasan a group of *Hikau khasut* are shown in their coats of many colours, being received by the nomarch Khnumhotep in his capacity as Governor of the Eastern Desert in

94

94 Part of a painting of a group of Western Asiatics trading eyepaint with Khnumhotep, the governor of the Eastern Desert in the reign of Sesostris II. The women are preceded by a youth carrying a spear, the usual Asiatic weapon (cf. ill. 135). Their ethnic physiognomy, bright multicoloured garments and leather boots have been faithfully recorded.

the reign of Sesostris II, *c.* 1890 BC. Such bedouin were no more than wandering Semites trading their products with Egypt, or going down there for sanctuary, or to buy corn, or water their flocks according to an age-old tradition referred to in *The Prophecy of Neferti*. The story of Joseph reveals how some of these Asiatics may have arrived, sold into slavery for corn in time of famine, or offering themselves as menials in return for food and shelter. By the Thirteenth Dynasty, the number of Asiatics, even in Upper Egypt, was considerable. They acted as cooks, brewers, seamstresses, vine-dressers and the like. One official, for instance, had no fewer than forty-five Asiatics in his household. Such people were classed as 'slaves', a comparatively new element in Egyptian society, but one that was destined to prevail for a long time as wholesale migrations and foreign wars brought many aliens into Egypt. Their children often took Egyptian names and so fade from our sight. Asiatic dancers and a doorkeeper in a temple of Sesostris II are known, showing that these foreigners attained positions of importance and trust. It is not difficult to see that by the middle of the Thirteenth Dynasty the lively and industrious Semites could be in the same positions of responsibility in the Egyptian state as Greek freedmen were to enjoy in the government of Imperial Rome. Famine or ethnic movements leading to large-scale infiltrations into the Delta of Semites, mixed perhaps with Hurrian elements, especially during the anarchy into which the Middle Kingdom lapsed, could have resulted in the founding of a Lower Egyptian state with an Asiatic chieftain and officials taking over imperceptibly all the functions and machinery of pharaonic government. At a later stage there must have appeared upon the scene a war-leader similar to a number of condottieri who at this time with their aristocracy of chariot warriors were seizing power and founding military states all over Western Asia. According to Josephus, quoting Manetho, this was Salatis (whose precise identification with a king in the monumental record is uncertain), who seized Memphis and turned the ancient site of Avaris into a formidable stronghold.

A rather different immigration was also evident at the other end of the country. Nomadic warlike tribes from the eastern highlands of Nubia, particularly the Medjay, entered Egypt as mercenary soldiers and took service with the Theban princelings. They have left traces of their sojourn in the scanty ruins of their settlements, and especially in the characteristic shallow round or oval graves of pan-like formation at various sites in the desert verges of Upper Egypt. These pan-graves contain the contracted bodies of warrior immigrants dressed in leather garments and simple barbaric jewellery, accompanied by weapons of Egyptian design and make. They were clearly of a more primitive culture than their Egyptian hosts. In time, their burials lose their characteristic features and by the end of this period are indistinguishable from native Egyptian.

The movement of the Medjay into Egypt may not have been unconnected with ethnic movements elsewhere in Nubia and the Lower Sudan. The pharaohs of the Middle Kingdom had subjugated these territories as far as

95 Part of a statue of the nomarch Hepdjefi of Asyut in the reign of Sesostris I was found, together with this statue of Sennu his wife, in the burial mound of a local Kushite ruler at Kerma during the Second Intermediate Period. The statue of Sennu is superior in size and quality to most private statues of the Twelfth Dynasty, and doubtless came from a royal workshop. How it reached Kerma is problematic.

the Second Cataract and had established some kind of outpost as far as Kerma near the Third Cataract. Kerma was probably at this time the capital of Kush, a civilization of native origin but greatly influenced by Egyptian importations. Here a curious hybrid culture flourished, employing Egyptian techniques in faience and metal, yet also using such alien materials as mica and shell, and native-inspired designs. But the more primitive nature of this culture is seen in the *sati* burials of its local rulers under great circular tumuli, enclosing subsidiary graves of hundreds of servants and women who had been drugged and suffocated to accompany their masters into the hereafter. Egyptian statues, and other treasures looted or traded from sites further north, were also buried as part of the funerary equipment.

95

The conquest of Nubia and its organization had been the work of the pharaohs, particularly of Sesostris III, and as soon as their interest in their southern appanage began to wane in the face of more potent threats in the north, the decay of Egyptian power in Nubia was inevitable. The great forts were gradually abandoned, some of them being fired, perhaps by their garrisons they left, and were occupied by native pastoralists, squatting among the ruins. The acceptance by the Theban rulers in Upper Egypt of the suzerainty of the Hyksos overlords completed the work of disengagement. The Prince of Kush became an independent kinglet, ruling perhaps with the aid of Egyptian officials, entering into trading relations with the Hyksos, and being recognized as in some kind of alliance with them.

Hyksos and Thebans, *c.* 1650–1550 BC

By the 17th century BC Lower Egypt was ruled from Avaris by a line of Hyksos kings with their vassals who had wrested Memphis from the tired hands of the last feeble monarch of the Thirteenth Dynasty. They adopted Egyptian titularies, costume and traditions, writing their outlandish personal names, such as Yakobher and Khyan, in hieroglyphs and selecting Egyptian throne-names. They dutifully worshipped Re of Heliopolis, as well as Seth or Sutekh, the Egyptian equivalent of their Baal. That they were regarded as legitimate sovereigns in Lower Egypt at least is clear from their inclusion in the Turin king-list written as late as Ramesside times, and in other documents.

The six 'Great Hyksos' kings of the Sixteenth Dynasty who ruled Lower Egypt from Avaris, probably with the assistance of Egyptian collaborators as well as Asiatic officials, inherited all the prestige and responsibilities of the Egyptian pharaoh, and exerted an influence beyond the Delta over territories in Sinai and Palestine. Upper Egypt, from Elephantine to Cusae north of Asyut, enjoyed an uneasy independence under its princes ruling at Thebes by paying tribute to the Hyksos overlord. We can perhaps see in this partition the first movements of a political arrangement which had been conceived when a Governor of Upper Egypt had been appointed in the Fifth Dynasty, and which was to emerge fully at the end of the New Kingdom. A separate Upper Egyptian principality was created, with the ruler of Thebes at its head, but owing allegiance to the pharaoh in Lower Egypt, and united to him by marriage ties. Names of princesses have survived which already at this time arouse the suspicion that the Hyksos and the Thebans were connected by intermarriage.

While to Manetho the Hyksos seizure of supreme power seemed an unmitigated disaster, we can recognize it as one of the great seminal influences in Egyptian civilization, rescuing it from political decline, bringing new ideas into the Nile Valley and ensuring that Egypt played a full part in the development of Bronze Age culture in the eastern Mediterranean. A problematic example of the Mediterranean connections of the Hyksos is provided by the series of Cretan Minoan frescoes found in the ruins of Avaris. The earliest of their kind found anywhere, their interpretation remains uncertain, although clearly showing the depth of contracts between the north of Egypt and the Aegean. A number of innovations appear in the archaeological record. Even at the end of the Old Kingdom, a curious perforated hemispherical seal, known to archaeologists as a button-seal or design amulet, made its appearance. During the Middle Kingdom this was transformed into the characteristic Egyptian scarab, perhaps more of an amulet than a seal, and this artifact was adopted with enthusiasm by the Hyksos who produced them in enormous numbers. With the increase in Asiatic influence during the Middle Kingdom, bronze comes into general use. It was easier to work than copper and more effective for weapons and hardware. It had already been used for casting statues in the reign of Ammenemes III, a technique not possible with copper which was hammered over a wooden core in the only two large examples surviving from the Old Kingdom. Silver, too, of a purity which shows that it was not of native origin but smelted from argentiferous ores, was now imported from Asia in increasing amounts.

In the later phase of the war of liberation that developed between the Hyksos and the Thebans at the end of our period, a whole range of novel weapons was introduced from Asia, such as the horse-drawn chariot, scale armour, the composite bow and new designs of daggers, swords and scimitars. It is doubtful whether such weapons as the horse-drawn chariot were fully effective in Egypt where the inundation and topography gave a greater importance to water-borne operations; but the Thebans certainly adopted all these weapons in their wars against the Hyksos both in Egypt and Palestine. The Asiatic origin of the chariot was preserved in the different woods used in its construction, the Canaanite names for its various parts, and by the tradition of retaining Asiatics to drive and maintain some of them at least. A war helmet, probably made of leather sewn with gilded metal disks, was added to the pharaoh's regalia and is known to Egyptologists as the *khepresh*, the Blue, or War Crown.

More important than these weapons of destruction were certain abiding inventions of peace, such as improved methods of spinning and weaving, using an upright loom; new musical instruments, a lyre, the long-necked lute, the oboe and tambourine. Hump-backed bulls were imported from an Asiatic source, probably brought by ship with the greatly increased trade that the Hyksos fostered. Other importations included the olive and pomegranate tree.

In Thebes during this period, the poverty and lack of good timber encouraged further changes in funerary customs and the self-contained burial comes into fashion. There had indeed been a shift of emphasis during the last quarter of the Twelfth Dynasty when a new expression creeps into the funerary prayers to indicate that the deceased was regarded less as a materialization than as a spirit. At the same time, under the impact of the Osiris cult, the coffin as a sort of rectangular wooden house is replaced by the anthropomorphic case decorated to represent the deceased as the masked, mummified and bandaged Osiris, or as the human-headed *ba* bird, a form of the spirit.

With the appearance of this type of coffin, the tomb-statue, already greatly reduced, either disappears or is transformed into the funerary statuette or shawabti (later ushabti) figure. Such objects do not make their appearance before the Eleventh Dynasty and the first examples are in wax, but by the end of the Middle Kingdom they were being made of stone or the wood of the persea (shawab) tree, and inscribed with the full shawabti chapter from the so-called *Book of the Dead*, a collection of funerary prayers and spells written on linen shrouds and later on papyrus rolls which replaced the Coffin Texts as the rectangular sarcophagi were discarded. The shawabti figure was a specialized form of the servant statue which had disappeared with the triumph of the Osiris faith. Its purpose was to act as a substitute for the deceased whenever onerous toil had to be performed in the fields of the

96

Osirian underworld. As we have already mentioned, from the earliest times a corvée had existed whereby labourers could be drafted *en masse* for public works at critical moments during the inundation. Similar duties were naturally expected in the agricultural realms of Osiris, and it was to exempt the deceased from such forced labour that the shawabti was provided. By the end of this period even the king, who on death was assimilated to Osiris, was thought to be subject to this same conscription, and royal shawabtis are many and elaborate.

96 A shawabti of the Overseer of Works Huy holds a pick, hoe and baskets for carrying spoil. The inscription from *The Book of the Dead* is a spell which will ensure that this substitute will answer for Huy whenever a muster of the corvée is made in the afterlife.

The lack of good timber as well as changes in doctrine hastened the disappearance of the rectangular outer coffin and the sole anthropoid containers were now dug out of local trees and are invariably ill-shaped and crude. They were painted with a characteristic feathered decoration representing the wings of the sky-mother, Nut, who, according to a pastiche of several brief spells from the Pyramid Texts regularly found on the coffin-lids of the next dynasty, is exhorted to embrace the deceased with her winged arms so that he might not die a second time but be placed among the Imperishable Stars which were in her.

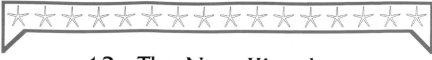

12 · The New Kingdom

The military state

About the year 1600 BC, a certain Tetisheri, the daughter of commoners, was married to Taa I (Senakhtenre), the Prince of Thebes who recognized the suzerainty of the Hyksos king in Avaris. By the time that she died as a little, white-haired, partially bald old woman, her grandson, Amosis, was the pharaoh of a united Egypt and the greatest prince of his age. This dramatic rise from obscurity to supremacy was not achieved without a bitter struggle. A novelette of later years relates how her son Taa II (Seqenenre) fought a diplomatic battle of words with the Hyksos overlord Apophis, who had challenged his pretentions in Upper Egypt. Although the end of the story is missing we are to assume that the verbal victory lay with the Theban.

This is the same Taa II who was less successful on a more active field, for his shattered skull shows that he met a violent end, either in battle or at the hands of assassins. It was probably at this critical juncture that his widow Queen Ahhotep took over the reins of government, for a later stela erected in her honour praises her for cherishing Egypt, for tending her soldiers and rallying her fugitives, 'She has pacified Upper Egypt and cast out its rebels.'

It was left to Kamose, the successor of Taa II, to begin a war of liberation in earnest, and we are fortunate in having his account of the opening of the

97 Head of a parade axe found in the coffin of Queen Ahhotep by Mariette's agents in 1859. It is of bronze overlaid with gold and electrum, and inlaid with carnelian and blue and green frit. The scene shows King Amosis wearing one of the earliest representations of the new-fangled Blue Crown despatching a rebel. Such weapons were given as rewards to warriors for valour in the field. This example was probably given to the queen by Amosis for having earlier saved the Thebans at a crisis in their fortunes.

campaign in two texts, the second of which came to light only in 1954 upon a stela among the foundations supporting a later colossus at Karnak. We learn that in his third regnal year, the new king sailed downstream with his forces and stormed the stronghold of a Hyksos collaborator, Teti, near Hermopolis, pushing his boundary to within a short distance of the entrance to the Faiyum. Kamose, however, did not live to see the end of the affair, and it was Amosis, the next in line to the Theban principality, who carried on the struggle, eventually reducing the Hyksos capital Avaris after a long siege. In order to deter further Asiatic incursions into Egypt, another campaign was necessary, and this was mounted as far as the town of Sharuhen in south-western Palestine which was destroyed, thus advertising to the Asiatic princes the arrival of a vigorous new actor upon the international scene. This incursion into Palestine, however, was not followed up till later in the reign when the land of the Syrian *Fenkhu* was invaded and their hump-backed cattle imported into Egypt.

After his capture of Sharuhen, Amosis was able to turn his attention to 97 consolidating his position in Egypt by replacing the last of the Hyksos col-laborators with his own men, and by restating claims upon the southern ter-ritories, Nubia and Kush. Kamose had already campaigned in this region, and had evidently pushed the frontier southwards from Elephantine to beyond Toshka. It was the work of Amosis to suppress all opposition, rebuild the fortress of Buhen at the northern end of the Second Cataract, and appoint his own nominee to the position formerly occupied by the Prince of Kush.

Both Egypt and Kush were reorganized upon the bureaucratic system of government which had been developed during the last reigns of the Twelfth Dynasty, but with a new logistical efficiency appropriate to a military state. The feudal nomarchs had long since disappeared from political life and no rivals to the supreme rule of the pharaoh were to be tolerated by Amosis and his successors. His soldiers, both Egyptians and their Medjay auxiliaries, were rewarded for their services by modest grants of land, with prisoners as slaves, and with valuable gold decorations and parade weapons; but the large estates in Lower Egypt were kept in the possession of the king and his family.

From the days of Menes, it had been the founder of an epoch that set the pattern for the culture that developed subsequently, and gave it its impetus. Amosis (*c.* 1550–1524 BC), the son of the last rulers of the Seventeenth Dynasty, was honoured by subsequent generations as the founder of a new line and a glorious chapter in Egyptian history. The policies which he initi-ated were followed by his successors, and during the Eighteenth Dynasty this was a recipe for unparalleled prosperity and imperial expansion in Palestine, Syria and Kush. It was from the last-named region that new sup-plies of gold were procured that made Egypt rich and influential among the nations of antiquity. The Hyksos interlude had destroyed for ever the Egyptians' belief in their uniqueness and superiority. Their pharaoh, tradi-tionally the incarnation of the god that had created their world and ruled its

98 The three entertainers are playing the double oboe, the long-necked lute and the large standing harp. Two are in their finery: the lutenist has discarded her outer robe to perform a dance with twists and turns, revealing an unusual frontal aspect. Only her amuletic girdle has been retained. The painting is full of the novelties of the Eighteenth Dynasty – the lavish jewellery and the floral adornments worn by the fashionable beauties, the Asiatic musical instruments, the cult of nudity, even the varnish on the central figure which though colourless on application has now discoloured to an opaque orange tone.

extent as far as the circuit of the sun, inherited from the Hyksos the leadership of vassal states in Palestine and Syria, but he also shared his sovereignty with 'brother' monarchs in Cyprus, Babylonia and Assyria and the Hittite and Mitannian lands in Anatolia. The triumph of Amosis on the field of battle introduced a new idea of the pharaoh as the national hero, a personification of Egypt itself, sitting as Kamose expressed it between an Asiatic in the north and a black Nubian in the south. In challenging the Hyksos power, Amosis had to adopt all the weapons and panoply of the new warfare and along with it the new social order to which it gave rise. The pharaoh was now regarded as the incarnation of some warrior-god, Baal or Seth or Mentu, at the head of a caste of professional military leaders, chariot-warriors accomplished in athletic feats, the management of horses and all the skills of a new mobile warfare.

Imperial designs

The Asiatic component in the civilization of the New Kingdom is considerable, extending even to an alteration in the racial type of the Egyptian ruling class. The men and women of the New Kingdom have lost the heavy physiques of their Old Kingdom counterparts and the dour solemnity of their Middle Kingdom forerunners. The countenances of the men are

98 bland, often faintly smiling. The women are slight, their features delicate, with great gala wigs and tip-tilted noses and long almond eyes. An erotic element enters the art of the Eighteenth Dynasty, perhaps as a result of the introduction of the cults of nude goddesses from Asia. The luxury of the age finds expression in the colourful jewels made in new materials, such as polychrome faience and glass, worn by both sexes.

The initial Egyptian forays into Western Asia brought her armies into sustained contact with the great cultures of the Near East. Against the unified power of Egypt, under the command of a warlord, were opposed loose federations of Syrian and Canaanite principalities lacking cohesion. In Palestine, Lebanon and Syria, the political unit was the city state, ruling over the territories in its vicinity and receiving within its walls the local populace in times of trouble. These states, like their equivalents in Renaissance Italy, were in constant rivalry with each other. Occasionally, under the leadership of a prince more energetic and crafty than his fellows, a coalition of powers would win some stability, but too great a success would engender its own reaction and the federation would dissolve and re-form in another direction.

These various states hardly welcomed the interference of a great power in their rivalry with each other, their main aims being to preserve their autonomy, and to extend their frontiers at the expense of their neighbours. They were, however, only too ready to turn intervention to their own advantage, following the power whose star was in the ascendant and seeking its assistance in promoting their own local ambitions. But sometimes it was doubtful to whom fortune would incline the supremacy, and in such cases one big power was played off against the other, vows of loyalty given to both, and sides changed and re-changed with little compunction. This is the world of Palestine and Syria that has been revealed to us from the Amarna diplomatic correspondence, which also apprises us of the intrusions of a mysterious people known as the Sa-Gaz or Apiru, whom some scholars regard as the immediate ancestors of the Hebrews. Apiru appear to have been displaced persons of both sexes moving around like robber-bands and probably

99 Bearded Asiatics in their long robes make obeisance as they bring gold and silver vessels, an oil-horn, a quiver and slave-children as gifts to the pharaoh. The last bearer in the lower register carries an eagle-headed rhyton upon a bowl, an object of Minoan design probably acquired by trade with the Aegean.

keeping to difficult country away from the military high-roads, and intervening in the local politics by accepting service as mercenaries when they were not fighting on their own account.

Egyptian campaigns in Western Asia quickly made their impression on the local rulers who hastened to show their submission by sending tribute. But by the time Tuthmosis III attained to sole rule (c. 1457 BC), the Egyptian position in Asia was threatened by a confederation of petty kingdoms under the leadership of the Mitanni, a Hurrian people ruled by an Aryan-speaking aristocracy who worshipped Indo-European gods and inhabited the land of Nahrina, the watershed of the Euphrates. On the east they were bounded by the young nation of Assyria and on the west by the Hittites, a mixed people occupying most of Anatolia, with an Indo-European ruling class speaking a language akin to Greek and Latin. At the beginning of our period the Mitanni were the dominant power in north Syria, having conquered the eastern Hittite territories.

100   Tuthmosis III found it necessary to fight seventeen campaigns over a period of some twenty years before his claims in Palestine and Syria could be recognized and the pretensions of the Mitanni checked. In the course of these wars Egypt was forced to organize her Asiatic sphere of influence into a virtual dependency, forming garrison-towns at strategic points and removing the sons of local rulers to Egypt as hostages for their fathers' good behaviour. These sons were brought up with the Egyptian royal children 'to serve their lord and stand at the portal of the king'. Eventually they went back to rule their states after having been anointed by the pharaoh himself.

As part of his foreign policy, Tuthmosis III had concluded a treaty with the Hittites, the rivals of the Mitanni, and a similar strategy was pursued by his successors. A pact of mutual assistance was also negotiated with Babylonia to keep the Canaanite vassals in check. Such treaties were cemented by marriages between the daughters of the various royal houses and the pharaoh. Even the daughters of less exalted princes also entered the royal harems and played their part in the diplomacy of the age. This traffic was all in one direction. When the King of Babylon attempted to make a reciprocal arrangement, he was haughtily reminded that it was not the custom for Egyptian princesses to be married to foreigners.

After the conclusion of peace between Egypt and the Mitanni, such treaties brought a century of comparative calm and stability to Palestine and south Syria during the middle reigns of the Eighteenth Dynasty, when the Egyptian district-commissioners, with the aid of loyalist levies and troops from their garrison-towns in Asia, were able to keep the more factious
99   princelings in order, and to repress the Shasu bedouin and the Apiru marauders who posed a threat to law and order.

This balance of power was however upset by the accession of the energetic and able King Suppiluliumas to the Hittite throne (c. 1350 BC). He was to remould the political structure of the region for the next century. The struggle between the Hittites and the Mitanni was renewed. After a long

100 Tuthmosis III wears the White Crown of Upper Egypt and treads upon nine bows symbolizing the traditional foreign foes of the pharaoh. The portrait is an idealized rendering of the features of the king in his early years when he was co-regent with his step-mother Hatshepsut.

contest, the Mitanni capital was sacked and its king subsequently assassinated. Syria came under the dominance of the Hittites who fostered intrigue and dissension farther south by means of their vassals, all anxious to take advantage of a situation that once more had become fluid. At this moment, the pharaoh, the ally of the Mitanni, issued no effective challenge to the Hittite threat, an indifference which has been accredited to the preoccupation of the religious reformer Akhenaten with events at home. Egypt, however, had treaties with both powers, and it may have been of little account to the pharaoh which of the two rivals had authority over north Syria. His chief concern was in preserving Egyptian influence in a coastal trading region stretching from Byblos in the south to Ugarit in the north. In this, however, the Egyptians were thwarted by the wily Amorite vassals of the Hittites, whose domains straddled the area; and although a serious attempt to win back territory and influence was undertaken by the immediate successors of Akhenaten, they did not achieve any lasting success. The powerful kingdom of the Mitanni riven by civil strife became a mere satellite of the Hittites and was eventually incorporated into the expanding state of Assyria on the death of Suppiluliumas, and disappears from history.

While events in Asia followed a fluctuating course, the more important southern dependencies of Nubia and Kush, the Biblical 'Ethiopia', came under effective Egyptian government as never before. The first kings of the Eighteenth Dynasty had campaigned regularly in these regions and extended the southernmost frontier to Napata near modern Gebel Barkal. The entire territory was now put in charge of a high official or viceroy, 'the King's son (=Prince) of Kush', appointed by the pharaoh and responsible to him alone. Under a peaceful and efficient rule, the region prospered; irrigation works improved the fertility of the soil; new cities were founded and at least a dozen new temples built, some of them of great size, such as the one erected by Amenophis III at Sulb. The Egyptianization of Nubia and Kush was so effective that at the end of the New Kingdom, c. 1075 BC, the viceroy intervened decisively in the affairs of Egypt proper in the name of law and order. The products of Nubia and Kush added greatly to the wealth of Egypt, particularly gold, ivory, ebony, cattle, gums, resins and semi-precious stones.

Most of these same commodities were also obtained by trading ventures to Punt, always an indication of the health and vigour of the Egyptian state, and during this period such voyages became commonplace. The first of these expeditions during the Eighteenth Dynasty, in the reign of Hatshepsut, is the most noteworthy for the detailed representation of it carved in relief on the Queen's funerary temple at Deir el Bahri. This is the first known example of an anthropological study of an alien culture, with its record of the flora and fauna of the region, the human types, their physique, dress and habitations. The Egyptians were mainly in search of myrrh, in the form of either the living tree or its dried resinous exudations. In exchange for this they offered the trade goods of all such African adventurers ever since – strings of beads, bangles and weapons. The final sequence in the scenes shows the triumphant return from Punt with gold, ivory, apes and precious myrrh-trees, their root-balls carefully protected in baskets, and the dedication of measured heaps of myrrh to Amun of Thebes.

The advent c. 1298 BC of the Nineteenth Dynasty, a family of evident Semitic descent from the eastern Delta, brought a new dynamic into the affairs of Western Asia, and in the first year of his reign Sethos I set forth to follow the sacrosanct patterns of the campaigns of Tuthmosis III and win back the Syrian dominions. While Sethos was successful in re-establishing Egyptian authority in Canaan and in capturing the key fortress of Qadesh on the Orontes, his battle with the Hittites was inconclusive; and it was left to his impetuous son Ramesses II to try conclusions with the prime enemy. In the latter's fifth regnal year (c. 1274 BC) the Egyptian forces fell into a trap set by the astute Hittite king north of Qadesh and were extricated from disaster only by the chance arrival of one of their army corps and by the

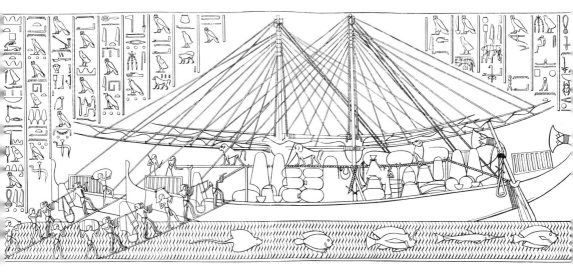

101 Two ships of the Egyptian expedition are being loaded in Punt with myrrh-resin in sacks, myrrh-trees, their root-balls protected by baskets, ebony, ivory, gold, incense-woods, apes, dogs, leopard skins, natives and their children. In the water below swim specimens of the local fish.

personal valour of Ramesses in persistently charging the enemy to rally his demoralized forces. Thereafter no serious challenge was made to Hittite ascendancy in northern Syria. The two powers in fact entered into increasingly friendly relations culminating in a defensive alliance between them which is an important landmark in the history of diplomacy. In the treaty, of which a Hittite copy exists as well as Egyptian versions of the original inscribed silver tablet, both powers act as equals; their spheres of influence are carefully defined, south Syria going to Egypt and the north to the Hittites; each pledges the other not to support its enemies, and there are provisions for the extradition of criminals or emigrés.

The treaty was sealed by a marriage between Ramesses and the daughter of the Hittite king, an affair which breathed fresh inspiration into a continuous romance of the Near East, celebrated alike in the scarab of regnal year ten of Amenophis III, when he was married to the daughter of the King of Nahrina, and in the story of Solomon and the Queen of Sheba, though in the case of the Hittite princess, we have a more tangible memorial in a scrap of papyrus found by Petrie at Gurob, listing part of her wardrobe.

Loss of empire

It may be that both powers realized the futility of warring against each other in the face of a common menace. Neither side could foresee that they were both on the threshold of a new era in the Eastern Mediterranean that was to sweep their order away and replace it by the world of the Old Testament and the long Dark Age of Greece. But there had already been portents. In his

102 The relief shows members of the king's clean-shaven Shardana bodyguard with their characteristic weapons, a long sword, circular buckler, spear and hemispherical helmet with horns and a disk on a spike. This resembles the garb found later on statuettes from sites in Sardinia to which the Shardana may have given their name.

102   second regnal year, Ramesses II had captured in the Delta a force of Shardana freebooters, roving at large over the Levant from a homeland in north Syria. They immediately took service in the Egyptian armies and formed a *corps d'élite* around the pharaoh, being reinforced with fresh intakes during the next century. They had almost certainly been meddling in affairs in the Western Delta where unrest among the Libyan border tribes had earlier obliged Sethos I to take the field against them. Ramesses II had also campaigned in the area, capturing many prisoners, and found it advisable to reinforce considerably his defences in the Western Desert.

103   It was, however, in the fifth regnal year of his successor Merenptah, *c.* 1207 BC, that the threat took a more aggressive and perilous shape. New tribes of Libyans appeared in force on the western frontier, penetrating the defences as far as the oasis of Farafra and the Canopic branch of the Nile. This was no plundering incursion, but a migration of peoples moving with their families, cattle, household goods and treasure to settle in the rich pastures of the Delta, in the face of increasing aridity in their own lands. Merenptah's forces drove them back with great losses. This heavy defeat gave Egypt nearly half a century of uneasy peace; but in his time Ramesses III (*c.* 1185–1153 BC), the first effective king of the Twentieth Dynasty and the last great pharaoh of Egypt, was called upon to repulse two more desperate invasions of immigrants from Libya, again accompanied by their families, cattle and possessions. Even these disasters did not deter these land-hungry peoples from settling in Egypt. Throughout the Twentieth Dynasty, wandering bands of Libyans filtered across the western borders,

striking terror in the Valley-dwellers as far south as Thebes and Aswan. Many of them took service with the Egyptian armies, and as veterans were eventually settled on the land. Their descendants constituted an influential military caste and later became powerful enough to intervene decisively in Egyptian affairs and form several dynasties of pharaohs.

These various incursions from Libya had a feature that was new and soon to prove of a calamitous significance. The Libyans who had invaded the Delta in the reign of Merenptah had been accompanied by foreign contingents of 'northerners coming from all lands', bearing such names as Lukka, Teresh, Shekelesh and Akawash in addition to more Shardana. We can recognize in these names the toponyms of the lands they eventually occupied, Lycia, Etruria, Sicily and Sardinia. Similar groups of piratical adventurers, some bearing the same names, appear again in strength in the next great crisis that Ramesses III had to meet, the invasions of the Sea Peoples *c.* 1177 BC. This is a name which the Egyptians themselves applied to the loose federation of roving corsairs that now overwhelmed the old nations of the Levant and cast them into a newer mould. According to the only account of these events, given in bombastic language and none-too-explicit reliefs on the walls of the mortuary temple of Ramesses III at Medinet Habu, a league of these northern peoples had evidently been formed to replace sporadic raiding by a concerted drive against the great powers of Anatolia, Syria and

103 The foemen fallen in the two invasions of Egypt during the reign of Ramesses III have the ethnic appearance of Libyans with their side-locks, beards and long robes, though on both occasions they were accompanied by Sea Peoples.

104 Egyptian warship with a lion head at the prow, its oarsmen shielded by raised gunwales, and manned by soldiers in padded armour, a slinger in the crow's nest, engage a boat of different design full of warriors wearing 'feathered' helmets with neckguards. Such head protection was worn by the Peleset contingent of the Sea Peoples, in whom may be recognized the later Philistines.

Palestine. 'All at once', says Ramesses, 'these peoples were on the move . . . No country could stand up to them. The Hittites, Cilicia, Carchemish, Cyprus and others were cut off. A camp was established in Amor, and they desolated its people and annihilated its land. Their confederacy was Peleset, Tjeker, Shekelesh, Denyen and Weshesh . . .' Egypt lay before them rich in spoils and ripe for settlement. Ramesses met the invasion on two fronts. A fierce land battle was fought near the Egyptian frontier in Palestine. The Egyptians with their auxiliaries claimed a great victory. The second assault 104 was fought upon the sea; and evidently, in order to avoid single scattered actions, the enemy were enticed, 'like birds into a clap-net', to enter the Nile mouths where boomships had been stationed, and a single decisive engagement could be fought. Once more Egypt was victorious and the dire threat dispelled.

Much has to be read between the lines of the Egyptian account, but the victory seems to have been complete. The Egyptian strategy was correct in tempting these essentially small, individual bands of marauders to commit their forces to a concerted attack against which a unified command would have the advantage. But while the Egyptian frontiers may have been preserved, the map of the Near East was considerably altered in the process. Priam's Troy had traditionally fallen to the Achaeans a year or two before the advent of Ramesses III. The Hittite empire now disappeared from Anatolia together with its maritime vassals Ugarit and Amor. Despite the total victory claimed by Ramesses III over the land forces of the Sea Peoples, accompanied by their women and children in bullock carts, the Peleset and the Tjeker settled in the coastal towns of Palestine during the next half-century. The former are often equated with the Philistines, and the latter with the Teucri of the Troad. The identification of the Denyen also poses problems, though a daring case has been made out for their being the Biblical tribe of Dan. Whether the Weshesh originated in Illios (Troy), and the Akawash were Mycenaean Greeks, may be beyond all conjecture; but what is more evident is that the 12th century BC in the Levant was a time of the breaking of nations, when in the words of the Egyptians, their peoples were on the march, scattered in war.

This was indeed a proto-Armageddon, the end of an epoch. During the last three centuries of the Bronze Age, there had been estbablished all over the Near East great and little principalities of indigenous farmers ruled by divine warlords and their *maryannu*, an aristocracy of chariot-using warriors, dedicated to the service of their leaders. These élites were usually Aryan-speaking and devoted to such military sports as shooting with the composite bow, hurling the javelin, taming horses and fighting from the chariot. The character of these stratified societies is as much revealed in the epics of Homer as in the Amarna Letters. They were feudal, contentious, boastful and aggressive, living in splendid palaces and cultivating the luxurious arts. Their leaders engaged in commerce, but were dependent upon a palace bureaucracy for organizing their trading ventures as much for prestige as profit. They exchanged their oil, corn, copper and timber for such luxury goods as gold and silver, lapis lazuli, fine furniture and ivory carvings, rich needlework, ornate chariots and spirited horses.

In the 13th century BC this world began to disintegrate. The reasons are complex; probably climatic change, leading to drought and the movement of starving peoples, was at the root of the deterioration. Plague had been endemic in Anatolia since the 14th century, doubtless reducing the farming community and restricting the supply of grain. Merenptah had to relieve the famine in the Hittite lands in his second regnal year (c. 1211 BC) with supplies of corn. The area was also subject to severe earthquakes, and the enormous volcanic eruption on Thera, but Troy VI and Ugarit were also destroyed by earthquakes, as were Kition and Enkomi in Cyprus at the end of this phase. Such catastrophes had their political effects upon settled communities, and the commerce in which they were engaged. As trade began to decline, maritime adventurers unable to trade as before took to piracy, an endemic feature of the Mediterranean seaways until very recent times. Such assaults led to reprisals and ever bolder brigandage. A governing caste that had been nurtured upon the military arts knew only how to fight and plunder. The kings of men became the sackers of cities. From this boiling cauldron of nations on the move, the Mediterranean lands were eventually colonized by warrior groups preserving legends of a former greatness when their heroic ancestors were in pursuit of glory.

The decline and fall of the divine kings of Asia and their *maryannu* had its repercussions upon the position of the pharaoh who shared the same ideals. The prestige of the pharaoh waned in the later years of the Twentieth Dynasty when revolt against authority was in fashion. There was trouble on the frontiers in the north and west and a need for constant vigilance. Late in the reign of Ramesses XI, the last pharaoh of the New Kingdom, civil war broke out between the king and Pinhasi, his viceroy of Kush, whom Ramesses had earlier called upon to put down disorder in Thebes. Pinhasi was driven out of Thebes by the king's generals Herihor and Piankh, not without inflicting deplorable damage in the process, and retired to Kush where he kept up such an effective resistance that the province was thereafter permanently lost to Egypt. Asia had been abandoned a little earlier, probably in the reign of Ramesses VI; and the Faiyum, and possibly other northern oases, had become indefensible through Libyan raids. By the end of the New Kingdom, Egypt was back behind her old frontiers.

The cultural heritage

The civilization of the New Kingdom seems the most golden of all the epochs of Egyptian history, and the nearest to us, probably because of the wealth of its remains. Its great pharaohs are more than mere names; we have many of their personal possessions, their sceptres, weapons, chariots, jewels and finery, their very paint-boxes and toys. We can even look upon the now shrunken features that once held the world in awe. Its voices are many and varied: we have the measured strophes of the great paeans of Tuthmosis III and Merenptah, the psalm-like sentiments of Akhenaten's hymns to the Aten, and the nearest approach to an epic that the Egyptian poet ever achieved in the account of the valour of Ramesses II at the Battle of Qadesh. There are joyous poems in praise of the coronations of kings and the wonderful cities they had built: and lyric verses to be sung to the lute describing the pangs of separated lovers, or their delight in each other's company in some Oriental pleasance.

A more satirical note is struck in allegories such as *The Blinding of Truth by Falsehood* or *The Dispute between Body and Head* or in the miscellanies praising the profession of the scribe at the expense of other callings, or in *A Literary Controversy* which exposes the pretensions of one pundit and the learning of his rival. In a more irreverent vein are the vulgarizations in the form of folk-tales of religious myths such as *The Tale of Two Brothers*, *The Outwitting of Re by Isis* and the Rabelaisian *Contendings of Horus and Seth*. The wars of liberation and conquest engendered a crop of popular historical romances such as *Apophis and Sekenenre* and *The Taking of Joppa*, besides the fairy-tales set in Syria such as *The Foredoomed Prince*. In addition to these literary works, there are autobiographies, model letters, books of proverbs

105 (*right*) The temple of Luxor, looking through the pylon built by Ramesses II to the colonnade of Amenophis III. The colossi that flank the gate bear the names of Ramesses but, like many other sculptures, may originally have been made for Amenophis III and re-carved for the later king.

and maxims in the tradition of the 'teachings' of earlier ages, accounts, taxation-rolls, horoscopes, dream interpretations, a sadly damaged list of kings (the Turin Canon), and a body of juridical papyri dealing with lawsuits, wills, marriage settlements, a curious case of adoption, the reports of a royal commission which investigated the harem conspiracy that may have ended the life of Ramesses III, and the proceedings of other tribunals which looked into allegations of widespread tomb-robbery during the reigns of the last Ramessides. Probably in the same category is *The Adventures of Wenamun*, an account of misfortunes that befell a priest of Amun when he set forth for Lebanon in the sunset years of the New Kingdom to buy cedarwood for the barque of Amun. For its vivid character-drawing and descriptive force, this narrative is unequalled in the literature of the pre-Classical world.

106 Oil-flask in the form of a Nile fish made of dark blue glass decorated with white and yellow dragged-glass threads simulating scales and fins. Such elegant baubles in polychrome glass were a feature of the luxurious rococo taste of the ruling families of the late Bronze Age.

105   The artistic legacy is vast, from colossal statues in granite and quartzite to small articles of luxury in ivory and gold. New materials make their appearance. A factory for the manufacture of vessels in brilliant polychrome 106   glass seems to have been attached to the royal palaces; and great skill was shown in casting glass to imitate semi-precious stones for inlay in jewellery and furniture. Fine work in various coloured faiences is a prominent feature of architectural decoration especially during Ramesside times. The art of the goldsmith hardly reaches the high standard of the court jewellers of the Middle Kingdom, but a process of colouring gold in tones from pink to crimson was invented during this period. Tapestry-weaving and needlework embroidery were employed for the new and luxurious fashions of dress, though the surviving examples are in poor condition. The rich store of trea- *Frontispiece*   sure from the tomb of Tutankhamun has given us a dazzling conspectus of court art at the period of its most opulent development, and acquainted us with the skill and resource of the craftsmen of the day whose taste was often a little too exuberant.

All this heritage has survived by the accident that the founders of the New Kingdom were princes of Thebes who made that city the virtual capital of Upper Egypt and lavished much of their wealth upon its god Amun who had promoted their success. Above all, they returned to the birthplace of their dynasty after death, to the tombs that had been prepared for them there. The tradition begun by Amenophis I or Tuthmosis I (late 16th century BC) of abandoning the pyramid in favour of a rock-hewn sepulchre in the crags of Western Thebes was followed by their successors, who for the next four centuries cut their tombs in the lonely Valley of the Kings and built their mortuary temples on the plain below. Other wadis were subsequently used for the tombs of some queens and princes. In the adjacent hills, overlooking the mortuary temples of the kings they had served, the court officials were granted burial in the old tradition, and the painted walls of their chapels have bequeathed us a most lively picture of life in the Eighteenth Dynasty – the reception by the pharaoh at his accession and jubilees of ambassadors bringing gifts from Nubia, Syria, Palestine and the Aegean; the royal investitures; scenes of military life and the professional occupations of the owners; besides such traditional subjects as the hunt in marsh and wadi, the procession to the tomb and the last rites. After the Amarna interlude, the subjects lose their pagan delight in the world and its joys and show a more sombre preoccupation with funerary scenes and magic rites, in this probably being influenced by the decoration of contemporary royal tombs as well as by a change of mood. To cater for the construction of the royal tombs, a village was established at what is now Deir el Medina housing generations of necropolis workers; and it is from the ruins of this hamlet that many of the Theban objects in our museums have come. We owe the preservation of the New Kingdom past almost entirely to the dry climate of Thebes.

The new ideal of the pharaoh as the heroic champion of Egypt is expressed in representations of him on a colossal scale. Huge statues and reliefs of kings, and sometimes of their queens, dominate the ancient sites.   107 The ambitions and tastes of the kings and their courtiers instigated the building of great temples to the gods in the main towns, and to the royal funerary cult at Western Thebes. All were richly furnished with equipment and handsomely endowed. There were two main reasons for this growth in the size and volume of such works, apart from the great increase in wealth and the *folie de grandeur* of the entire contemporary world. The reorganization of the government of Egypt as a military autocracy, with its bureaucracy reshaped to deal with the logistics of a military state, meant that a large professional standing army could be used at home as a labour corps whenever field operations were in abeyance. Reinforced with criminals and prisoners captured in the imperial wars, it provided the means of exploiting the new gold mines in Nubia and Kush on which so much of the prestige of the new Egyptian state depended. The use of the army ensured that a disciplined labour force could function without affecting vital agricutural operations.

The second factor was the use of sandstone in place of limestone as the prime building material, allowing wider spaces to be spanned. The opening of new quarries at Gebel es Silsila on the very banks of the Nile, enabled fine-quality sandstone to be easily extracted and transported in great quantities and sizes with comparatively little effort. Access to this plentiful building material made it possible to erect enormous buildings in a relatively short time.

107 (*left*) Figure of a queen carved in front of the legs of a standing colossus in the First Court of the Great Temple at Karnak. There has been much debate as to whether the statue was made in the New Kingdom (perhaps begun by Amenophis III and finished by Ramesses II) and usurped by Pinudjem I of the Twenty-First Dynasty, or made by Pinudjem from a block quarried by Ramesses II. If the latter, the queen is Henttawy, later the mother of Psusennes I.

108 (*above*) The Temple of Hatshepsut at Deir el Bahri. Although built in terraces it conforms to the usual plan of New Kingdom mortuary temples, with a central sanctuary of Amun, flanked on the left by a chapel of the dead ruler, and on the right by one of the sun.

109 (*right*) This statue, which is unique in its material and scale among the series produced for the funerary temple of Hatshepsut, probably came from the queen's own chapel in the uppermost court. Although it shows her in all the trappings of a pharaoh, such as she assumed on the death of her husband Tuthmosis II, full justice is done to her feminine figure and appearance.

110 (*left*) By Roman times the northern of the two colossi that stood at the entrance to the vanished mortuary temple of Amenophis III was thought to represent the Homeric Memnon, slain at Troy by Achilles. About AD 200 an earth tremor demolished its fissured upper part, and it was crudely repaired with blocks of quartzite in the reign of Septimius Severus (193–211).

111 The youthful Amenophis III, a detail from a dyad in hard yellow limestone showing him being presented with the sign of life by the crocodile god Sobek. The group was found in a well near the ruins of the temple of Sobek at the ancient Sumenu, 20 miles south of Luxor, and is excellently preserved.

It is in fact the great temples of the New Kingdom that reveal the full extent of the wealth and power of the reformed state, whether they be the additions that each pharaoh made to earlier foundations, or the complete temples which he built on new sites, as at Sulb, Amarna, Abu Simbel and Western Thebes. The tradition began with Queen Hatshepsut who, after dutifully serving for seven years as regent for her young nephew Tuthmosis III, assumed pharaonic titles and ruled as his co-regent for a further fifteen years. She was particularly devoted to the worship of Amun of Thebes, whose oracles doubtless sanctioned her seizure of power, and she built a splendid temple dedicated to him and to her own funerary cult at Deir el Bahri. Her architect and favourite, Senenmut, was obviously influenced by the adjacent temple of Mentuhotep II, and also used limestone for his own construction, but he transformed the design of his predecessor into a more satisfactory architectural unity. Despite modern re-constructions by three different missions, it still impresses by its skilful exploitation of the site. The reliefs which embellish the colonnades commemorate the great events of Hatshepsut's reign, in conformity with the heroic ideals of the age, and show her expedition to Punt (p. 154 above), her divine birth and the erection at Thebes of colossal granite obelisks brought from Aswan by river transport.

112 The colonnade of Amenophis III in the temple of Luxor. It was originally equipped with high side-walls bearing scenes from the Festival of Opet. Beyond is the courtyard of Ramesses II and the same king's pylon.

In addition, over 200 statues in various stones of different sizes were furnished for the temple precincts.

The architects and sculptors trained on the queen's pioneer constructions were available for the undertakings of Tuthmosis III in his sole reign, during whose long tenure the buoyancy of the new Egypt, confident and wealthy as a result of its military successes, is expressed in widespread building. The climax of this development was reached in the reign of Amenophis III who devoted most of his reign of nearly forty years to the arts of peace. His buildings at Thebes are still impressive, even in their ruin, though they were once lavishly decorated with gold and silver. Thus we read of 'numerous royal statues in granite of Elephantine, in quartzite and every splendid and costly stone, established as everlasting memorials and shining in the sight of men like the morning sun'. He furnished the temple of Mut, the consort of Amun, with some 600 statues of the lion-headed goddess Sekhmet; and examples of these sculptures, usually usurped by later kings, are in nearly every Egyptological collection. With him statuary on an enormous scale makes its appearance, the most notable perhaps being the pair of colossi, the so-called Colossi of Memnon, still dominating the Theban plain before the vanished portal of his funerary temple, much of whose stonework was

reused by Merenptah. The temple of Amenophis III at Luxor is still stand-   112
ing, and the fame of this and other great monuments won for the king's
master of works, Amenophis-son-of-Hapu, the unprecedented honour of a
funerary temple in his lifetime and deification in the Ptolemaic Period.

The reformed sun cult

A feature of the age was the greatly enhanced influence of the cult of the sun
god Re-Herakhty of Heliopolis. During the Middle Kingdom, the name Re
had already been compounded with those of many other gods, such as
Mentu, Sobek and Amun in the Theban region. A more tangible effect is
now evident upon the religious architecture of the New Kingdom. The
worship of the sun god was observed at an altar under the open sky within
a colonnaded court, and such adjuncts were now added to every primal
temple containing the sanctuary of the original local god and his associated
deities. Above all, two symbolic hills forming the towers flanking a main
entrance to the colonnaded court were erected to represent the twin mountains of Bakhu and Manu between which the sun god rose daily to shine
upon the temple and bring it to life.

Another testimony to the fresh currents circulating in religious thought,
perhaps as a result of ideas coming from Asia, were the new theological
works that decorate the tombs of the kings at Thebes, *The Book of What is
in the Underworld*, *The Litany of the Sun*, and *The Book of Gates*. These writings reveal a new emphasis upon a monotheistic syncretism of ancient
beliefs. Re is not only the sun god, he is also the universe, having made
himself for eternity. He is 'the sole god who has made myriads from himself:
all gods came into being from him'. He is invoked as 'he whose active forms
are his eternal transformations when he assumes the aspect of his Great
Disk'. This disk, or Aten, which illumines the world of the dead as well as
the living, and daily brings both to life from death or sleep, is the constant
element in these transformations which the active day-sun undergoes to
become the inert night-sun and vice versa. The power immanent in the disk
is Re, the supreme god whose son, the pharaoh, his representative on earth,
will return to him on death. The design of the royal tomb gradually evolves
to become a model of the caverns of the underworld through which the
night-sun is drawn to a transformation in the burial chamber at each dawn,
as the texts and scheme of decoration make evident.

The effect of these doctrines is seen in the sun worship which the pharaoh
Akhenaten introduced at his advent. He departed from the pundits of the
orthodox sun cult in placing a little more emphasis upon the Aten, or visible
manifestation of godhead, than he did upon Re-Herakhty, the hidden power
that motivated it. Where he differed from the sun cult was that instead of
incorporating all the old gods in his sole deity, he rigidly excluded them in
an uncompromising monotheism. Where this idea came from in a world
which tolerated so many diverse forms of godhead is unknown. They were

presumably Akhenaten's own, the logical result of regarding the Aten as a self-created heavenly king, whose son, the pharaoh, was also 'unique, without a peer'. The Aten was made the supreme state-god, achieving the position of a heavenly pharaoh, who like his earthly counterpart, had his names inscribed in two cartouches, assumed titles and epithets and celebrated jubilees.

113   The cult of the Aten became more uncompromising as the reign of Akhenaten wore on. Almost from the first, the Aten ceased to be represented in the old iconic form of Re-Herakhty, but was symbolized as the abstract glyph for sunlight, a rayed disk, each sunbeam ending in a ministering hand. Other gods, particularly the influential Amun and Osiris, were abolished, their images smashed, their names excised, their temples abandoned, their revenues impounded. The plural form of the word for god was suppressed. At the same time, however, the prayers to the Aten were usually addressed through the intermediary of the king; and the icons of the new faith in the tombs which he gave to his followers are concerned only with the doings of the royal family. The participation of the tomb owner, even the most exalted, is minimal and subsidiary.

This increase in the power and glory of the kingship, in conformity with the spirit of the time, was the inevitable outcome of Akhenaten's religious ideas. The closing of the temples would have had the effect of transferring all their property and income to the ownership of the pharaoh, doubtless to the advantage of his deity, the Aten. The administration of this great accession of property evidently ceased to be in the hands of the many local temple officials for fiscal purposes; and the king had to call upon the army as the only source of manpower capable of enforcing tax collection in the absence of the former officials. Without proper supervision, and the sanction of traditional practice, corruption, arbitrary exactions and other malpractices soon took a firm hold and had to be savagely suppressed by subsequent kings in restoring the former system of taxation.

The rapid building of new temples to the Aten at Karnak and on other major sites, and particularly the erection of a new residence-city on virgin ground at Amarna, must have drained the land of its labour and economic resources. The lavish offerings to the Aten that were such a feature of the daily worship in the temples at Amarna, and doubtless elsewhere as well, must have hastened economic collapse that probably more than anything ensured the abandonment of Akhenaten's religious ideas immediately after his death. Even in his own capital city of Akhetaten, his ambitions outran his resources. Only two of the tombs he lavished upon his followers were completely cut and decorated: even his own sepulchre is unfinished. He also defaulted on supplies of gold that had been promised to his ally, the king of the Mitanni. When his successor, Tutankhamun, attempted to return to the policies that had succeeded in the past, he reported that the temples of the land, from one end to the other, were abandoned, weeds grew in their sanctuaries and their courts were as a trodden path. If one petitioned a god or

113 The royal family at Tell el Amarna stand before altars heaped with offerings while the Aten sun-disk radiates light upon them. Akhenaten and Nefertiti present perfume holders: the daughters assist in the worship by rattling their sistra.

goddess, one's prayers went unanswered for they were angry at what had been done. His remedial measures were to restore the morale of the nation by appeasing the offended gods whose resentment would have put a blight on all human enterprises. Temples were therefore to be cleaned and repaired, new images to be made, priesthoods to be appointed and endowments restored.

Decline of the pharaonate

Despite this rehabilitation, and reforms in the army and fiscal service later introduced by Horemheb, it was left to the Ramessides of the next dynasty to repair much of the damage, Sethos I restoring desecrated buildings at Thebes and embellishing Abydos and other centres. His son, Ramesses II, was the most vigorous builder to have worn the Double Crown, nearly half the temples remaining in Egypt dating from his reign. His mortuary temple at Thebes, popularly known as the Ramesseum, the huge Hypostyle Hall at Karnak, the rock-hewn temple at Abu Simbel, and many other erections, would have contented lesser men: but in addition he usurped a great deal of the work of earlier kings to adorn the new capital city of Pi-Ramesse on which he expended so much treasure. These appropriations have won him the reputation in modern times of being the arch-plunderer of others' monuments. This judgment, however, is too harsh. According to Egyptian beliefs a statue that had not received its annual consecration was deprived of its virtue, and belonged to no one. There were still many monuments remaining from the reign of Akhenaten that had lain neglected and required reconsecration on new sites during the reign of Ramesses II. Much of his work, particularly of the latter half of his long reign, is coarse, tasteless and

114, 115

tired, and involved the usurpation of much earlier work, particularly that of Amenophis III, but he left so universal and impressive a legend of super-human qualities that his successors could only attempt a pale reflection of it. Ramesses III, for instance, named his sons after those of his idol, and in his mortuary temple at Medinet Habu copied much of the decoration and texts of the Ramesseum, a little to the north of Medinet Habu. The reliefs on the later site, however, showing the king hunting wild bulls and human foes, seem to be original in design. This temple included in its complex a palace, administrative buildings, military quarters, store-rooms, gardens and pools. It was enclosed by a great wall and the main entrance was a fortified gate-building like a Syrian *migdol*. It served, in fact, as a fortress for the protection of the population of West Thebes in times of trouble during the later years of the Twentieth Dynasty when it was stormed at least twice in the fighting that broke out between the forces of Pinhasi and Herihor (p. 160 above). Despite an evident decline in enterprise and invention during this dynasty, the royal sepulchres continue to be vast excavations, such as those of Ramesses VI. A ritual plan of the tomb of Ramesses IV, which has survived on a torn strip of papyrus at Turin, shows that it was designed to be equipped with a full set of furniture, including five gold-covered enclo-sures around the sarcophagus similar to the opulent provision made for Tutankhamun. The fine granite sarcophagus made for Ramesses IV, and the one made for his father Ramesses III, testify to the vigour of the pharaonic tradition which could still command such resources in what seems to be a period of decline.

116

114 Osiride statues in the ruined second court of the Ramesseum at Thebes. In this mortuary temple of Ramesses II the dead king is identified with the god Osiris. The cliffs of Western Thebes can be seen in the background, honeycombed with the tombs of the royal officials.

115 The great Hypostyle Hall at Karnak, with its roof upheld by a forest of columns with papyrus-bud capitals, represents the primeval marsh and would be in elemental darkness were it not for the central aisle of taller columns with open papyrus-umbel capitals. The space between the architraves at different levels is filled by a clerestory perforated by a window between each row, of which one has been restored in this example. The transition from the sunlight of the open court to the darkness of the sanctuary is thus made through a hall in half shade.

116 The girdle wall of the mortuary temple of Ramesses III at Medinet Habu was pierced by a gatehouse in the middle of its western and eastern sides, the latter remaining largely intact. The design of this fortified entrance is based upon that of a contemporary North Syrian *migdol* or fortress. Since Priam's Troy was traditionally destroyed a little before the advent of Ramesses III, it is at Medinet Habu, before the Eastern Gatehouse, rather than at present-day Hissarlik in Turkey, that the visitor can receive his most vivid impression of the walls of Homeric Ilion.

Under their fighting pharaohs, the Egyptians in the early Eighteenth Dynasty had shown a new-found zest for war and conquest. The professional soldier, as distinct from the unwilling conscripted peasant, had made a sudden appearance. The Asiatic campaigns introduced many exotic novelties into the Nile Valley, strange people, fashions of dress, Canaanite words and phrases, and foreign religious cults. It was from Syria that Tuthmosis III imported curious plants, animals and birds, represented in reliefs adorning a chamber of his great festival temple at Karnak. In all this, Egyptian horizons were widened and an optimistic spirit prevailed. The Egyptians shared in the delight in personal greatness and the pride in worldly success which is the spirit abroad over the entire civilized Near East in the Late Bronze Age. The procession to grandeur reached its apogee with the reign of Akhenaten who revived the old concept of the sun king, the patron of the dead as well as the living. After the failure of his policies both at home and abroad, a loss of self-confidence can be sensed in the Egyptian psyche. The military career tended to be left to foreigners, mercenaries from Nubia, the Sudan, Canaan, Libya and the lands of the Sea Peoples. The Egyptians turned more to the professions of scribe and priest, especially with the great increase in the wealth of Amun of Thebes, being content to fill or create some comfortable office which they could hand on to their sons.

The loss of Asia, Kush and some of the western oases turned the vision of the Egyptians inwards upon themselves, and their pharaoh ceased to be regarded as the heroic champion of the entire nation, successfully challenging the insolent foreigner. The story of Wenamun (c. 1070 BC), in his ill-starred mission to Byblos to buy cedarwood at the prompting of Herihor and the oracle of Amun, shows how far the mighty had fallen in the estimation of former vassals and clients.

The change in the Egyptian outlook is reflected in the tomb-chapels of the age where gay, painted scenes of everyday life are discarded in favour of the icons of a funerary mythology permeated with magic. The self-contained burial within the coffin of Hyksos times had been elaborated in the wealthy days of the Eighteenth Dynasty to comprise nests of coffins, stone sarcophagi, Canopic chests, copies of *The Book of the Dead*, and the personal possessions of the deceased housed in the burial chamber. But in the necessitous times that followed the reign of Ramesses II, there was a return to the former practice; only a coffin or a set of coffins was provided, painted with selected religious scenes and short extracts from *The Book of the Dead*. This vogue, with variations in style and elaboration, persisted thereafter, in all but the wealthiest burials, even into the Christian period. At the same time, there was a tendency to create family burial places by making intrusive interments in the ancestral tomb, or in loculi within its precincts. Intrusive burial in fact became very much the common practice at Thebes, after the wholesale pillaging of the necropoleis during the disorders at the end of the New Kingdom. Very many of the earlier tombs had been desecrated and were then standing open ready for appropriation. Even the despoiled bodies of past royalty were to be hidden away in this manner during the following decades in two or more mass-burials.

13 · The Third Intermediate and Late Periods

Upper and Lower Egypt

The troubles at the end of the Twentieth Dynasty left the Thebaid and much of the southern part of Egypt under the control of the military-priestly regime installed by Piankh and Herihor. The descendants of Piankh combined the offices of High Priest of Amun and Commander-in-Chief of the Army, and for a time at least had a residence at el Hiba, the fortress town on their northern border.

The nominal kingship of the whole of Egypt had passed from the last Ramesside (XI) to his son-in-law, Smendes, Governor of the Delta city of Tanis, whose authority was recognized by the Thebans. However, for the second part of his reign, the former Theban High Priest, Pinudjem I, had also taken pharaonic titles, and soon after Smendes' death, Pinudjem's son, Psusennes I, became pharaoh in Tanis. Thus, for most of the Twenty-First Dynasty, the soldier-priests of Thebes and the pharaohs in Tanis were closely related, and for a period were even brothers.

The city of Tanis, originally a dependency of Pi-Ramesse, was greatly embellished with new temples, mostly constructed with stone salvaged from the older town, whose functions had transferred to the upstart. It was here that the Tanite kings were buried, in stone tombs sunk in the courtyard of the great temple of Amun-re. One of these tombs, that of Psusennes I himself, was found intact in 1939, and shows us the mixture of riches and poverty that characterizes the Third Intermediate Period: although the king lay in a silver coffin, a gold mask upon his face, his granite outer coffin and sarcophagus were both second-hand, the latter coming from the tomb of Merenptah in the Valley of the Kings.

Libyan Dynasts

About 974 BC, a family of Libyan descent who had eventually settled at Bubastis became influential enough to secure the throne after the death of King Amenemopet. Osokhor, the first of these kings, may not have been able to retain the throne for the next generation, but around 948 BC Shoshenq I (the Biblical Shishak) was able to establish a new dynasty, the Twenty-Second. An energetic ruler, he invaded Palestine in about 930 BC and

117 The court in front of the Second Pylon which admits to the great Hypostyle Hall of the temple of Amun at Karnak (see ill. 115) also encloses such subsidiary buildings as a temple of Ramesses III, and a triple barque-shrine of Sethos II. Of later constructions little now exists, but this stately entrance to the court on its south side still remains, and has been given the name of the Bubastite Portal from the reliefs and inscriptions that were carved upon it by Shoshenq I, Osorkon I and other notables of the Twenty-Second Dynasty who otherwise have left few memorials.

118 (*right*) This solid gold statuette is of high quality, suggesting that it came from a tabernacle within a temple. Amun holds the scimitar of power in his right hand, and the sign of life in his left.

plundered Solomon's temple of its rich treasure (2 Chronicles 12, 2–9), restoring some of Egypt's prestige. He also renewed contacts with Byblos, and may have sent an expedition into Nubia to recover lost ground in that region of gold and fighting men. The plunder from his raid into Israel and Judah enabled him to undertake new additions to the temple of Amun at Karnak, and especially in the forecourt. However, only the Bubastite Portal was anywhere close to completion at his death.

117, 118

During the next century, the successors of Shoshenq managed to maintain something of his original impetus in the affairs of Egypt. Temples and many of the great centres of the land were richly endowed with furniture and other treasures in gold and silver. However, around 867 BC, Thebes once again obtained its own king, the former High Priest Harsiese, and, for the next one-and-a-half centuries, each half of Egypt had its own separate pharaoh. The Theban kingdom was soon wracked with internal disputes, with a number of claimants fighting for the throne. Matters were only resolved following the victory of Osorkon III around 800 BC, when he overthrew the last of the usurpers.

In the north, Tanite power waned in the years following the definitive decoupling of Thebes around 840 BC. Various fiefdoms were assigned to members of the royal family, which gradually became hereditary princedoms that owed but nominal allegiance to the king. Thus, by the latter part of the 8th century BC, Lower Egypt was a patchwork of independent polities, of which the old national capital territory of Tanis was but one of many. Middle Egypt now had its own pharaoh as well, making, together with a king in Leontopolis, a total of four individuals claiming the ancient titles of Egyptian kingship. This may have been the natural result of the Libyan heritage of the royal family, one which had a lesser appreciation of centralized rule than earlier monarchs of native stock.

119 The craftsmen employed by the Kushite king Taharqa on his buildings at Kawa, some 30 miles south of Kerma, came from Memphis and brought with them their recollection of the pharaoh in his aspect of a protective lion, a concept which had appeared earlier in the similar lions of Ammenemes III found at Tanis. The forbidding mien of these statues has here been intensified by emphasizing the king's negroid features. The two uraci signify the sovereignty of Taharqa over Egypt as well as Kush.

Kushite intervention

Since the end of the Twentieth Dynasty, Kush, including its northern province of Nubia, had secured independence from Egypt, its kings ruling from Napata near the Fourth Cataract. When the Kushite king Piye (formerly rendered as Piankhy) marched from Napata to subdue Egypt in the name of order and orthodoxy, he met with no resistance in Upper Egypt, and was in fact welcomed deliriously in Thebes during the great Festival of Opet. His armies defeated one by one the petty kings of Lower Egypt who submitted to him abjectly, though Tefnakhte of Sais was able to maintain some nominal independence as Prince of the Western Delta.

On the death of Piye at Napata in 717 BC, his successor Shabaka found it necessary to undertake the re-conquest of Egypt, and this task he achieved by his second regnal year, in the process capturing and executing Bokkhoris, who had succeeded Tefnakhte as the organizer of resistance to Kushite rule.

The pious Kushite kings favoured a provincial version of the Egyptian culture of a purer past, harking back to the classical arts of the Middle and

120 (*below*) This graceful statue of Queen Karomama, originally holding sistra, was cast in bronze for her chapel at Karnak by an official of the Divine Consort of Amun called Ahentefnakht, who signed his work. The details of the floral collar and embroidered gown are inlaid with gold, silver and electrum. This is one of the masterpieces in which the metalsmiths of the Libyan Period were particularly expert.

121 Detail of a heroic statue of Mentuemhet who as the High Steward of the Divine Consort of Amun governed Thebes in the difficult days of the Assyrian capture of the city, and the subsequent rule of the Saite kings in the North. He was the foremost patron of the art and antiquarianism of the age.

122 The Divine Consort Shepenwepet II is represented as a sphinx in the manner of such statues of queens in the Middle Kingdom (cf. ill. 3), but her features are set in the severe mould of the Kushite rulers. She holds in her human forearms a libation vessel with a lid in the form of the head of the ram of Amun.

New Kingdoms. They proved energetic builders, particularly at Thebes, where they restored and repaired many of the monuments of earlier times. They brought some long-needed direction into the affairs of Egypt, though the country was far from being united under their sway as the prophet Isaiah knew well enough (Isaiah, 19, 2). Like their Libyan predecessors they attempted to interfere in the politics of Palestine, proceedings which aroused the enmity of Assyria, the now dominant power in the region. The intrigues of Taharqa, the third successor of Piye, at length brought about a long-delayed open confrontation with the Assyrians whose forces twice marched into Egypt, eventually sacking Thebes (663 BC) and driving Taharqa's successor, Tanutamun, into his own Kushite domains, where he and his successors became more and more Africanized and ceased to play any direct role in Egyptian affairs.

119

The southern theocracy

The Kushites continued a policy, begun by their predecessor, Osorkon III, of neutralizing the powerful *imperium in imperio* of the High Priests of Amun of Thebes by appointing one of the royal women as the Divine Consort of Amun. From the beginning of the Eighteenth Dynasty, Ahmose-Nefertiry, the chief queen of Amosis, had also held this position of Divine Consort of Amun, a wealthy sacerdotal office with great estates and a powerful establishment which rose to paramount importance as the High Priests became more and more involved in their military and political roles. The tradition of appointing an heiress daughter of the pharaoh, like a Vestal Virgin, to the position of Divine Consort was continued by the Kushites when Piye obliged the Libyan princess Shepenwepet I to adopt his sister Amenirdas I as her successor. Such 'god's wives', together with the oracle of Amun to whom they were 'married', ruled the Thebaid with the administrative assistance of their high stewards. The most notable of these latter was Mentuemhet, the fourth prophet of Amun, who governed Thebes in the difficult days of the Assyrian invasions and was one of the chief patrons of the new art that flourished in the Kushite Period and the following dynasty. When the Kushites were displaced by a family of Libyan extraction originating from Sais, the first effective pharaoh of a reunited Upper and Lower Egypt, Psammetikhos I (664–610 BC), in turn compelled Shepenwepet II, the reigning Divine Consort, to adopt his eldest daughter Nitokris as her junior partner and eventual successor. In her later years about 595 BC, Nitokris adopted Ankhnesneferibre, the daughter of Psammetikhos II, and she proved to be the last incumbent of this important religious and political office before it lapsed with her death in Persian times.

120

121

122

The King and the Gods

Apart from the universal worship of Amun as a state god, not only in Upper Egypt, but also in newly developed Delta sites, the tendency was for the populace to turn to their local gods for spiritual support and succour, as they had done in similar situations since the First Intermediate Period. The reason was the same, the sharp decline in the power and prestige of the pharaoh. Since the Egyptian found it difficult to direct his religious feeling to mere abstractions, he tended to worship tangible manifestations of godhead, and for preference something animate. In the Late Periods there was a vast increase in the worship of divinities incarnate in animals. This feature of Egyptian cultic practice had always been present as a dark warp in the richly coloured fabric of its religious life, even the monotheist Akhenaten had not proscribed the worship of the Mnevis bull, but now it erupted in force, to earn the bewilderment of Greek observers, and the contempt of such Roman satirists as Juvenal. The ruling groups of both Upper and Lower Egypt, however, adhered to the worship of Amun-re, the oracles of the god, in fact, so far determining the government of Upper Egypt that it became a theocratic state. The pharaohs in addition extended their patronage to the gods of their residences, such as the cat goddess Bast of Bubastis, the archer goddess Neith of Sais, and Ptah of Memphis. The cult of Osiris, the hope of salvation for all mortals, never lost its impact throughout the period, though the worship of his wife Isis and the child Horus steadily increased in popularity until they had entirely overshadowed him by Roman times.

The Amosids, at the beginning of the New Kingdom, had found it difficult to rule Egypt from distant Thebes and transferred their capital to Memphis. Subsequent dynasties found it convenient to move their seats of power even nearer to the Mediterranean littoral where the action was. The dynasties of the Late Period show a general pattern: they began with vigour and promise, reviving the old dream of exercising suzerainty over Palestine and Phoenicia and so preventing another invasion from Asia across their northeastern borders. As the Old Testament reveals, they did not hesitate to interfere in the turbulent politics of the area as opportunity served. Their campaigns, however, were little better than armed raids in search of plunder and the replacement of hostile princes by willing collaborators. Whenever their forces came up against battle-trained and united enemies with superior weapons, such as the Assyrians, Babylonians and Persians, they invariably suffered defeat despite often valiant efforts. Constant defeat could not but produce further discouragement at home, as well as the reputation abroad of being a broken reed.

The northern merchant princes, 664–525 BC

The Saite kings brought more than a century of order and prosperity to a troubled Egypt. The first Psammetikhos freed himself from the overlordship of Assyria which was now beset with its own troubles. In their stirring days the Saites were to see the sack of their own 'populous No [Thebes] that was situate among the rivers' (Nahum, 3, 8) repeated in the destruction of

123 Amasis was the general of the army who overthrew his predecessor Apries (the Biblical Pharaoh-Hophra) and ruled in his stead. During his long rule he controlled the coasts of the Levant with a strong fleet and captured Cyprus. At the end of his prosperous reign, the rising power of Persia threatened troubles which broke in the first year of his successor.

Nineveh and Babylon. Psammetikhos I appointed his own men to key positions in Edfu and Herakleopolis to keep Thebes in check. He also curbed the power of the military caste by employing Ionian, Carian and Lydian mercenaries. With this *corps d'élite* and the possession of a strong fleet, probably largely Phoenician, the Saites ruled as merchant princes, restoring prosperity by active commercial ventures, forming factories for Milesians at Daphnae and Naukratis in the Delta, and setting a precedent for the export of Egyptian corn and wool which was to be followed with greater intensity by the Ptolemies. In the interests of trade, Nekho II (610–595 BC) began a canal from the Nile to the Red Sea and commissioned Phoenicians to circumnavigate Africa. But the Saites never won the wholehearted co-operation of their subjects by these policies. The favouritism shown to Greek oracles, wives, traders and soldiers aroused jealousy and revolt in outbursts of xenophobia, and when the Persian Kambyses invaded the country in 525 BC it fell into his hands without much trouble. The Persians, who organized their empire with a thoroughness lacking in previous conquerors, ruled Egypt with the aid of efficient satraps and collaborators for nearly two centuries, except for an interlude when native princes with Greek aid were able to snatch half a century of uneasy independence (404–343 BC). This was, however, the last twitch of dying pharaonic Egypt, and it was only the embalmed corpse that then passed in turn to the Persian kings, the Greek Ptolemies, and the Roman emperors. After Alexander the Great had defeated Darius on the plain of Issus in 333 BC, the western satrapies of the vast Persian empire fell into his hands without any great struggle, and Egypt thereafter became a part of the Hellenistic world.

Since the residence-cities of Third Intermediate and Late Period kings have suffered almost total destruction or lie beneath Delta silt, the absence of material remains from the palace sites is apt to sharpen our impression of

123

124 The gold face-piece from the mummy mask of Shoshenq II, beaten from a single sheet of gold, in the idealized royal portraiture of the Third Intermediate Period. The remainder of the mask will have been formed from cartonnage.

decline and poverty. Yet there are indications that whenever a new dynasty attained to vigour and wealth, court patronage could still command sufficient resources to undertake rehabilitation and ambitious building schemes at Thebes, Bubastis, Tanis, Memphis and other sites, requiring a proper complement of reliefs, statues and furnishings. Such enterprises once more stimulated the cunning fingers of Egyptian craftsmen to produce works of art which are often of considerable merit and high technical excellence. The royal burials at Tanis have shown that besides heirlooms and usurpations of an earlier age, the contemporary art could still maintain a good standard of design and technique. During the Libyan dynasties a school of palace artists flourished who showed considerable skill in the working of bronze, silver and gold, though little of the latter work has survived. It was probably under the inspiration of such luxury articles that green and blue faience footed cups or 'chalices' were also produced. These vessels are strongly influenced by the shape and design of engraved metal prototypes, which are of such excellence that they have often been accredited to the New Kingdom, though a specimen in Berlin and a fragment at Eton with names of Libyan kings show their true age.

124

The Kushite kings with their conservative tastes for classical standards are usually adjudged to be the instigators of the antiquarian study of the past which is such a feature of the following dynasties, but the movement began earlier. Looking back in nostalgia to the golden past is, in fact, the malaise of the entire Late Period, which recalled the glorious achievements of former days, without any deep commitment to their inner meaning. Not only were the styles of the Old, Middle and New Kingdoms copied with a more searching technique, but eclectic confections were made by antiquarians almost for other connoisseurs to appreciate. The Pyramid Texts and the Coffin Texts were revived for funerary inscriptions. Reliefs were inspired by those of Hatshepsut at Deir el Bahri; and fashions of dress and coiffure long out of date were revived. Burial was sought near such hallowed sites as the Step Pyramid at Saqqara, in the vicinity of which its now legendary architect had been buried, or near the Great Pyramid at Giza.

The intensive copying of the past is a prominent feature of the Saite Age – though the tomb-reliefs of Mentuemhet and his temple statues had already set the fashion with sculpture in the style and dress of all periods. As an idealistic academic art it has its appeal. Its technique, especially in the cutting of inscriptions in hard stones, is faultless, but as in all art where style has become more important than content, a tendency to emphasize the abstractions underlying form leads to a distinctive mannerism. Egypt had invariably gone back to her past as a point of vigorous departure, but now her return was a permanent retreat from the world of her decline. That monasticism which is so characteristic of Christian Egypt is already inherent in the outlook of the Late Period. In Persian and especially in Ptolemaic times, the dying embers of this art were to glow for a brief interval when a realistic portraiture was grafted on the idealistic and abstract forms of Saite art, but that manifestation lies outside the scope of this survey.

125

125 This relief of professional mourners from the tomb of the Vizier Nespekashuti (fl. *c.* 610 BC) is inspired by paintings dating to seven centuries earlier; but the artist is more concerned with recalling the conventions of a past age than with eternal grief. The demeanour of the women, even the one on the extreme left, is not expressive of sorrow: their gestures, like their long coiffures, have become the rhythms of an abstract pattern.

14 · Egyptian social groups

The pharaoh

While Egypt may have been in the epigram of Hecataeus, 'the gift of the Nile', the Egyptian state was the creation of the pharaoh, the divine king whose evolution has been traced in the foregoing pages. Other civilizations had risen and flourished in river valleys elsewhere in the Near East, and enjoyed economies based upon agriculture, and had a unifying system of communications afforded by a great river. They too had discovered the art of writing and keeping records, without which no civilization can flourish, yet for the most part they remained a congeries of rival city states, whereas Egypt displayed a national conformity under the leadership of a deity. So powerful, so successful a ruler could not fail to impress other nations with the charisma of his office, and they vied with each other in sending embassies loaded with gifts to beg his blessing at the advent of each new king.

For the pharaoh is a prime example of the god incarnate as king. A tangible deity, whose sole authority could produce results by the exercise of the divine attributes of 'creative utterance', superhuman 'understanding' and 'rightness' (*ma'et*), appealed to the Egyptian mentality and gave the nation confidence to overcome daunting obstacles.

The prehistoric origins of the king as a pastoral chieftain and rain-maker have been outlined above. Even in more sophisticated times his control of water, 'which begets all living things, and all things which this earth yields', was often stressed. Akhenaten was apostrophized as 'this myriad of Niles'. Ramesses II is regarded as being able to make rain fall even in the far-off Hittite lands, or to withhold it at his pleasure. The advents of Merenptah and Ramesses IV are occasions for rejoicing as the Nile then carried a high flood from its source. The connection between the pharaoh and the Nile is particularly evident in the peripteral stone kiosks that Tuthmosis III, Amenophis II and Amenophis III built on Elephantine Island to celebrate their second jubilees, when Khnum of Elephantine was specially honoured as the god who brought forth the Nile from his cavern under the island. At this particular time he was already beginning to be associated with Osiris, later to move to Bigga and become Lord of the Inundation. Even when the king was dead, he was believed to exercise a control over the Nile still, since he was then assimilated to Osiris who floated in the river at flood time.

Several instances exist where pharaohs acted as water diviners when wells had to be dug in desert places. Sethos I is credited in the Wadi Abad with having saved his gold miners from death from thirst by finding water at Kanayis where his well still has water in its depths. It is significant that on the nearby rocks are prehistoric drawings of animals, probably indicating an ancient water-hole, and acting as an indication to the diviners that water was in the vicinity despite the general aridity. Similarly Ramesses II boasted of having found water for his miners in the Wadi Alaki at a depth of twelve cubits.

As the controller of the Nile and its water, the pharaoh was also a fertility king, an incarnation of the god who had created the Egyptian universe at the First Time, and to whom he would return on death. This demiurge varied from time to time and from place to place, though the sacrosanct traditions of the myth ensured that its fundamentals would not change. Thus the king was an incarnation of Horus, the Remote One, a prehistoric sky-god who was also manifest as a falcon. This identification of the pharaoh with the falcon is frequently encountered. The king is said to 'rule while he was yet in the egg', and his death is spoken of in such terms as, 'the falcon has flown to the horizon'. On solemn occasions he may wear garments decorated with a feathered pattern. Statues of him also exist in which the human and avian aspects have been combined.

When the sun cult conceived of its active god as a heavenly king, reflecting the political system on earth, they united their lord of the day-sky with the sky-god Horus in the concept Re-Herakhty. The king became the son of Re. The idea was probably engendered in the Fourth Dynasty that the birth of the king was theogamous, and we have already seen that the myth was invoked for the appearance of the first three kings of the Fifth Dynasty; but the earliest surviving plastic representation of the Divine Marriage occurs in the reliefs in the temple of Hatshepsut at Deir el Bahri. Here we see that the god takes the form of the pharaoh and fills the chief queen with the divine afflatus by holding the sign of life to her nostrils. As a result of this union the heir apparent will be born. Thoth, the messenger of the gods, is dispatched to announce the good news to the queen. The Creator in his active aspect of Khnum is instructed to fashion the child and its spirit on his potter's wheel, a poetic device for symbolizing the growth of the foetus within the womb. Guardian spirits and birth-gods come to attend the birth. Lastly the infant is recognized by its divine father and nursed by the seven Hathors. Other representations of this myth are carved in similar low relief on walls of the temple of Luxor and in the birth-house of Nektanebo I at Dendera. In all cases it is the sun god in his aspect of the Upper Egyptian Amun who acts the role of the progenitor.

Similarly the coronation of the king, though conducted on earth by chamberlains who had the royal insignia in their charge, was thought to take place in heaven and to be performed by the gods, as is represented on so many temple walls. Tuthmosis III claimed that it was Amun of Thebes who recognized him as his son while the young prince was serving as a mere acolyte

126 The gods Horus of Lower Egypt on the left, and Seth of Upper Egypt on the right, knot the plants of the North and the South around the symbol of union which supports the cartouche of Sesostris I.

in the temple at Karnak, whereupon he flew like a divine falcon to heaven and was crowned by the sun god, though this is probably a fanciful way of saying that it was his earthly father Tuthmosis II who crowned him in the sanctuary of the temple ('the heaven') as his co-regent. It was this same king's southern vizier, Rekhmire, who affirmed the divinity of his lord in two asseverations: 'Every king of Egypt is a god by whose guidance men live. He is the father and the mother of all men, alone by himself, without a peer,' and 'I saw his person in his [true] form, Re the lord of heaven the King of the Two Lands when he shines forth, the Aten when he reveals himself.'

The harmony between this divine kingship and the natural world is evident not only in the intimate connection between the pharaoh and the Nile, on which the prosperity of Egypt depended, but also on the timing of the various royal ceremonies to conform to the cycle of the agricultural year. Thus the coronation of the king traditionally took place at a time which was heralded by the rising of Sirius at the beginning of the inundation. This moment was the auspicious point for the sympathetic rising of a new king and a new Egypt out of the old land drowned in the chaotic waters of the Nile flood in which the old king as Osiris was now believed to float.

Each king therefore at his advent was regarded as recreating the old universe anew in the primal pattern that had come down intact from the time when the gods had ruled the earth. Their son and incarnation was on the Horus throne of the living, and when he died and was assimilated to Osiris, the king of the dead, his son the new Horus would reign in his stead. Thus Egypt was eternally under the beneficent rule of God. The idea of this god incarnate, his birth and coronation, bequeathed a legend and a tradition to the nations of the Near East which persisted for centuries.

The chasm that separated the pharaoh from the rest of society was not only symbolized by his pyramid with its gilded capstone, he also underwent ceremonies at his coronation that ensured that his human nature would be entirely absorbed by his divine aspect. As the protector of the land, he combined within his person two rival forces, Horus the god of Lower Egypt, and Seth the god of Upper Egypt. This duality is expressed in the different crowns he wore, and the titles he assumed. The throne he sat upon had the quality of rendering him divine and royal, and was itself personified by the goddess Isis. At his advent, craftsmen from all parts of the kingdom were set the task of preparing a complete outfit for him with the exception of the White and Red Crowns which were holy objects, goddesses in their own right, kept in shrines in the charge of special chamberlains. His garments, weapons, sceptres, jewels and furniture, everything used by him, were designed for his use alone and consecrated at a special ceremony similar to that which was observed when the image of a god was installed with its ancillary equipment in a newly built shrine.

126

127 View of part of the remains of the second palace of Ramesses III at Medinet Habu, from the top of the pylon of his mortuary temple. The throne-room still remains the stone podium with its staircases on which the royal throne was placed between two columns. A bathroom adjoins the throne-room on the right.

The protocol that governed his life was as punctilious as that which attended the daily service of a god in a temple. The throne-rooms of the royal palaces at Memphis and Medinet Habu have the effect of isolating the 127 king within his baldachin as the statue of a god was contained within its shrine. The strict regulation of his life is confirmed in the words of Diodorus; 'For there was a set time not only for his holding audience or rendering judgments, but even for his taking a walk, bathing and sleeping with his wife; in short, for every act of his life.'

This concept of the king as the supreme god Horus incarnate reached its fullest development in the Archaic Period and the early Old Kingdom; and probably the Step Pyramid and the pyramids of Giza stand as its greatest memorials when the entire nation undertook the tremendous travail involved in raising and equipping these huge monuments not for the sole benefit of their human ruler, but to ensure the persistence of their greatest divinity. By the Fourth Dynasty, the thinkers of Heliopolis were beginning to make their influence felt, and became dominant in the next dynasty. The king was now regarded as a descendant of the sun god Re-Herakhty who had ruled Egypt in the beginning, but weary of mankind had retired to the remote heavens, leaving the pharaoh as his earthly representative to govern in his stead.

The prestige of the pharaoh received a severe blow during the First Intermediate Period when droughts and low Niles destroyed belief in the supreme divinity of the pharaoh which had instigated the Egyptian state machine. The exclusiveness of the pharaoh was replaced by a multiplicity of local kinglets who boasted less of their magic powers than of their ability to preserve their people by their temporal might. This concern for the material well-being of their subjects was carried over into the tenets of government during the Middle Kingdom when the idea took hold that the king tended his subjects as a good shepherd watched his flock. 'God has made me the herdsman of this land, for he knew that I would maintain it in order for him,' said Sesostris I to his assembled courtiers. 'He is full of graciousness, rich in benignity, and through love has he conquered,' said Sinuhe of this same king. Though the pharaohs of the Twelfth Dynasty restored the prestige of the kingship, it was more as a powerful champion than as a god that the 'living Horus' was esteemed. Much of the reverence for the king as the best hope of immortality for those who were 'known' to him had passed to that deification of kingship, Osiris, despite the weight of tradition that still gave the terrestrial ruler and his family sumptuous burial in a pyramid tomb.

The pharaohs of the New Kingdom, true to the ideals of the contemporary warrior society with its aristocracy of armoured chariot fighters, had to hack their way to power by feats of arms, and the character of their rule is distinctly martial. The pharaoh himself took the field at the head of his troops, the Champion of Egypt, an incarnation of a warrior god Mentu or Baal, as well as a sun god. His heroic stature is emphasized by his skill in rowing, shooting, riding and hunting. To the traditional garb of a prehistoric pastoral chieftain, he adds a new headgear, the Blue Crown or Crown of Victory, a kind of war helmet, and replaces the old mace with a modern scimitar which even becomes a sceptre, like the pastoral 'crook' and so-called flail. His trophies are the foes he has vanquished and stripped of their inlaid armour, the prisoners he has taken, the rich booty he has captured. Such heroes had to have memorials that not only sustained their mortuary cults but left some record of their great deeds to posterity: and the ruined funerary temples on the west bank at Thebes bear witness to these ambitions.

The age reached its climax in the reign of Amenophis III when the imperial bounds were widest, the state coffers the richest, the monuments the most colossal and numerous. Thereafter, only a decline was possible in step with the decay of the heroic age all over the Near East, culminating in the forays of the Sea Peoples, and the movements of new settlers in Syria, Anatolia, the Lebanon and Palestine in the 12th century BC.

In the Late Periods the kingship became but a prize for which foreigners – Libyans, Kushites, Persians and Greeks – fought each other. While the weight of traditional thought made it certain that there would always be tremendous respect paid to the kingship especially in court circles, the fact is that men turned more to the worship of gods in the form of kings, to Amun, Re-Herakhty and Osiris. Prayers were addressed to gods less and less through the intermediary of the king and more through the agency of the city god; while for the great mass of the people, as the cult of the god incarnate in the king declined, the worship of animals increased to grotesque proportions. The greatness of ancient Egypt was indissolubly bound up with her kings who had created it: they rose and fell together.

The royal family

When Sesostris I encourages the fugitive Sinuhe to return to Egypt he holds out the inducement that Queen Nofru, whom Sinuhe served, still inhabited the palace and was alive and well. She played her part in the government of the realm and her children were in the council chamber. The position of the chief queen of the pharaoh is thus incidentally defined. A sidelight on her part in the government of the realm is cast by the cuneiform tablets from Amarna and the Hittite capital, which reveal that such queens as Tiye, Tuia and Nefertari, at least, in the reigns of Amenophis III, Akhenaten and Ramesses II, held correspondence with the rulers of the Mitanni and the Hittites.

If the king was the incarnation of the supreme god, the queen was also regarded as embodying the goddess Hathor, 'the Mansion of Horus', i.e. the 128 mother of the sky-god Horus. She was early assimilated to Isis, another goddess of kingship, and also to a very ancient goddess of the sky in the form of a cow, her body speckled with stars. The attributes of Hathor, her headdress with cow-horns, sun-disk and tall plumes, were worn by queens upon their crowns. Her symbols, the sistrum rattle, and the necklace with its *menyet* counterpoise, were carried by her priestesses, of whom the queen was the leader. Both had the power of bestowing a propitiatory blessing upon all to whom they were held.

128 A priestess of Hathor welcomes the nomarch Senbi of Cusae with her sistrum and the necklace with its *menyet* counterpoise which she holds out to him with a greeting such as, 'For your spirit, behold the *menyet* of your mother Hathor! May she make you flourish for as long as you desire!'

The chief queen was a lady of great sanctity, and in a number of cases left a greater impression on posterity than her husband. Besides her biological role, her office carried politico-religious functions, which in some cases led to the title being bestowed upon certain kings' daughters, after their mother or stepmother's death. Whether this always implied a sexual relationship between the pharaoh and his daughter remains the subject of debate.

Alongside the chief queen, however, a king maintained a 'harem' of other women, some of whom held the title that we conventionally translate as 'queen'. Ideally, the heir to the throne was the eldest son by the chief queen, but where such a child was lacking, or had died prematurely, the offspring of one of the 'junior' wives would be elevated to the status of Crown Prince. The queen who had conceived the pharaoh of the divine seed was exceptionally privileged among the royal women as the king's mother, even if she had not previously been the late ruler's chief wife.

It appears that the designation of the heir to the throne was the subject of a public declaration by the king. Where there was an eldest son by the chief queen, this must have been a formality, but where a child of a lesser lady was involved, there may have been some jockeying for position to define who was actually the senior prince. Even more significant would have been the declaration when no son of the reigning king's body survived. It is unclear how the succession was formally determined in such cases, but indications are that senior political or military figures were the most likely nominees.

Where someone had royal blood, or had married into the royal family, their qualification for the purple was clearly increased.

A number of pharaohs married their full- or half-sisters, which once led to a theory that the royal inheritance passed down the female line, princes having to marry the 'heiress' to qualify for the throne of pharaoh. It is now quite clear that this was not the case, far too many chief queens being of demonstrably plebeian birth to permit such a conclusion. A more likely explanation for consanguineous marriages is the fact that within all systems where a king is divine, a supernatural potential exists in all his progeny. From this would derive a desirability that this be kept within the royal house, and not spread too far outside. However, a number of nobles certainly married royal daughters, and many other cases are doubtless hidden from us: it seems to have been much more acceptable to proclaim one's politico-social relationship with royalty than one's close physical relationship.

Naturally, however, where a queen was also a royal daughter, her status was further elevated, something which can be particularly traced in the early Eighteenth Dynasty, though data are unfortunately missing which would enable evaluation of how far the situation is exceptional or conforms to the general rule. The prominence of Ahhotep, one of the first of a line of such queens during the Seventeenth and Eighteenth Dynasties, has already been mentioned in the honours paid to her as the Saviour of Upper Egypt at a time of crisis. Her daughter Ahmose-Nefertiry, married to her son, Amosis, was even more influential, being the first queen to hold the important post of Divine Consort of Amun, before it was limited to virgin incumbents. She was later deified and became one of the great Theban deities for as long as the New Kingdom lasted. Later queens of the dynasty, however, include numerous ladies of non-royal birth – the principal wives of Tuthmosis III, Amenophis II, Amenophis III and Akhenaten were in no case kings' daughters. In spite of this lack of lineage, Tiye, spouse of Amenophis III, and Nefertiti, wife of Akhenaten, attained a prominence almost unparalleled by their earlier sisters, in the case of Nefertiti verging on kingly status. Under the Nineteenth Dynasty, yet another commoner, Nefertari, became a pivotal figure as chief queen of Ramesses II; royal blood was thus not a determining factor in the careers of those holding the highest official female status in the pharaonic state.

The very highest office of all, that of king, was not nominally open to females. However, at least four women obtained pharaonic titles prior to the Ptolemaic Period; on the other hand, in the two best known cases, those of Hatshepsut and Tawosret, the ladies had first come to power as regents for child-kings, and obtained pharaonic status for political reasons that do not seem to have been accepted by posterity.

We are ill-informed about the careers of royal sons, and particularly crown princes before the Nineteenth Dynasty. They were usually brought up by high-ranking wet-nurses and formed strong attachments to their milk-brothers who often became companions of their youth and maturity, holding important positions in their households. Royal sons were instructed in the military arts by army veterans appointed for the purpose; military scribes were engaged to teach reading and writing. Princesses also learnt to write and paint in watercolour, judging from the ivory writing-palettes of two daughters of Akhenaten that have survived, showing signs of use. Female nurses and male tutors or major-domos were also appointed to attend upon them. Some of the highest officials in the land filled such posts, presumably after they had retired from a more active role.

It would appear that all the royal sons received the education of a potential pharaoh since no one could know whom fate had in store for the succession. There are many instances of heirs apparent who did not survive infancy. Tuthmosis III while still a child was singled out for kingship by the oracle of Amun. Tuthmosis IV was similarly promised the succession by Re-Herakhty. In the first case it is highly probable that we have a simple declaration of the heir by the king; in the latter, however, there is a suspicion that Tuthmosis' known elder brothers may have been removed from the scene to ease his way to the throne.

There are occasions on which a king associated his eldest son on the throne with him as co-regent and the system is well attested for the Twelfth Dynasty in which every king ruled for his later years with a junior partner. Double datings exist to prove the circumstance, and from these, it is possible to affirm that Sesostris I ruled with his father Ammenemes I for the first ten years of his reign. At other periods a different system of co-regency appears to have prevailed, and double datings were avoided. For this reason there are scholars who in the absence of such proof would deny the existence of co-regency as an institution. As the official statements are very reticent and vague about a practice in which the god incarnate shared in some undefined way his sovereignty with another, the problem is a very thorny one, the little evidence that exists being largely circumstantial. The difficulties are likely to remain unresolved until definite proof is unearthed, assuming that it has in fact survived.

The officers of state

In theory all government was by the kings: in practice, of course, he ruled through officials. In the earliest dynasties these appear to have been his near relatives; for, since authority came from the gods, those who partook even in some small degree of the divine essence were best qualified for subordinate rule. In time, offices tended to become hereditary as the Egyptian ideal of appointing the heir to his father's place was generally followed. Veritable dynasties of officials existed by the side of the kings they served; and the genealogies of some may be traced for several generations, particularly in the New Kingdom and Libyan Period. During the First Intermediate Period and earlier Middle Kingdom the local governors duplicated the royal

129 The great sage Amenophis-son-of-Hapu is shown writing on the papyrus roll open upon his lap, his head bowed in reverence before the god who inspires his words. In his later years he served as the major-domo of Sitamun, the wife and daughter of Amenophis III.

administration on a smaller scale with their stewards, priests and henchmen. The military state of the New Kingdom, however, was much more highly organized by a bureaucracy which is usually regarded as having no connection with the ruling house, though the proofs are lacking. At least many of the officials had daughters in the royal harem. No particular specialization was demanded in earlier times: thus Weni of the Sixth Dynasty, whose training was as a steward, became in turn a judge, general, master of works and hydraulic engineer. Ability as an organizer was apparently of more value than technical knowledge; and this remained true throughout Egyptian history. Amenophis-son-of-Hapu, for instance, whose primary office was an administrative post in the army, was also the architect who moved 'mountains of quartzite', as he put it, in erecting the colossal monuments of Amenophis III.

129

The king as the origin and fount of all law was the final court of appeal. Death sentences could apparently be confirmed only by him and he must also have exercised prerogatives of mercy. Though his deputy was the vizier, nominally the king was at once the legislator, judiciary and executive; but in such a state as Egypt, where the pattern of government was constantly repeated, precedent must have played a cardinal role, and a body of decisions with all the sanctity of holy writ must have been available to form the climate of royal opinion, if not actually to affect judgments in individual cases. Even in the reign of Tuthmosis III, decisions taken by a vizier who had lived some

130 The palace officials of Tutankhamun wearing white mourning bands around their brows draw the catafalque of their king to his tomb. They comprise the high officers of state who assisted the king to govern. In the penultimate row are the two viziers of Upper and Lower Egypt with their shaven heads and voluminous gowns.

five centuries earlier, were still recalled. There were also the *Instructions* which as we have seen several kings wrote for the guidance of their posterity, and these too would form a sort of *aide-mémoire*, to give them no higher function. The king's creative power to make laws at his will evidently did not affect the main body of precedent. In the 13th century BC a lawsuit brought by a scribe before the king's vizier, regarding an estate near Memphis which had been given to his ancestor by King Amosis three centuries earlier, went through a long process of litigation over several reigns, leading to claim, counter-claim, appeals, eviction and eventual vindication. This intricate case reveals that records of earlier judgments were filed in central archives over a long period, that bribery and collusion could be successfully challenged and *ex cathedra* decisions overcome by a kind of affidavit supported by sworn witnesses. While the case does little to elucidate the full extent and limits of the law in ancient Egypt, it does make clear that men and women were equal before it and enjoyed an equal degree of proprietorship.

In the New Kingdom, it was the officials of the palace who acted as a kind of privy council and helped the king to govern. They were the Egyptian equivalent of the *maryannu* who formed the military aristocracy of great states elsewhere. They are depicted walking in the funerary procession painted in the tomb-chapel of the vizier Ramose at Thebes, accompanied by the governors of Thebes where the tomb had been prepared. In particular, they are represented, like pall bearers, in the burial chamber of the tomb of Tutankhamun wearing mourning bands around their brows as they haul the catafalque of their dead lord. Included in the cortège would have been the two Overseers of the Treasury, concerned with the reception and allocation

130

131 (*below*) The Chief of the Treasury hands over the king's signet to Huy on his being appointed the Viceroy of Kush by Tutankhamun.

132 Relief of the High Priest of Amun, Amenhotep, being rewarded with gold collars in the presence of a statue of Ramesses IX in the absence of the king himself. Some twenty years after the carving of this triumphal scene Amenhotep was to undergo great tribulations, beginning with his ejection from office.

of raw materials and finished goods, tribute, plunder and other commodities. Also important was the Overseer of the Granaries of Upper and Lower Egypt whose responsibility was the harvesting, recording and storage of the annual crops of wheat and barley. There were several other court posts such as the Chief Steward, the Master of the Horse, the Scribe of the Recruits, the Superintendent of Works, the First and Second Heralds, the King's Secretary and Butler, besides a host of underlings, chamberlains, pages and fan-bearers, though the title of 'fan-bearer on the right of the king' was claimed as a great honorific by the highest officers in the land.

Two officials during the New Kingdom were of especial importance. The first, a new post, was the Viceroy of Kush, the king's deputy in Nubia and the Lower Sudan as far as the Fourth Cataract. His seat of government was at Aniba, whence he was responsible for territories that stretched from Elkab in Egypt proper to Gebel Barkal in the Sudan. In this task he was assisted by two deputies, one for Wawat (Nubia), also stationed at Aniba, and the other for Kush with his base at Amara. The viceroy appears to have inherited the title and office, formerly held by the Prince of Kush in the later years of the Seventeenth Dynasty, but he differed from his predecessor in being an Egyptian and a nominee of the pharaoh, receiving his signet as a token of his delegated power. The office, like others in Egypt, however, had a

131

195

tendency to be handed down from father to son. In one documented case, in the Nineteenth Dynasty, the office seems to have been held by the son of the Crown Prince, but whether this was a common instance is unclear.

The other important official was the First Prophet, or High Priest of Amun at Thebes, whose temples received such enormous endowments and gifts from grateful pharaohs that four senior prophets were required to administer its considerable revenues. Of these priests, the Second Prophet appears to have been a close relation of the king or his chief queen, since the days of Amosis. In later Ramesside times the First Prophet became the virtual ruler of Upper Egypt of which Amun was by then the state god. The last incumbents of the office were in turn sons of a predecessor, though the ultimate high priest before the appointment of Herihor was apparently dismissed from office by a rival. This suppression began a contest that eventually resulted in a civil war, the eclipse of Western Thebes, the pillaging of the royal necropoleis and the loss of Nubia and Kush.

The chief official under the king, however, was still the vizier whose office goes back to the dawn of history and persisted until the 4th century BC. Generally, there were two viziers, one serving in Upper, the other in Lower, Egypt. Three viziers from the same family who succeeded each other during the long reign of Tuthmosis III have left in their tombs detailed accounts of their duties, though all the records are regrettably much damaged. The vizier's responsibilities, in which he was assisted by a legion of scribes, stewards, runners and guards, included not only a daily report to his sovereign on the state of the nation but also the delivering of judgments in his audience hall, the receiving and issuing of instructions to the various branches of central government, and the making and rescinding of appointments.

He was chiefly concerned with the collection of taxes in Upper and Lower Egypt, but he also mobilized the king's personal bodyguard; saw to the cutting of timber and general irrigation; directed village headmen as to summer cultivation; made a weekly inspection of the water resources; considered the state of the fortresses on the borders; took measures against raids by robbers and nomads; and saw to the fitting out of ships. He presided over important civil cases referred to him from lower courts; he dealt with questions of land tenure and the witnessing of wills; and he considered criminal cases requiring heavy sentences, all in his capacity as Chief Justice. He also received foreign embassies, and supervised workshops and building enterprises including the work on the royal tomb. No wonder that the pharaoh, in delivering the homily that it was customary to address to high officials when they took office, should say:

Look to the office of the vizier. Be vigilant about what is done in it, for it is the mainstay of the entire land. As to the vizierate, it is not sweet, indeed, but it is bitter as gall. For the vizier is hard copper enclosing the gold of his master's house.

The king went on to warn the new incumbent against using his rank to further his own interests. He is to show favour to no one. He must be scrupulous in administering the law, neither favouring friends, nor judging their cases more harshly because they were his friends, 'for that would be more than justice'.

Such officials were to be well rewarded; as *The Instruction for King Merykare* explains, a poorly paid official is open to corruption. In his reforming zeal after the Amarna interlude, King Horemheb decreed that he was appointing reliable men to the vizierate, and adjuring them not to fraternize with other persons, nor to accept bribes or gifts from them. Those judges who performed their duties conscientiously were to be honoured by being rewarded periodically by the king in person. But if any member of the district councils was found to be practising injustice, he was to answer a capital charge.

The armed forces

The king, as the Narmer palette makes clear right from the start, was the protector of Egypt, producing concord at home and making the state enemies his footstool abroad. His divine might alone was sufficient to conquer: in the face of his superior right, his opponents became weak and submissive. In practice, the pharaoh was assisted in police and military matters by an army. During the later Old Kingdom, this probably consisted of local levies under their regional commanders; and it was but a short step from these to the feudal lords and their retainers that brought the miseries of civil strife to the kingdom at the collapse of the Sixth Dynasty. There must also have been a royal corps or bodyguard of Egyptian and Nubian troops stronger than any equivalent local force. The duties of such levies were concerned largely with police work on the frontiers, quarrying operations in Sinai, the Wadi Hammamat and elsewhere, and in trading expeditions to Punt. They combined the duties of a labour corps and a protective force.

During the Middle Kingdom immense fortress building on the frontiers 133 became symptomatic of the current military thinking. The frontiers of Egypt were to be strengthened against unauthorized entry. Trade with Asia and tropical Africa was to be strictly regulated. The massive mud-brick forts built in the region of the Second Cataract, with their stone foundations, protected water-stairs, fire-ports, curtain walls, glacis, ditches, barbicans and drawbridges were extremely strong, and if resolutely defended almost impregnable. The scenes of warfare in the Middle Kingdom tombs at Beni Hasan all centre around attacks upon some such fortresses, and probably refer to conditions during the First Intermediate Period. The private armies of this age of internecine strife were still tolerated until the reign of Sesostris III. The expeditions which the first three kings of the Twelfth Dynasty led into Upper Nubia were accompanied by the nomarchs of the Oryx and Hare

133 The fortress at Buhen in Nubia below the Second Cataract was built as the main entrepot for the protection of the Southern frontier and the regulation of imports from tropical Africa. The view shows the north-west line of the fortifications in the Middle Kingdom after the removal of later accretions.

nomes together with their contingents. It is presumed that the central force of the pharaoh was just such a body of feudal levies, but organized on a larger scale with a quota of Nubian volunteers around a nucleus of the personal retainers of the king. This army, which campaigned on a regular basis in Nubia where it also garrisoned the trading-forts, was much more highly organized than the forces of former days. Its duties still included public works and quarrying operations, besides field-service.

The armies of the Old and Middle Kingdoms, however, have a thoroughly amateur appearance beside the large professional forces of the New Kingdom with their chariotry, infantry, scouts and marines. We have already referred to the heroic age that was ushered in with the horse-drawn chariot and the new social order that it fostered. A return was made to a mobile warfare with its own peculiar rules and disciplines. The champion who distinguishes himself in single combat, or announces the day of battle, makes his appearance. The age is notable for its paladins and their exploits: the two Ahmose of Elkab; Djehuti who took the town of Joppa by a stratagem; Amenemhab who defeated a ruse of the prince of Qadesh by despatching his decoy mare before it could throw the stallions of the Egyptian chariots into confusion.

With the chariot came new arms and armour, new methods of warfare and a military aristocracy, as we have mentioned earlier. The small standing army of the Old and Middle Kingdom was expanded into a large professional organization with squadrons of chariots, each manned by a driver and fighter, and armed with such new weapons as the composite bow, the heavy bronze falchion, the battle-axe and the light javelin impelled by a spearthrower.

Military standards enabled units to be readily located on the field of battle and instructions could be signalled by means of the war trumpet. Engagements became more than the shock of armed bodies meeting in a general melée. Strategy and tactics became the concern of the pharaohs and their war councils; and if we are to believe the official accounts it was, for instance, the plan of battle devised by Tuthmosis III that was responsible for his great victory at Megiddo *c.* 1456 BC over a confederation of Asiatic princes, though the indiscipline of his raw troops lost him the early fruits of victory.

Kings, or their sons, were nominated as in command of the armies, or their chariot forces, when they were mere children, as in the case of several of the sons of Ramesses III who died in childhood. Bakenkhons was in charge of the training-stable of Sethos I before his twelfth year.

The Egyptian forces, under the supreme command of the pharaoh or his deputy, were divided into four armies named after the principal gods. There was an elaborate chain of field command from the generals and battalion commanders through the standard-bearers to the platoon leaders.

The highest staff posts in the army, however, were open only to the educated man who might begin his career as a simple scribe acting either at home or in the field as a sort of pay-clerk. From having charge of accounts and stores, he would pass to chief army-clerk, concerned with keeping the war-diary, with reports and general secretarial work. A further elevation would be to scribe of recruits, a very important post held for example by Amenophis-son-of-Hapu, who superintended conscription and the allocation of recruits to various services, either in the army proper or the public works for which the army supplied labour, such as the quarrying of stone, the working of the gold and turquoise mines and the erection of great monuments. The general staff was concerned more with logistics than strategy. Before a campaign the pharaoh consulted a war council of general officers and high state officials, though the bold and successful plan is accredited entirely to the king. The general staff gained an unrivalled experience in the handling of large numbers of men and in complex organization and methods.

In the earlier part of the Eighteenth Dynasty, the armies were manned by native Egyptians and Nubian auxiliaries who followed the family calling. But the pick of the young men called up for service in the general corvée were also conscripted particularly for the labour force: 'Every man is called up, and the best are chosen. The adult is made into an infantryman, and the youth into a cadet.' A career in the army in fact was the only opportunity for an enterprising but uneducated man, either Egyptian or alien, to achieve a

134

position of importance or affluence. By the reign of Amenophis III, even foreign captives were being drafted into the Egyptian forces, and so winning their eventual freedom. From this time onwards the Egyptian armies were manned more and more by foreigners – Libyans, Sudanis, Shardana and 135 other Sea Peoples, and finally by Carian, Ionian and Greek mercenaries. The Wilbour Papyrus lists a number of cultivators in Middle Egypt during the 12th century BC who bear foreign names and were evidently veteran soldiers who had been settled on the land.

An army career in fact appealed so strongly to adventurous youth that the master-scribes had to paint a lurid picture of its drawbacks in order to keep their pupils at their dull tasks of learning to read and write:

> Come, let me tell you how the soldier fares with his many superiors – the general, the commander of the auxiliaries, the standard-bearer, the lieutenant, the captains of fifty, and the commander of the garrison

134 (*above*) The officer Userhet had a number of scenes of military life painted on the walls of his tomb chapel, including the reception of the new intake of recruits, with men having their hair trimmed into a natural resilient helmet, and the distribution of rations in the barracks.

135 The painting on a stela in Berlin shows an Asiatic mercenary, a spearman, seated on a faldstool with his wife at her ease opposite him. Their Egyptian servant helps his master to drink a beverage, probably *seremt*, from a jar on a stand by means of a reed syphon.

troops. Come let me tell you how he marches over the mountains to Palestine. His bread and water are carried on his back like the load of an ass. His drink is foul water. He falls out only to go on picket duty. When he reaches the enemy he is like a pinioned bird and has no strength in his limbs. If he returns to Egypt he is like worm-eaten wood. He is brought back upon an ass: his kit has been stolen and his servant has run off.

The lot of the aristocratic charioteer was no better:

He squanders his patrimony on an expensive chariot which he drives furiously. When he has acquired a fine span of horses he is overjoyed and tears madly around his home town with them. But he does not know what is in store for him. When he reaches the mountains he has to cast his expensive chariot into a thicket and go on foot. When he reports back he is beaten with a hundred blows. (After Erman 1966, pp. 194–7.)

Despite what the satirist had to say about the miserable life of the soldier, its rewards were considerable. Warriors who had shown bravery in the field were promoted to officers, given prisoners as serfs and decorated with 'the gold of valour'. Such awards took the form of massive flies in gold, gold or silver weapons and jewellery of considerable intrinsic value.

Even the less distinguished solder shared in the cattle, weapons, clothing, ornaments and other loot captured from luxurious Asiatic enemies. He was pensioned off with grants of livestock, serfs and land, from the royal domains, on which he paid taxes but which continued to be held by his family as long as they had an able-bodied male available for military service. Such soldiers formed a privileged class, devoted to the tradition of service in the armed forces. In times of peace they dwelt in comfortable settlements.

Experienced military scribes and officers were appointed to positions in the foreign service as ambassadors or district commissioners, and to such court posts as stewards of the royal estates, butlers, fan-bearers, police-chiefs and instructors to the young princes or even major-domos to the king's daughters. Whenever the hereditary succession to the throne died out at the end of a dynasty, it was these warrior intimates of the king who stepped into his empty sandals.

The scribes

For all these posts in the highly centralized administration, officials were required who could read and write; and the first necessity of any man who wished to follow a professional career was that he should be properly educated in one of the schools attached to the great departments of state such as the palace, the treasury and the army, or to the 'House of Life', the scriptoria of the larger temples where books were copied and inscriptions compiled. Humbler village scribes would doubtless teach their own children, and might also take a number of pupils from near relatives. The wealth of school exercises that has survived at Deir el Medina and elsewhere suggests that the scribes found time to take advanced pupils as well as follow their calling. Probably they were their sons or nephews, since education in Egypt was largely on the master and apprentice system.

The training of a scribe began at a very early age, and if we are to judge by the career of the high priest Bakenkhons in the reign of Ramesses II, was completed twelve years later when he reached manhood. In learning the classical utterance of the Middle Kingdom which was used for some monumental and religious purposes down to Roman times, the pupil often had to contend with a language which was already dead and which he understood only imperfectly as his copies of the classics clearly reveal. But it is often only in this garbled form that Egyptian literature has come down to us.

The pupil began by learning by heart the different glyphs grouped into various categories, and from that he progressed to words in the literary language selected according to meaning. From this stage he went on to copy extracts from the classics, sometimes translating them into the vernacular language. Papyrus was too expensive for beginners to spoil and potsherds and flakes of limestone (*ostraka*) had to serve instead. The instruction in reading and writing comprised other subjects as well. The writing of various glyphs demanded an ability to draw with the pen. Geography, mathematics, foreign words, articles of trade, travelling equipment, religious feasts, parts of the body, and so forth, were learnt incidentally in copying stock-letters, poems on the king and his residences, and the various exchanges in a literary controversy between two learned scribes. Learning without tears may have been the ideal in some respects, although the Egyptians also had a Tudor belief in the efficacy of corporal punishment and the pupil was told that if he was idle he would be soundly thrashed. It is not surprising that under such treatment, and obsessed with the tedium of learning, the schoolboy should have thought of running away to become a soldier or a baker or a farmer; and repeatedly by means of such homilies as *The Satire on Trades* the teacher sought to make his pupils stick to their dull tasks, comparing the easy lot of the trained scribe with the miseries of other callings. The theme is usually that the profession of scribe leads to a comfortable well-paid job; but some hint of the pleasure of learning for its own sake is given in the injunction to 'acquire this high calling of scribe; pleasant and fruitful are your pen and papyrus roll, and happy are you the livelong day'. There is evidence that some girls were taught to read and write, for profit as well as pleasure. A word for a female scribe exists by the time of the Middle Kingdom at least; a more emphatic expression is current in the Late Period, and there is a graffito in the Step Pyramid with a sneering reference to the literary efforts of women.

When the young scribe had graduated from school he had his foot upon the first rung of a career in the higher ranks of the army, the treasury or the palace. While a career open to all the talents was hardly possible in ancient Egypt, where the tradition was to appoint the son to the place of his father from the pharaoh down to the merest field labourer, it did sometimes happen that a man from humble circumstances attained to high office. In the exhortation to be a scribe which the master set his pupil to copy, the rewards of successful graduation are enticingly set forth. 'A man of worth is sought for, and you are found. The man that is skilled rises step by step until he has attained the position of a magistrate.'

It would help, of course, if he could follow his father in his chosen occupation, but occasionally an obscure man was able to rise by merit to a position of authority. Some of the high officers of state during the New Kingdom boast of their lowly birth, and though in most cases they exaggerate in order to flatter the king who had advanced them, nevertheless such a factotum as Senenmut did come from modest antecedents, his father having only a vague, and probably posthumous, title of 'worthy'.

A training as a scribe was also a necessary preliminary to a career in such professions as medicine, the priesthood, and art and architecture. A medical student would be apprenticed to a practitioner, almost always his father or some near relative; but an ability to read was necessary for learning the various prescriptions, spells and diagnoses contained in medical papyri, whether the work in question were a quasi-scientific treatise on surgery and fractures such as the Edwin Smith Papyrus, or a specialist work on gynaecology such as the Kahun Papyrus, or a mere collection of medico-magic recipes, nostrums and incantations such as the Ebers Papyrus.

During the Old and Middle Kingdoms the priesthood had been a largely amateur organization, the district worthy being the chief priest *ex officio* of the local god, though he may have been assisted by a number of full-time subordinate priests. During the New Kingdom, however, with the considerable resources that were lavished upon such state gods as Amun of Thebes, Ptah of Memphis, and Re-Herakhty of Heliopolis, the priesthood became a highly specialized profession. The chief priests are great secular administrators as well as ecclesiastics. Thus Amun had not only four prophets or high priests, and a host of minor officiants down to bearers of floral offerings, but a complete secular establishment, a chief steward and overseers of his granary, store-houses, cattle, huntsmen, peasants, weavers, craftsmen, goldsmiths, sculptors, shipwrights, draughtsmen, records and police, a veritable enclave within the pharaonic state. All these posts and their subordinate offices had to be filled with trained scribes, though the degree of their proficiency naturally varied.

It was through his command of writing in the hieroglyphic and hieratic scripts, and later in demotic, that the scribe for so long made ancient Egypt the most highly organized and prosperous state in the Near East. He was predominantly a civil servant concerned with keeping records of all kinds, but in addition to his accounts, reports, legal texts, letters, mathematical and surgical treatises, he also produced a wide literature – novels, poems, lyrics, hymns, meditations, instructions and lamentations, which directly influenced some of the writings of the Old Testament. That these were not the least esteemed of their writings is clear from a eulogy on the ancient authors written by a scribe in the 13th century BC:

> Their monuments have crumbled in pieces. Their mortuary priests have gone; their tombstones are covered with sand; their chambers forgotten. But their names are pronounced because of the good books that they wrote and their memory is for ever more. (After A. H. Gardiner, *Hieratic Papyri in the British Museum*, 3rd series, London 1935, pp. 38–9.)

Artists and craftsmen

It is more difficult to determine whether the training of a scribe was demanded of artists and craftsmen, who are so largely represented as working anonymously in studios attached to the palaces and temples. It is clear that sculptors and painters need not have been able to read or write so long as they could copy on a large scale what was drawn on an *ostrakon* or papyrus by a master-scribe or draughtsman. Models of hieroglyphs were supplied in plaster for ignorant workmen to copy at Amarna, and there is plenty of evidence from this same site that stock subjects and texts were copied mechanically from year to year even when they were out of date, and if corrected at all, only after they had been cut into the stone. During the Middle Kingdom many *ex votos* were mass-produced at Abydos, for instance, by craftsmen who could not write, the inscription usually being feebly scratched on by a hand more used to wielding a pen than a chisel. From this and other evidence it is usually argued that the artist was of little account, a despised and humble workman devilling away for a literate official who took all the credit. The fact is that especially in the earlier periods it was seldom that artists proclaimed their calling: they preferred to masquerade under such titles as the high priest of Ptah. Several court artists were given handsome tombs at Thebes by their grateful sovereigns. Parennefer (*c.* 1350 BC) was honoured by a tomb at Amarna as well as at Thebes where he is prouder of his title of the king's cupbearer than that of chief craftsman of the king. In his interesting biography, the Old Kingdom architect Nekhebu (*c.* 2250 BC) mentions only incidentally the fact that he began his career by acting as secretary to his brother, an overseer of works; and the evidence that he had received the training of a scribe is missing from the list of his many titles.

Kings themselves did not disdain to be considered as artists. Bek, the chief sculptor of Akhenaten, claims that he was taught by his king; while there is a passing reference to the designing by Tuthmosis III of a set of metal vessels. If the names of only a mere handful of ancient Egyptian artists are known and pictures of them are very rare, and above all if we are unable to accredit nearly all the surviving works of art to particular artists, that is only what we should expect. In Egypt the artist worked under the same anonymity that prevailed in the early Middle Ages. He was considered

136

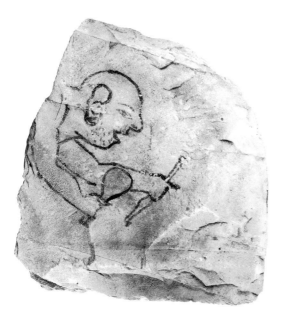

136 A burly, bald, ill-shaven quarryman, his mouth open with the effort, hammers away with his chisel and mallet at the Theban hillside. This study, drawn upon a flake of the discarded limestone with a few rapid strokes, gives a vivid impression of a stone-mason in action, and is a testimony to the humorous observation of the workmate who sketched him.

primarily as a craftsman; and sculptors and painters are often shown at work in the same studios as joiners, metalworkers, potters and other artisans.

The individuality of the artist was of no importance. What mattered was his ability to render faultlessly the ageless conventions, which he had imbibed from his master and would impart in turn to his pupil. But despite all the forces that operated to ensure that a statue or painting should repeat only the primal pattern, Egyptian art did move. The wonder is that it should change so much; and it is often possible for the expert to date a specimen to within a few years by its stylistic features alone.

How could such artistic changes come about in the conservative and traditional milieu of the Egyptian craftsman? The answer lies in the qualities of the designers of Egyptian art. In the early days when the centre of Egyptian culture was at the capital of Memphis, it was Ptah, the god who had brought all things into being by his creative utterance, who was also the creator of all artistic enterprises. His high priest bore the title of 'Greatest of Craftsmen', and it was such literate men who designed the buildings, their decoration and their contents. They it was who guided the hands of the builders, stonemasons, painters, jewellers, joiners and other artisans who made and embellished the works that they conceived. Such humbler craftsmen were isolated in workshops attached to the palaces, the houses of the great feudal lords, or the temples of the gods to whom nearly all their lives were dedicated. Only in their leisure hours could they make something for themselves or for modest patrons. Communities of craftsmen resided at several of the sites of major construction as at Giza, Lahun, Amarna and, most significantly, Deir el Medina in Western Thebes.

This last-mentioned location was occupied by the workmen who hewed and decorated the tombs of the kings and their families, at Thebes during the New Kingdom. The excavation of their walled village has recovered many articles and documents which tell us much of their lives and work. Generations of artisans and their families lived in this village, their employment being hereditary. They enjoyed a fair measure of independence and self-government, but the vizier or a king's butler visited the site from time to time to inspect progress, impart news and listen to any requests or complaints. During the Twentieth Dynasty these were not infrequent and mostly concerned irregularities in the supply of their rations. When protests had no effect the workmen downed tools. A strike in the last year of Ramesses III caused especial consternation.

The community was divided into two 'crews' or gangs, each in the charge of a foreman and his deputy. A scribe kept their records and acted as their secretary. He also kept a diary of the work done, noting each day the names of absentees and the reasons for their non-attendance. Work went on throughout the year, but at the end of every week of ten days the men enjoyed a rest day; and they also celebrated many festivals of the gods, some of these lasting for several days. Workmen were also part-time priests of the local gods and officiated in the village shrines.

The workmen were paid in kind, though payments of silver are also recorded at the beginning of a new reign. Their rations consisted of emmer wheat and barley, for making the staple bread and beer. The manual workers were given more generous allowances than the clerks and porters. In addition they regularly received vegetables and fish and a supply of wood for fuel. Occasionally, salt, wine, sweet beer and other luxuries were distributed.

Each family occupied a house built of mud brick on stone foundations. Inter-marriages between members of the community was the normal practice. The callings that the various workmen professed, stone-masons, quarrymen, plasterers, draughtsmen, painters, sculptors, coppersmiths, scribes, were hereditary. They had enough free time in which to cut and decorate tombs for their own use in the neighbourhood of their village. The heyday of these workmen's tombs was in the reign of Ramesses II. After that, their descendants generally ceased to make tombs for themselves but added loculi to earlier tombs, thus turning them into family burial places.

The workmen had a labouring force of servants and serfs to assist them and minister to their wants. These were literally hewers of wood and drawers of water, the former to supply fuel for the baking ovens of the village, the latter to bring up a constant supply of water on donkey-back from the Nile about 3 miles away. Laundresses were supplied to wash their clothes, and a few slave women to grind their corn. Each gang had a fisherman to supply them with a stated quantity of fish every week. The community's affairs were managed by a village council which changed its composition from time to time, though usually one of the foremen and a scribe were members. Other representatives were the elder workmen and their wives. They settled disputes and awarded punishments; but severe penalties had to be sanctioned by the vizier who also granted pardons.

In view of the popular idea that the monuments of ancient Egypt were built only by the blood and sweat of expendable slaves, it is sobering to learn that these artisans worked for four hours in the morning before knocking off for a meal and a nap. The rest of their working day consisted of another four-hour stint in the afternoon. Even so, absenteeism was common.

Peasants and labourers

The peasantry of ancient Egypt formed the largest and most enduring component of the population, but because it was illiterate has never spoken with its own voice. Instead, we have that view of the countryman which the more sophisticated townee, the scribe or the artist, has everywhere presented of him, as uncouth, clumsy, living close to the soil and his animals, doltish and crippled with excessive toil or disease.

From the moment when the flood water came hissing through the parched channels at the beginning of the inundation, giving rise to the belief that the water snake in the cavern under Elephantine Island was on its way to Heliopolis in the north, the year began for the farmer and his family. His work included the draining of the marshy verges of the river, extending the cultivation, clearing the irrigation channels, removing wind-blown sand from fertile fields, and the laborious watering by hand of the higher-lying fields. The satiric scribe draws a woeful picture of him contending with drought, grubs, locusts, vermin, thieves and the tax collector; but compared with the other cultivators of the eastern Mediterranean his lot was favoured. Each year he planted his seeds or dibbled his seedlings into virgin soil that 137 had been freshly deposited and watered by the beneficent Nile. The plough was used not for breaking a hard pan and producing a tilth, but merely for turning in the scattered grain. This was just as well done by driving animals over the fields to tread in the seed or by dragging a log over the ground. Deep ploughing in fact was not required on the alluvial soil lest the under-lying sand should be brought to the surface. Instead, mulches of rotting vegetation were used for building up the organic structure and providing

137 The village headman (second left) receiving two bags of seed corn from the clerk to the Overseer of the Granary, sowing the irrigated land and turning in the seed with a shallow plough drawn by two heifers yoked at their horns.

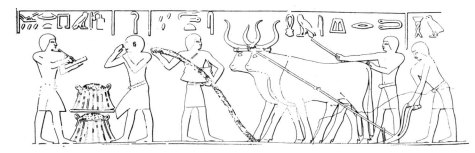

138 An assessor measures the standing crops with a knotted cord to determine the yield and the tax upon it. A tenant farmer, hand upon his little son's head, introduces him to the assessor. His wife and an elder son, right, offer a corndolly and refreshment.

nitrogenous matter, just as in recent times the fellah has used *sebakh*, decayed mud brick, for this purpose, and demolished the ruins of entire ancient cities in the process. Most of the labour was devoted to the irrigation of crops, whether in digging or cleaning water channels, or in transporting the river by means of the *shaduf* or in pots slung on a yoke, since the *sakiyah* water-wheel operated by an animal was not introduced until Persian times.

For the most part the peasants lived in their village around a nucleus of families, or camped out with their flocks and herds under simple shelters among the pastures and rushy thickets of the Delta. It is probable that like the artisans of Amarna, Thebes and other residence centres, they lived fairly independent lives in their communities, their affairs managed by a headman and the village scribe, with a council of elders from the principal families. But the impact of a more remote but more powerful authority was felt at certain times of the year, principally when the inundation flooded their fields and made cultivation impossible, and also when the harvest was ready for gathering, and taxes had to be paid to the central state.

The essential wealth of Egypt was well understood to lie in its agriculture. Low Niles from time to time served to remind those in authority how dependent a large civilized nation was upon the skill and industry of its farmers. Nothing could therefore be allowed to stand in the way of securing a proper yield of produce each year. A great number of workmen not concerned with the cultivation of the land were yet wholly dependent upon the products of farms for their livelihood, such as weavers of linen and wool, butchers and leatherworkers, brewers, basket-, mat- and rope-makers, woodworkers, and so forth, not to mention the hosts of priests, scribes and other officials

139 Labourers measure the heaps of threshed grain in standard tubs, while a scribe keeps the tally on his fingers and his fellows enter the amounts on their writing boards.

necessary for running the state machinery. In agricultural work, personal liberties and predilections were subordinated to the common weal. A time-honoured institution for dealing with crises that demanded a concerted effort in a limited space of time was the corvée, whereby all the able-bodied citizenry were called up with their picks, hoes and baskets to labour on such tasks as the maintenance of the irrigation system, the weeding of crops, or the gathering of the harvest.

In this work, scarcely anybody was in theory exempt, even priests were conscripted, and high officials could be called upon to supervise the labouring force. Some kind of selection, however, appears to have been exercised in using the census returns for forming the local labour corps. A similar system was expected to prevail in the Elysian Fields of the Osirian hereafter, where the wheat grew to a height of nine cubits, and even the king was not exempted from the operation of the corvée. To avoid such future inconvenience, the deceased provided himself with shawabti figures (see p. 146). These images would undertake the agricultural labour of the afterlife by virtue of a magic spell whenever he was called up and registered for work which had to be done in the otherworld, 'as a man is bound to do, whether it be to cultivate the fields, to dig out the channels, to move soil, etc.' During the celestial mustering, when the name of the deceased was called, the shawabti was expected to reply, 'Here I am,' and take his place. In real life, a sufficiently affluent Egyptian would be able to hire a proxy, possibly at a standard rate, and so avoid the operation of the corvée in his case. In such a system it was inevitable that the labouring force should have been composed mainly of slaves and those members of the community who could not afford to hire a substitute.

It was the corvée that made major undertakings possible, although in the New Kingdom the army was largely conscripted for labouring in mines and quarries. The hydraulic works made necessary by the inundation were the main business of the corvée. After the flood waters had retreated, the old boundaries of fields had to be re-established and the surveyors then appeared to take measurements and replace any stone markers that may have been shifted, according to their cadastral records.

138, 139   The second great encounter between the farmer and the central authority came at harvest time when commissioners arrived to measure the standing crops and calculate what taxes they should yield. A little later the tax collector accompanied by a posse of police would arrive to secure the imposts. Censuses of cattle, geese and other livestock would also be made and the yearly increase taxed accordingly. As no money in ancient Egypt existed in the form of coin until Persian times, all commerce was conducted by barter, and taxation was also exacted in kind. Besides the imposts collected on grain, cattle and poultry, contributions were required from orchards, groves of palm trees, vineyards, weaving-sheds, hives and every commodity that the earth provided and the craftsman manufactured. As far as the cultivator was concerned, his taxes were heavy; at least half of all produce went in exactions, and often he was left only with the bare necessities for himself and his family. It was these taxes however that maintained the rest of the population, and if they were not collected in their entirety, either because of crop failure or peculation, someone else went hungry, as for instance the workmen of the king's tomb at Thebes in year twenty-nine of Ramesses III, c. 1156 BC.

As elsewhere, tax-farming was employed as the most convenient way of gathering in the imposts, and such taxpayers ranged in importance from the managers of large estates and officials in charge of whole districts, through mayors of towns, to individual cultivators. All enjoyed the privilege of extracting from their plots produce in excess of the taxes required by the state.

In theory, the pharaoh owned all the land, though in practice the management of the great estates was vested in such institutions as the departments of the palace, the state granaries, or the temples great and small. The temple of Khnum at Elephantine, for instance, had estates as far afield as the marshes of the Delta, from which it drew revenues and on which it paid taxes. As the king was the final owner of all land and property and industries, the labourers on these enterprises were referred to as 'king's servants', even though most of them worked not directly on the royal estates, but for the individuals and institutions to whom responsibility had been delegated by the pharaoh. Such labourers, the hewers of wood and the drawers of water, were registered in the census lists and it was from such lists that the corvées were marshalled. The lowest grade in this labouring force were the serfs or slaves who were particularly numerous from the later Middle Kingdom until the end of the New Kingdom. They were mostly foreigners from Asia and Kush who had been sold into slavery or captured in war, and as early as the middle of the 2nd millennium BC it is possible to see already established an institution which existed in the Near East until the end of the last century. Such people enjoyed fewer privileges than their fellows. They could not enter temple courts, being ritually impure; and it was only when the local god was brought from his shrine and paraded around his estate on a veiled litter during feast days that they could take a modest part in the worship. The observance of some local cult at a wayside shrine where a godling such as Bes or Toeris could be petitioned was the limit of their religious devotions. Too poor to afford a tomb or burial in family plots, their corpses were evidently thrown into the Nile for 'the eater of the dead' to scavenge and so assimilate them to that primeval force that came out of the waters of Chaos in the form of a crocodile.

But the slavery system also required that in life they should be reasonably well treated. In addition to food and lodging, they received a yearly allowance of clothing, oils and linen. Their working hours were reduced when the weather was hot. Captives were assigned as serfs to the temples and private estates and to the households of army officers who had distinguished themselves on the battlefield. But the demarcation between slave and citizen was fluid. The personal slave of a high ranking Egyptian would be more affluent than most of the native peasantry. By Ramesside times, foreigners held important posts in the palace administration and in the army. A stela from the earlier Amarna days shows a Syrian mercenary soldier being waited upon by a native Egyptian. While slaves could be bought or sold, or hired out, the Wilbour Papyrus makes it clear that they could also rent and cultivate land on the same conditions as an army officer, priest or other tenant-farmer. A simple declaration by the owner before witnesses was apparently sufficient to make a slave into a 'freedman of the land of Pharaoh', and one document has survived in which a woman adopted as her heirs the offspring of her dead husband and a female slave they had purchased, in preference to nearer relatives. Another case exists of a barber who married his orphan niece to a slave to whom he bequeathed his business.

The satirist, in painting a woeful picture of the lot of the peasant, describes the tax collector as arriving on the farm with his apparitors armed with sticks and palm-ribs. They demand corn and when none is forthcoming, because of drought or other misfortune, they stretch out the luckless peasant and thrash him thoroughly. This account reflects the scenes in the Old Kingdom mastabas of peasants being beaten at the whipping-post, and in New Kingdom tomb-paintings of farmers being bastinadoed by the police. Thus, it is claimed, even tenant farmers, as distinct from the mere serfs, received little or no consideration from their superiors and could be cruelly maltreated when they failed to deliver the full amount of the oppressive taxes imposed upon them. It may be just as likely, however, that a wily and obstinate cultivator ultimately required punishment of this nature, or the threat of it, before he would disgorge what he owed to the state.

There is also another side to the picture. Adjacent to such scenes, there are representations of a less abrasive relationship. A farmer, his wife and sons greet the tax collector with a corn-dolly and refreshments. Field workers are shown during a break in their work, sitting under the trees and taking a pull from a water-skin, or playing the flute, or just snoozing. A herdsman bringing cattle for registering is told by his companion not to waste time arguing with the scribe, 'he is a fair man and will assess you properly, he is not hard on folk'. A sage advises that the official should act considerately towards the cultivator: 'if a poor man is in arrears with his taxes, remit two thirds of them.' Examples of such leniency are seen in actual accounts where an eight-per-cent deficit in the harvest tax of one farmer is ignored; and in the case of another, nearly half the quota of corn was not delivered, and eighty sacks of grain were allowed as seed for the following season.

The authorities in fact appear to have treated the peasant community with some respect. Many of them were veterans who had been settled on the land by grateful kings after their military service was over, though their sons might be called up to serve in their stead. The importance of not alienating such cultivators is seen in the stern measures which were introduced by Horemheb to stamp out the exploitation that had arisen during the preceding reigns. While doubtless the system, like most human institutions, did not always operate with justice and efficiency, the general impression is that for the most part it worked tolerably well. The cultivator had a weapon in his armoury for use as a last resort. If a farmer was driven too hard he could give up the cultivation of his fields and take to a hunting and marauding life like the bedouin of the Eastern Desert, as was often the case in Roman and Turkish times. Fields that once went out of cultivation could rapidly revert to desert.

The most wretched of pharaoh's subjects were the criminals, some of them officials who had been found guilty of corruption; they were banished to the lonely frontier fortress of Tjel, or forced to labour in the mines of Sinai and Nubia, often after losing their noses.

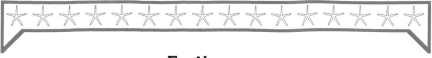

Epilogue

In the foregoing pages we have incidentally touched upon the ideology that determined the character of ancient Egyptian civilization. No understanding of its development, however, would approach completeness without a more profound study of the complex religious beliefs of the Egyptians than is possible here. Indeed, in a strictly theological sense any such exposition is out of the question since the dogma of Egyptian religion was never committed to writing. Such works as the Pyramid and Coffin Texts, and later compilations, may give the impression that sacred books did in fact exist, but their purpose was not to confirm faith with divine revelation. Rather they were no more than a collection of prayers and spells for ensuring the persistence of the personality after death, or its assimilation in the demiurge.

The lack of an authoritative doctrine is not surprising in a milieu where so many local gods were tolerated. A universal creed could be formulated and accepted only in a context of monotheism, and it is noteworthy that while the monotheistic king Akhenaten spoke of his 'teaching', it is nowhere expounded in the texts that his monuments have bequeathed to us.

Conversely, however, we do not lack for information on the cult. Prayers, myths, ritual, the forms of divinity, the gestures of worship, are all represented in the temples and tombs and expressed in writings. The gods of ancient Egypt, mostly manifestations of two or three universal concepts, were tangible entities that had their seats in local shrines which reproduced in their architecture that world of the First Time when the Creator arose from the waters of Chaos. In his 'house' upon the primeval mound the god had existed from the beginning in the form of a graven image. Like a human grandee he was tended in his habitation by 'servants' (the priests), secure from all profane and unclean contact, and protected by magic from the assaults of Evil in whatever form it should come.

From the time of the New Kingdom, when an immense development in temple building took place, the great temples and their personnel became part of the machinery of state. They administered the religious foundations of the pharaohs, or local governors, and as tenants of the royal domains assessed the paid taxes on their extensive and scattered estates. Their granaries, stockyards and store-rooms became part of the national exchequer, playing a prime role in the economic organization of the country. The prosperity of the temple and its god was therefore indissoluble from the prosperity of the state. The pharaoh, in fact, was nominally the chief prophet of every god, the intermediary between man and the divinity, as his statues at the entrance to the temple made plain. The priesthoods were also the theologians whose worship and speculations kept the work of divine creation continuously alive. Some of these cults, particularly that of the sun god at Heliopolis, attained to great power and influence, largely for political reasons, and dominated the thinking of other priesthoods, such as that of Amun at Thebes.

While the official religion had its purpose in promoting the intervention of divine power for the benefit of the state with the pharaoh at its head, there were also many cults with a less intellectual and professional priesthood which were more concerned with the personal well-being of the worshipper. Such modest cults were usually centred around some unpretentious godling, such as the household protectors Bes and Toeris, or a spirit inhabiting a hill-top, or a tree, or the statue of a king or great man, or the like. The worship of such powers was in the nature of private communion, and because it was observed by humble folk was not generally expressed in writing. But the vagaries of chance have handed down to us from the end of the New Kingdom a number of prayers from lowly petitioners, probably written for them by one more literate than his fellows, which reveal a personal relationship between the god and his devotee (Erman 1966, pp. 307–12). They tell of suffering, physical and spiritual, that was relieved by the god; or of punishment in the form of sickness or blindness that was visited upon the suppliant as a result of his transgressions, and they appeal for the god's mercy or succour. 'Forgive me my many trespasses,' prays one, 'I am a foolish man.' 'Thou givest breath to him who is afflicted, and thou deliverest me who am in bondage . . . for while it is in the nature of Man to sin, it is the nature of God to relent,' declares another. 'Come unto me, deliver me in this year of wretchedness,' cries a third.

In these humble prayers the piety and faith of the worshipper shine through his invocations: 'Herakhty, the Saviour of him who cries out to thee,' 'Amun, the upright Judge of the wretched . . . beloved god who hearkens to the humble . . . who stretches out his hand to the poor man and who saves the wearied.'

Such testaments have surfaced imperfectly from a limited period only; but they serve to show that beneath the elaborate and daunting structure of the official religion with its apparatus of sacerdotal power, lavish offerings, choral hymns, oracles and sympathetic magic, there must also have existed in Egypt an essentially simpler faith which has survived with varying changes in the name of deity down to the present day.

Chronology and List of Kings of Egypt

Conjectural Dates BC

PREDYNASTIC PERIOD CULTURES

LOWER EGYPT	*UPPER EGYPT*	
Fayum A/Merimda	Badarian	5500–4000
?Omari A	Amratian (Naqada I)	4000–3500
?Omari B	Early Gerzean (Naqada II)	3500–3300
Maadi		3300–3050
	Late Gerzean A (Naqada II)	3300–3150
	Late Gerzean B (Naqada III)	3200–3050

ARCHAIC PERIOD

Dynasty I 3050–2813

Narmer (Menes?)
Aha (Menes?)
Djer
Djet
Den
Anedjib
Semerkhet
Qaa

Dynasty II 2813–2663

Hotepsekhemwy
Nebre
Ninetjer
Weneg
Sened
Sekhemib/Peribsen
Neferkare
Neferkasokar
Khasekhem/Khasekhemwy

OLD KINGDOM

Dynasty III

Sanakht 2663–2654
Djoser 2654–2635
Sekhemkhet 2635–2629
Khaba 2629–2623
Nebkare 2623–2621
Huni 2621–2597

Dynasty IV

Snoferu 2597–2547
Kheops (Khufu) 2547–2524

Djedefre 2524–2516
Khephren (Khafre) 2516–2493
Mykerinus (Menkaure) 2493–2475
Shepseskaf 2475–2471

Dynasty V

Userkaf 2471–2464
Sahure 2464–2452
Neferirkare 2452–2442
Shepseskare 2442–2435
Neferefre 2435–2432
Niuserre 2432–2421
Menkauhor 2421–2413
Isesi 2413–2385
Unas 2385–2355

Dynasty VI

Teti 2355–2343
Pepy I 2343–2297
Nemtyemsaf I (Merenre) 2297–2290
Pepy II 2290–2196
Nemtyemsaf II 2196–2195

FIRST INTERMEDIATE PERIOD

Dynasty VII/VIII 2195–2160

Netjerkare
Nitokris
Neferkare
Neby
Shemay
Khendu
Merenhor
Nikare
Tereru
Neferkahor

Pepysonbe
Neferkamin
Ibi
Wadjkare
Khuihapy
Neferirkare

Dynasties IX/X 2160–2040

Akhtoy I
Neferkare
Akhtoy II (Wahkare)
Senenen
Akhtoy III
Akhtoy IV
Meryhathor
Akhtoy V
Merykare

Dynasty XIa

Mentuhotep I 2160– . . . .
Inyotef I . . . .–2123
Inyotef II 2123–2074
Inyotef III 2074–2066

MIDDLE KINGDOM

Dynasty XIb

Mentuhotep II (Nebhepetre)
2066–2014
Mentuhotep III (S'ankhkare)
2014–2001
Mentuhotep IV 2001–1994

Dynasty XII

Ammenemes I 1994–1964
Sesostris I 1974–1929

Ammenemes II 1932–1896
Sesostris II 1900–1880
Sesostris III 1881–1840
Ammenemes III 1842–1794
Ammenemes IV 1798–1785
Sobekneferu 1785–1781

Dynasty XIII 1781–1650

Wegaf
Amenemhatsonbef
Sekhemre-khutowi
Ammenemes V
Ameny-Qemau
Ameny-Inyotef-Ammenemes VI
Nebnuni
Hornedjhiryotef-sa-Qemau
Swadjkare
Nedjemibre
Sobekhotep I
Rensonbe
Hor
Kay-Ammenemes VII
Sobekhotep II
Khendjer
Imyromesha
Inyotef IV
Sobekhotep III
Neferhotep I
Sihathor
Sobekhotep IV
Sobekhotep V
Iaib
Ay I
Sobekhotep VI
Neferhotep II
Sobekhotep VII
Dedumose
Senebmiu

SECOND INTERMEDIATE PERIOD

Dynasty XV (Hyksos) 1650–1535

Sheshi
Yakobher
Khyan
Yansas . . . .
Apophis 1585–1545
Khamudy 1545–1535

Dynasty XVII (Thebes) 1650–1550

Rehotep
Djehuty
Mentuhotep VII
Nebiriau I
Nebiriau II
Seuserenre

Sobekemsaf I
Inyotef V
Inyotef VI
Inyotef VII
Sobekemsaf II
Taa I (Senakhtenre)
Taa II (Seqenenre) 1558–1554
Kamose 1554–1550

NEW KINGDOM

Dynasty XVIII

Amosis 1550–1524
Amenophis I 1524–1503
Tuthmosis I 1503–1491
Tuthmosis II 1491–1479
Tuthmosis III 1479–1424
(Hatshepsut 1472–1457)
Amenophis II 1424–1398
Tuthmosis IV 1398–1388
Amenophis III 1388–1348
Amenophis IV/Akhenaten
   1360–1343
(Smenkhkare/Neferneferuaten
   1346–1343)
Tutankhaten/amun 1343–1333
Ay (II) 1333–1328
Horemheb 1328–1298

Dynasty XIX

Ramesses I 1298–1296
Sethos I 1296–1279
Ramesses II 1279–1212
Merenptah 1212–1201
Sethos II 1201–1195
(Amenmesse 1200–1196)
Siptah 1195–1189
Tawosret 1189–1187

Dynasty XX

Sethnakhte 1187–1185
Ramesses III 1185–1153
Ramesses IV 1153–1146
Ramesses V Amenhirkopshef I
   1146–1141
Ramesses VI Amenhirkopshef II
   1141–1133
Ramesses VII Itamun 1133–1125
Ramesses VIII Sethhirkopshef
   1125–1123
Ramesses IX Khaemwaset I
   1123–1104
Ramesses X Amenhirkopshef III
   1104–1094
Ramesses XI Khaemwaset II
   1094–1064

THIRD INTERMEDIATE PERIOD

Dynasty XXI

Smendes 1064–1038
Amenemnesu 1038–1034
(Pinudjem I 1049–1026)
Psusennes I 1034–981
Amenemopet 984–974
Osokhor 974–968
Siamun 968–948
(Psusennes II 945–940)

Dynasty XXII

Shoshenq I 948–927
Osorkon I 927–892
(Shoshenq II 895)
Takelot I 892–877
Osorkon II 877–838
Shoshenq III 838–798
Shoshenq IV 798–786
Pimay 786–780
Shoshenq V 780–743

'Theban Dynasty XXIII'

Harsiese 867–857
Takelot II 841–815
Pedubast I 830–799
(Iuput I 815–813)
Osorkon III 799–769
Takelot III 774–759
Rudamun 759–739
Iny 739–734
Peftjauawybast 734–724

Dynasty XXIII (Tanis)

Pedubast II 743–733
Osorkon IV 733–715

Dynasty XXIV (Sais)

Tefnakhte 731–723
Bokkhoris 723–717

Dynasty XXV

Piye 752–717
Shabaka 717–703
Shabataka 703–690
Taharqa 690–664
Tanutamun 664–656

SAITE PERIOD

Dynasty XXVI

Psammetikhos I 664–610
Nekho II 610–595

Psammetikhos II 595–589
Apries 589–570
Amasis 570–526
Psammetikhos III 526–525

LATE PERIOD

Dynasty XXVII (Persians)

Kambyses 525–522
Darius I 521–486
Xerxes I 486–465
Artaxerxes I 465–424
Xerxes II 424
Darius II 423–405

Dynasty XXVIII

Amyrtaios 404–399

Dynasty XXIX

Nepherites I 399–393
Psamuthis 393
Akhoris 393–380
Nepherites II 380

Dynasty XXX

Nektanebo I 380–362
Teos 362–360
Nektanebo II 360–342

Dynasty XXXI (Persians)

Artaxerxes III Okhos 342–338
Arses 338–336
Darius III 335–332

HELLENISTIC PERIOD

Dynasty of Macedonia

Alexander III 332–323
Philippos Arrhidaeos 323–317
Alexander IV 317–310

Dynasty of Ptolemy

Ptolemy I Soter 310–282
Ptolemy II Philadelphos 285–246
Ptolemy III Euergetes I 246–222
Ptolemy IV Philopator 222–205
Ptolemy V Epiphanes 205–180
Ptolemy VI Philometor 180–164
Ptolemy VIII Euergetes II 170–163
Ptolemy VI (again) 163–145
Ptolemy VII Neos Philopator 145
Ptolemy VIII (again) 145–116
Ptolemy IX Soter II 116–110
Ptolemy X Alexander I 110–109
Ptolemy IX (again) 109–107
Ptolemy X (again) 107–88
Ptolemy IX (again) 88–80

(Ptolemy XI 80)
Ptolemy XII Neos Dionysos 80–58
Ptolemy XII (again) 55–51
Kleopatra VII Philopator 51–30
Ptolemy XIII 51–57
(Ptolemy XIV 47–44)
(Ptolemy XV Kaisaros 41–30)

ROMAN PERIOD
30 BC–AD 395

BYZANTINE PERIOD
AD 395–640

ARAB PERIOD
AD 640–1517

OTTOMAN PERIOD
AD 1517–1805

KHEDEVAL PERIOD
AD 1805–1914

BRITISH PROTECTORATE
AD 1914–1922

MONARCHY
AD 1922–1953

REPUBLIC AD 1953–

Select Bibliography

The works marked with an asterisk (*) have extensive bibliographies to which the reader is referred for more advanced study.

General

ALDRED, C., *Egyptian Art in the Days of the Pharaohs*, London and New York, 1980.

BAINES, J. and J. MALEK, *Atlas of Ancient Egypt*, Oxford, 1980.

BREASTED, J. H., *Ancient Records of Egypt*, vols 1–5, Chicago, 1906.

Cambridge Ancient History (CAH), 3rd edition, Cambridge, 1970 ff.

CERNY, J., *Ancient Egyptian Religion*, London, 1952.

CLAYTON, P. A., *Chronicle of the Pharaohs*, London and New York, 1994.

DODSON, A. M., *Monarchs of the Nile*, London, 1995.

*DRIOTON, E. and J. VANDIER, *L'Égypte*, 4th edition, Paris, 1962.

GARDINER, A. H., *Egypt of the Pharaohs*, Oxford, 1961.

*GRIMAL, N.-C., *A History of Ancient Egypt*, Oxford, 1992.

*HAYES, W. C., *The Scepter of Egypt*, 2 vols, New York, 1953–9 (reprinted 1990).

HORNUNG, E., *Conceptions of God in Ancient Egypt*, London, 1983.

JAMES, T. G. H., *An Introduction to Ancient Egypt*, London, 1979.

Lexikon der Ägyptologie, 7 vols, Wiesbaden, 1975–92.

QUIRKE, S., *Ancient Egyptian Religion*, London, 1992.

SMITH, W. S., *The Art and Architecture of Ancient Egypt*, 2nd edition, revised by W. K. Simpson, Harmondsworth, 1981.

*TRIGGER, B. G., B. J. KEMP, D. O'CONNOR and A. B. LLOYD, *Ancient Egypt: A Social History*, Cambridge, 1983.

Introduction

PARKER, R. A., *The Calendars of Ancient Egypt*, Chicago, 1950.

QUIRKE, S., *Who were the Pharaohs?*, London, 1990.

Chapter 1

GREENER, L., *The Discovery of Egypt*, London, 1966.

JAMES, T. G. H., *Excavating in Egypt: The Egypt Exploration Society 1882–1982*, London 1982.

POPE, M., *The Story of Decipherment*, London and New York, 1975.

Chapter 2

EDWARDS, A. B., *A Thousand Miles up the Nile*, 2nd edition, London, 1891.

KEES, H. (ed. T. G. H. James), *Ancient Egypt: A Cultural Topography*, London, 1961.

NIMS, C. F., *Thebes of the Pharaohs*, London, 1966.

Chapter 3

ARNOLD, D., *Building in Egypt: Pharaonic Stone Masonry*, New York and Oxford, 1991.

JAMES, T. G. H., *Pharaoh's People*, Oxford, 1984.

LUCAS, A., *Ancient Egyptian Materials and Industries*, 4th edition, revised by J. R. Harris, London, 1962.

MERZ, B., *Red Land, Black Land*, New York, 1966.

Chapters 4, 5 and 6

ADAMS, B., *Predynastic Egypt*, Princes Risborough, 1988.

ADAMS, W. Y., *Nubia: Corridor to Africa*, Harmondsworth 1984.

BUTZER, K. W., *Early Hydraulic Civilization in Egypt: A Study in Cultural Ecology*, Chicago, 1976.

DODSON, A. M., 'The Mysterious Second Dynasty', in *KMT* 7:2 (1996), pp. 17–31.

EMERY, W. B., *Archaic Egypt*, Harmondsworth, 1961.

HOFFMAN, M. A., *Egypt Before the Pharaohs*, London, 1979.

SPENCER, A. J., *Early Egypt: The Rise of Civilisation in the Nile Valley*, London, 1993.

Chapters 7 and 8

ALDRED, C., *Egypt to the End of the Old Kingdom*, London and New York, 1965.

*EDWARDS, I. E. S., *The Pyramids of Egypt*, 3rd edition, Harmondsworth, 1985.

FAKHRY, A., *The Pyramids*, 2nd edition, Chicago, 1969.

LAUER, J.-Ph., *Saqqara, the Royal Cemetery of Memphis: Excavations and Discoveries since 1850*, London and New York, 1976.

LEHNER, M., *The Complete Pyramids*, London and New York, 1997.

ROTHENBURG, B. *et al.*, *Sinai: Pharaohs, Miners, Pilgrims and Soldiers*, Berne, 1979.

STADELMANN, R., *Die ägyptischen Pyramiden: vom Ziegelbau zum Weltwunder*, Mainz-am-Rhein, 1991.

STRUDWICK, N., *The Administration of the Old Kingdom*, London, 1985.

VERNER, M., *Forgotten Pharaohs, Lost Pyramids: Abusir*, Prague, 1994.

Chapter 9

BELL, B., 'The Oldest Records of the Nile Floods', in *Geographical Journal*, 136 (1970), pp. 569–73.

—'The Dark Ages in Ancient History. I: The First Dark Age in Egypt', in *American Journal of Archaeology*, 75 (1971), p. 126.

WARD, W. A., *Egypt and the East Mediterranean World 2200–1900 BC*, Beirut, 1971.

Chapters 10 and 11

BELL, B., 'Climate and the History of Egypt: The Middle Kingdom', in *American Journal of Archaeology*, 79 (1975), pp. 223–69.

BIETAK, M., *Avaris: The Capital of the Hyksos*, London, 1996.

BOURRIAU, J. D., *Pharaohs and Mortals: Egyptian Art in the Middle Kingdom*, Cambridge, 1988.

DAVID, R., *Pyramid Builders of the Pharaohs*, London, 1987.

OTTO, E., *Egyptian Art and the Cults of Osiris and Amon*, London, 1968.

POSENER, G., *Littérature et politique dans l'Égypte de la XIIe dynastie*, Paris, 1956.

—'Les Asiatiques en Égypte sous les XIIe et XIIIe Dynasties', in *Syria*, 34 (1957), pp. 145–63.

QUIRKE, S. (ed.), *Middle Kingdom Studies*, New Malden, 1991.

REDFORD, D. B., *Egypt, Canaan and Israel in Ancient Times*, Princeton, 1992.

ROBINS, G. (ed.), *Beyond the Pyramids: Egyptian Regional Art from the Museo Egizio, Turin*, Atlanta, 1991.

*RYHOLT, K., *The Political Situation in Egypt during the Second Intermediate Period, c. 1800–1550 BC*, Copenhagen, 1997.

WINLOCK, H. E., *The Rise and Fall of the Middle Kingdom at Thebes*, New York, 1947.

—*Models of Daily Life in Ancient Egypt*, Cambridge Mass., 1955.

Chapter 12

ALDRED, C., *Akhenaten: King of Egypt*, London and New York, 1988.

—*Akhenaten and Nefertiti*, London, 1973.

BIERBRIER, M., *The Tomb-Builders of the Pharaohs*, London, 1982.

DESROCHES-NOBLECOURT, C., *Tutankhamen*, London, 1963.

DODSON, A. M., *After the Pyramids*, London, 1997.

*DORMAN, P. F., *The Monuments of Senenmut*, London, 1988.

HORNUNG, E., *The Valley of the Kings: Horizon of Eternity*, New York, 1990.

*KITCHEN, K. A. *Pharaoh Triumphant*, Warminster, 1982.

KOZLOFF, A. P. and B. M. BRYAN, *Egypt's Dazzling Sun: Amenhotep III and his World*, Cleveland, 1992.

MARTIN, G. T., *The Hidden Tombs of Memphis*, London and New York, 1991.

PEDEN, A. J., *The Reign of Ramesses IV*, Warminster, 1994.

REDFORD, D. B., *Akhenaten, the Heretic King*, Princeton, 1984.

REEVES, R., *The Complete Tutankhamun*, London and New York, 1990.

SANDARS, N. K., *The Sea Peoples: Warriors of the Ancient Mediterranean*, 2nd edition, London and New York, 1985.

Chapter 13

BOTHMER, B. V., *Egyptian Sculpture of the Late Period, 700 BC to AD 100*, New York, 1960.

BOWMAN, A. K., *Egypt after the Pharaohs*, London, 1986.

KIENITZ, F. K., *Die politische Geschichte Ägyptens vom 7. bis zum 4. Jahrhundert vor der Zeitwende*, Berlin, 1953.

*KITCHEN, K. A., *The Third Intermediate Period in Egypt*, 3rd edition, Warminster, 1996.

LEAHY, A. (ed.), *Libya and Egypt, c. 1300–750 BC*, London, 1990.

LLOYD, A. B., *Herodotus Book II, Commentary 1–98*, Leiden, 1976.

MORKOT, R., *The Black Pharaohs*, London, 1997.

Tanis: The Gold of the Pharaohs, Edinburgh, 1988.

Chapter 14

KEMP, B. J., *Ancient Egypt: Anatomy of a Civilization*, London, 1989.

ROBINS, G., *Women in Ancient Egypt*, London, 1993.

TROY, L., *Patterns of Queenship in Ancient Egypt*, Uppsala, 1986.

List of Illustrations

Index